London's
Mystical
Legacy

Published by
BRUTUS MEDIA

ISBN 978-0-9574061-2-4

CONTENTS

ACKNOWLEDGEMENTS

The authors would like to thank the following people in bringing this work to fruition: Ray & Meriel, for their continued help and support, Suzi (art) Jones for suggested artwork and Adrian Dobbie ever present editor and graphic designer. Thank you to Vera Rodriguez, international photo journalist, for patience in typing manuscript and photographing two very difficult subjects. Thank you also to Tricia Gill for her commonsense approach to the ancient British material.

This book owes its existence to the kindness and generosity to the following: Jimmy Lee Shreeve, Paul Woods, Philip Hestleton, the late Bill Wakefield, Simon Williams, Robert Goodman, the London Museum, the London Livery Companies, and Worthing Library.

This book is dedicated to the memory of Joan Newton who down the years has been an inspiration and given her wholehearted support to projects such as this book and would have approved and enjoyed the subject matter considerably.

CHAPTER ONE
Brutus the Briton

The Adventures of Aeneas

The legend of the ancient king Brutus is intimately bound up with centuries of British history and folklore, yet the true origins of this semi-mythical ruler began on other, far-flung shores.

The story tells us that Brutus was a Trojan from the Mediterranean lands who, upon being exiled, found his true destiny in Britain, or more specifically the region in which he would establish a new city – London.

The Trojan heritage of Brutus can be traced back to his Great Grandfather, Aeneas, whose legend became firmly ingrained in Trojan history and culture.

The historian Robert Graves comments in *The Greek Myths*, "If Hector was the hand of the Trojans, Aeneas was their soul".

The Adventures of Aeneas is as central to Greek mythology as the *Odyssey* itself, with stories of heroism, gods and monsters that follow the meanderings of the chief of the conquered Trojans.

After the sacking of Troy, Aeneas and the remnants of the Trojan populace took to the high seas in search of a new land in which to re-settle. Their craft came to rest on the island of Delos, birthplace of Apollo and Diana, which was once a floating land mass until the god Jupiter fastened it with chains to the ocean floor. Here on Delos, Aeneas consulted the oracle of Apollo which answered him saying "seek your ancient mother; there the race of Aeneas shall dwell and reduce all other nations to their sway".

The exact geography of his destination may not have been explicit but the message in its meaning was clear enough. This was not the first time that Aeneas had been the central figure of a prophecy.

Prior to his birth, Aeneas' mother Aphrodite had told his father Anchisis that they would have a son, "who will rule over the Trojans and sons will be born to his sons and so on for all of eternity". This prophecy clearly described a dynasty of some importance. Aeneas' lineage and therefore Brutus' own can be traced back to the founder of Troy, Dardanus, whose origins are less well defined. One version has him being born on Samothrace now Samothraki, an island in the north-east Aegean near Turkey. This became a significant location as it was here that the Phoenician Cabiri practised their worship of the dark goddess Hekate before they arrived in Britain themselves.

1

However, we are told that Aeneas believed Dardanus and his mother were natives of Crete, so he set out for the island in the hope of finding a new home for his people.

In his quest, Aeneas and his Trojan crew encountered many of the hazards that had befallen Jason and the Argonauts in their pursuit of the Golden Fleece. In fact there are parallels that can be drawn between Aeneas' story and that of his Great Grandson Brutus, except perhaps for one very important difference. Aeneas never found his special island that the prophecies had told him to seek out – but Brutus did.

However, Aeneas did eventually triumph over those who would try to thwart him. He was able to establish his city of 'Lavinium', named after his wife Lavinia. One of their sons created Alba Longa, the birthplace of Romulus and Remus, who themselves were also descended from Aeneas. Alba Longa became known as the cradle of Rome itself. These accounts are mostly derived from Virgil, but his poem the *Aenid* makes no mention of Aeneas other than the sons of Ascanius, spawning any offspring himself.

It is in the annals of British folklore that we first hear of the legend of Brutus.

It appears that when Aeneas finally settled in Italy, he fathered a son called Ascanius who in turn bore a son named Silvius, who inherited the throne of Alba. Silvius had two sons, Aeneas and Brutus, but it is only the name of Aeneas that is recorded in classical accounts and the genealogy of mediterranean mythology. We must therefore ask if the story of Brutus was a later fabrication designed to give Britain mythical ties to the great city of Troy, or whether the existence of Brutus was deliberately left out of all classical texts relating to Aeneas, and if so, why?

The Legend of Brutus

The name of Brutus in connection with Britain first appears in the early 9th Century work, the *Historia Brittonium*, written in Latin by a Welsh monk from Bangor known simply as Nennius. He provides Brutus, Britto, or Brute as he was also known had a family tree which dates back to Japhet who was also equated with Atlas.

The genealogy of Aeneas can also be traced back to Atlas and his union with Pleione in Pierre Grimaldi's *Dictionary of Classical Mythology* (Presses Universitaire de France, 1951). Prior to the birth of Brutus, seers foretold that he "would be the death of his parents but rise in high honour".

Brutus' mother then died during childbirth and when Brutus had grown to adulthood, he accidentally shot and killed his own father Silvius with an arrow whilst they were both hunting.

After unwittingly perpetrating the death of his own father the King, Brutus was exiled from Italy to Greece where King Pandrasus was exploiting slaves who were direct descendants of Trojan war prisoners. Brutus began to roam the territory in a similar vein to his ancestor Aeneas but on land instead of on sea.

When the remnants of the Trojans learned of his pedigree, they gathered around Brutus and duly coerced him into becoming their leader.

Fortified with a newly founded army of followers, Brutus was able to actuate a revolution and take Pandrasus hostage. The Greek king was presented with a proposition in exchange for his release. This concordat involved Brutus being granted the hand of the king's daughter Ignoge in marriage along with a fleet of vessels in which the Trojan vestiges could seek out a suitable land for their resettlement. Pandrasus agreed to the terms and conditions and Brutus, together with his new bride and crew, was soon on his way to pastures new.

Within a couple of days after setting sail from Greece, the flotilla of craft made landfall upon an abandoned island. Here Brutus discovered a derelict city, at the centre of which, was a temple that had been erected in honour of the goddess Diana. At this sanctified site, Brutus made a suitable sacrificial offering to the goddess and in return he became the reciprocate of the moon goddess who materialised in a dream-like vision as part of the ritual invocation.

She spoke to him in a revelatory tone, telling him to seek out another island, a far greater one "towards the sunset out in the ocean". She also made mention of its occupants, referring to them as giants who were in the throws of dying out as a people. Diana said to him that this island was "beyond the realm of Gaul (France), fits thy people; you are to sail there Brutus and establish a city which will become another Troy. And Kings be born of thee, whose dreaded might shall awe the world and conquer nations bold," she continued. Brutus was also told that the new city was to maintain a world empire, but like ancient Troy it may suffer some perilous burning.

Stimulated by this quite specific prophetic command from Diana the moon goddess, Brutus and his crew of devotees set sail once more, this time turning up on the North African coast after a thirty day voyage.

In urgent need of replenishment and fresh supplies, they attacked the local residents of Mauritania before re-embarking on their journey. Having successfully navigated through the Pillars of Hercules, they came to the Tyrrhene Sea and to what is now known as Gibraltar.

But in these primeval times Gibraltar was under the Trojan control of Corineas who embraced Brutus and his fellow exiles and together they sailed to France.

Upon entering the mouth of the river Loire at Aquitaine, they soon encountered more trouble in the form of Gallic peoples who attacked them.

Brutus retaliated by inflicting total carnage upon the locals, which in turn prompted further reprisals from the kings of Gaul who threw everything that they could muster against the Trojan invaders. At first Brutus held out, driving the Gallic forces back inland but then he could also see that whilst the Gauls could replenish their own armies, the Trojan exiles could only reduce in size after each clash, suffering inevitable casualties.

Brutus decided to beat a timely retreat, so his flotilla set sail again in an undying quest for that special island that the goddess Diana had earmarked for them.

Soon a favoured wind blew him on his way and after many a passing day he arrived at the island of Albion, the name for ancient Britain. After sailing up the river Dart and weighing anchor, Brutus disembarked, took his first step on British soil and while standing a rock made a pronouncement.

"Here I am and here I rest. And this town shall be called Totnes."

All this happened approximately a century or more after his great-grandfather Aeneas had fled the burning buildings of Troy, carrying his father Anchises on his shoulders.

As for Brutus, the stone upon which he had first stood on British soil was to play a pivotal part in the mystical history of London. However, before going on to found that city, Brutus set up a community close to where he had landed in south west England. The former leader of the Gibraltarian Trojan community such as it was, became overlord of Cornwall, thus the county took its name from his.

Corineas was said to be immensely strong and after being set upon by some local inhabitants, he spared one of their number, Gogmagog, for a sporting challenge.

This wrestling encounter took place and ended with Corineas hoisting the giant Gogmagog over his head and hurling him over a cliff onto the rocks below. This event was commemorated when in 1494 the figures of two giants called Gog and Magog were cut in to the turf at Plymouth Hoe. This was the first mention of the two characters who were to play such a pivotal role as the Guildhall Guardians spanning 500 years in time. But as we shall see in the next chapter, there is far more to the symbolism and origins of this peculiar pair than the mere corruption of the name of a giant who met his end upon the rocks in the sea at the bottom of a Cornish cliff.

Brutus and his new Britons began to spread out, exploring their newly discovered kingdom. They went north and east, eventually arriving at the River Thames. Here Brutus walked along the river bank until he found a favoured location, where the River Fleet joined the Thames. Various accounts suggest that this spot was the Walbrook but the present authors prefer to plump for the Fleet. It was at this intersection of two rivers that

Brutus founded the city of London at what today is known as Ludgate Hill. The new city was originally known as 'Troia Nova' or New Troy. This was later corrupted to 'Trinovantum'. The Trinovantes were an Essex based tribe who had the option of collaborating with Queen Boudicca after they were no longer under the rule of arch rivals the Catuvellauni.

There were indications and suggestions that Trinovantes could have taken their name from Trinovantum, though the name Y Lin Troia, which is what the early Britons called themselves, does mean both 'Rose of Troy' and 'The Race of Troy'.

Apparently the old Celtic name for London was Llyn-Den but prefixed a hard C pronunciation. In 113 BC the city was rebuilt by Lud and renamed Caerludein, then Londinium.

London is first mentioned in actual historical records in the books of Tacitus. This is in connection with Boudicca and the Iceni uprising that occurred in 60 AD when it was said that Londonium was "a place not indeed distinguished by the title 'colony', but crowded with traders and a great centre of commerce".

Early historian Ammianes Marcellinus (circa 325–390 AD) mentions the city three times in total. Firstly he refers to it as 'Londinum', then 'Augusta' previously Londinium, and finally 'Augusta Trimobantum'.

The anonymous geographer of Ravenna, a 7th Century writer called the city 'Londinium Augusti'. In the 8th Century the chronicler Venerable Bede brings it virtually up to the present by referring to it as 'Londonia'.

One of the city's earliest sanctified sites of worship was where St Paul's Cathedral now stands, approximately 3000 years ago it was Brutus who first inaugurated a temple here – to his adored goddess Diana.

The legendary London Stone today left dishevelled behind in an iron grid in a poorly lit box on Cannon Street, is believed to be the same stone that Brutus first stepped upon after disembarking at Totnes, and marks the raising of another temple in London. (Full details of this and other stories and their surrounding legends are featured in the foregoing chapters). The final resting place of Brutus is said to be under the White Mound on Tower Hill along with another iconic figure, Bran the Blessed.

The Brutus Story – Fact or Fable?
William Dunbar (circa 1465–1530 AD), the finest Scottish poet of his time acquiesced fully to Brutus and the Trojan heritage of London as a historical certainty. Accompanying a diplomatic party sent by James IV of Scotland to the Court of Henry VII in London, Dunbar composed a special poem to present as a reading to the city of London. In the second verse there are a couple of lines which are of particular note:

"Gladdith anon, thou lusty Troy Novaunt Citie that some tyme cleped was New Troy". Dunbar wrote this in English as opposed to his native tongue Scottish. Someone who definitely wrote in English all the time was John Milton (1608-74 AD). In his *History of England* Milton writes "Brutus in a chosen place built Troia Nova changed in time to Trinovantum, now London."

However the principle chronicler of the Brutus story was Geoffrey of Monmouth in his *Historica Regum Brittanie*, or to give it its modern title, *History of the Kings of Britain*.

Conventional historians are, for the most part, a fairly sober, straight-laced, conservative-minded lot, except perhaps when their cages are being rattled and Geoffrey's book certainly has had that effect on many of them. The main sticking point is Geoffrey's claim that he sourced most of his material from a "most ancient book in the British language" given to him by Walter, Archdeacon of Oxford. This contention by Geoffrey has been fiercely disputed by the historical establishment who maintain that no such ancient secret work existed and that Geoffrey's writings are full of 'embroidered' chronicles.

His own background revealed that he did in fact have close associations with Oxford and may well have taught there for a while before being ordained as a Bishop in 1152 AD, just two years prior to his death in 1154 AD. Fast forward several centuries and enter the arrival of an unlikely vindicator for Geoffrey's works.

The US historian Acton Griscom called for a rudimentary re-evaluation of Geoffrey's work, by presenting new evidence to support his disputed claims. Griscom advances a theory that far from being non-existent the "ancient book in the British language" provided Geoffrey with other sources of ancient authority and historical value that were beyond the scope of his contemporaries at the time.

What made Griscom so sure of himself in this respect? In 1139 AD a certain Henry of Huntindon visited the Abbey of Bec where he was met by one of the housemonks, Robert of Torgini, who showed him a rare book containing those "Kings of the Britons who held our island before the English".

Robert gave Henry a summary of several passages containing events and incidents that were also in Geoffrey's *History*, which itself had been completed some years previously in circa 1135 AD. There were, however, substantial differences between the two works, but this is mainly due to the fact that Geoffrey did not follow the material solely from the ancient book, but drew from other sources in addition.

If Acton Griscom's researches are indeed correct – and there is no reason to suppose that they are not – then the inclination is more towards Brutus' narrative being based more on actuality than mythology.

But there is yet another facet to the fascinating tale of Brutus and his royal heritage, one that involves a middle eastern connection.

Dardanus and the House of Judah

British Israelites have claimed that Dardannus, the Trojan founder, is in fact Dara or Darda, a grandson of Judah, the founder of the Royal House of Judah which descends from Davidic line – from which the Rothschild dynasty also claims its pedigree.

They base their prognosis on Israelite tribal movements relating to the descendants of the twelve tribes of Israel. The origins of these tribes can be traced back to Jacob and Abraham before him. This lineage has, as its heart, the Royal House of Judah. These tribes apparently divided at one point in history, with some travelling to the lands north of the Black Sea in the northern region today covered by Russia, Ukraine, Moldova and Romania, while the rest remained behind.

The British Israelites believe that under God's covenant the lost tribes will one day be reunited with those who stayed behind, to form one kingdom in a Messianic era yet to come.

In his *Mythology of the British Isles* Geoffrey Ashe comments "This pedigree gives Brutus and his Trojans in general a collateral kinship with the chosen people, which would have qualified them to prepare Britain for the reconstitution of the Israelite work whenever the northern waves arrived".

Ashe also suggests that the word 'British' has its exact double in Hebrew, where British actually means 'Covenant Man'. The only reference to the birth of Dara is in the Biblical book of Chronicles, Chapter 2, Verse 6. Judah formed a liaison with his daughter-in-law Tamar of Kadesh, widow of the evil Er. This union bore them Pharez and Zerah, sons of Judah. Zerah had five sons, among them Dara. There are no further Biblical references to this grandson of Judah, perhaps due to his time coinciding with the missing generations of the Bible which are not chronicled. The British Israeli contingent who claim Dara's identity to be identical with Dardanus obviously have access to ancient manuscripts and other sources which are not available to other researchers. Enter into this yet another twist of the bloodline heritage.

The findings and conclusions of geneaologists and authors, Ralph Ellis, David Rohl and Sir Laurence Gardner, all point to in a similar direction on the question of the Davidic lineage of the Royal House of Judah. Namely that many Biblical figures including the forebears of the Royal House of Judah were deliberately cast as 'poor Israelites' by the Hebrew chroniclers in order to hide their true origins as seriously well connected Egyptians from the

Hyksos Pharaonic line – something that would of course been unacceptable to the vast majority of Jews.

In his book *The Lost Testament* leading Egyptologist David Rohl has a chapter entitled 'Abraham the Amourite' (Hyksos). Abraham is one of Jacob's ancestors. Ralph Ellis asserts that Jewish Jacob was actually Hyksos Jacoboam/Yakoboam in Egyptian, Abraham was really Maa-ab-ra Shesha – the first Pharoah from the Hyksos line. If one takes M as the first letter of his name – then reverses it to the end and add the letter h – we arrive at the name Abraham.

The official version of the Middle Eastern history is that the Hyksos kings were originally Amourites who invaded and subsequently occupied Egypt, circa 1720 BC, but Ellis along with others, maintains that they were already in residence well before that date.

According to Ellis, the Biblical exodus of the Israelites was actually a depiction of two mass expulsions from Egypt by Hyksos together with their apostates. This situation had mostly been incurred because of the divisions between the worship of the Bull and that of the Ram as instilled by the Heliopolis priesthood.

Even the Jewish writer Josephus referred to the departing Hyksos as "our ancestors". When the Hyksos were in Israel they sacked Jerusalem before returning to Egypt accompanied by the character of Joseph who is mentioned in the Old Testament book of Genesis, says Ellis. He also concludes, by presenting compelling evidence that King David of the Royal House of Judah, together with his son Solomon were both, in fact, yet another pair of Egyptian Pharaohs. King David, Ellis says, was actually Psusennes II, while Solomon was Sheshonq I. Psusennes II (David) was the last of the twenty-first dynasty Pharaohs. His seat of power was based in the eastern Delta lands at Tanis, the true location of the Temple of Solomon.

The Davidic bloodline has been charted from its inception in ancient Babylon and its progression through Nimrod, a Mesopotamian monarch who founded the ancient city, to his son Boethos (Hoetep-Sekhemwy) founder of the 2nd Dynasty of Egypt. It then came out of Egypt and into Israel before further progressing into Europe and the Royal House of Vere of Anjou. From France it became assimilated through various unions and marriages, and into the Scottish Stewarts and the Plantagenet Kings in England. The latter, in fact, were descended from Plantanu, a female from the junior branch of the Imperial House of Vere.

Geneologists and Egyptologists alike, not to mention Jewish historians, all have differering opinions as to the exact origins of the tribes that came out of Egypt. But all agree as much as they can, that the history of Egypt can offer more than many would care to concede.

Perhaps this is best illustrated by aspects of Egyptian symbolism that have been woven into the tapestry of the British nation state and the complex history of its capital city London. We shall return to this peculiar cultural infusion in some detail later.

The legend of London's founder Brutus is a story far more diverse than we had previously anticipated. Another intriguing facet of the Brutus story is the strange symbolism and the true identities of Gog and Magog, whose statues reside in the London Guildhall, the site of Brutus' original seat of power.

Gog and Magog have been referred to as champions of London, but their story first began over 2000 years before – in the Middle East.

CHAPTER TWO

Dragons, Griffins
& the Guildhall Guardians

The Scythian Link

We first the find Biblical reference to Magog in the Book of Genesis 10, in which he is cast as the sole descendant of a race or country. Most likely Magog refers to the land of Gog (or vice versa) as stated in the next Biblical reference, from the Book of Ezekiel, which mentions both. In Chapter 38 verse 2-3 it says,

"Son of Man, set thy face against Gog, the land of Magog, the chief prince of Meshesh and Tubal and prophesy against him. And say, Thus saith the Lord God; Behold, I am against thee, O Gog, the chief prince of Meshech and Tubal."

The Hebrew account is unclear as to whether Gog or Magog are identified as persons or locations. In Revelations, found in the New Testament, it is the latter, with Gog and Magog being revealed as nations in the far corners of the earth.

As St John's vision of the apocalypse unfolds, both Gog and Magog are enlisted by the unshackled Satan in the final reckoning. They are of course eventually routed by divine intervention, with the whole theme of Revelations being somewhat congruous with that of Ezekiel. They also make an appearance in the Qur'an, which has Gog and Magog escaping the confines of a great wall,

"But then Gog and Magog are let loose and they rush headlong down every height (or advantage). Then will the True Promise draw near." (Qu'ran 21:96-97).

Gog and Magog also play a part in the history of the Goths. Saint Isidore of Seville, said to be the highest authority on Goth history, claimed that the Goths and the Spanish Visigoths were all descended from Gog and Magog. In 387 AD, the Bishop of Milan associated the Goths with the Gog of Ezekiel's vision. There is also a geographical link, with old Armenian and European maps showing the place name of Gog, usually in the the area of the Caucasian mountains.

The story of the Goths dates back to 1500 BC when a number of individuals were expelled from the island of Gothland, near Scandza (Scandanavia). They sailed in three craft to Gothiscandza which is situated at the mouth of the river Vistula. From here they travelled further East towards Azerbaijan, eventually settling in Scythia whose name originates from Saka, the real name of the Goths. The early Jewish historian Josephus says that Gog and Magog were Scythians by race and were called so by name. This provides us with our most noteworthy link, perhaps also to the whole Gog/Magog scenario.

The Scythians were a Nordic/Aryan race who had moved into the Northern European territories from their Middle and Near Eastern origins. They travelled through the Caucasus Mountains and Sauromatia with a culture dominated by Priestess-Queens called Kurgans, who conducted rituals and used sacred cauldrons in the worship of goddess figurines.

The Scythians came to reign across Eurasian lands and as their name might suggest, the Scythians adopted the symbol of the scythe, which is sometimes associated with Saturn, the Roman equivalent of Kronos, and with the goddesses Rhea, Kali and Hekate. The scythe or moon-sickle is the symbol *par excellance* of the impermanence of life, reminding those who meditate on its meaning that all shall finally be cut down, just as the corn in the field is harvested at the swing of the scythe's blade.

To an extent, the Scythians acted as transporters of occult rituals and Aryan bloodlines. Before their exodus through the Caucasus Mountains, they were involved in the Trojan wars, with the legendary figure of Aeneas being said to have been a Trojan-Scythian lord.

In the Elysian account of Aeneas and the Trojan sacking, Aeneas travels to Italy in search of secret knowledge that will enable him to descend into the underworld and be granted an audience with his deceased father. In order to achieve this he must first bury a friend and then pluck the Golden Bough.

But a wise woman warns him that while he could enter the realm of Hades, few except the children of the Gods were able to return from the underworld. Accompanied by the wise woman, Aeneas begins his descent. Firstly he buries a fallen comrade, then he plucks the Mistletoe from the Golden Bough. Together they finish their quest and since Aeneas was a descendant of Atlas/Japhet who was founder of the Elven race, he was allowed safe passage from the underworld and therefore able to return.

Magog is said to be the Son of Japhet and would therefore be part of the same stock as Aeneas and Brutus. Gog was named in Ezekiel as the chief Prince of Meshech and Tubal, the other sons of Japhet. The parents of Japhet were Tubal Cain and Nin-banda (circa 3200 BC). Besides Japhet, Tubal Cain had another son, Ham. The grandson of Ham was King Nimrod of Babylon and from him we get the 2nd Dynasty of the Egyptian Pharaonic line.

In discussing the legend of a royal bloodline linked to the stories of the Holy Grail, Nicholas De Vere, in his book *The Dragon Legacy*, writes,

"...the Grail Dynasty from David and Solomon had progressed into the west, notably to the Merovingian Kings of Gaul while related branches established kingdoms in Ireland and Celtic Britain. These lines were linked through marriage and parallel Dragon strains from Ham, Japhet and Tubal Cain (which survived through the Royal Houses of Scythia and Anatolia). The families had forged their own marital links with the early princesses of the Egyptian succession".

The legend of the Grail bloodline goes back further than that to ancient Babylon and Sumeria and its inception by Tiamet, the Dragon Queen and the Grand Council of the Annunaki, or Grigori. This mythical race of so-called fallen angels were said to have mated with mortal women, which sounds very similar to the Biblical tale of a hybrid race of the Nephilim, described in Genesis 6:4.

From the remotest districts of the deepest parts of the African continent, to the summit of the Mediterranean coastline, people still speak in reverential whispers about recounted stories of the serpent headed or dragon race that were once known to their ancient ancestors. Accounts of these mythical beings, the Annunaki/Grigori/Nephilim were initially fundamental to the early religions of Babylon, Mesopotamia and Sumer.

Were the origins of Gog and Magog to be found here?

The Gaelic word 'Sumaire' pronounced 'Shimarie' translates variously as 'vortex', 'labyrinth', 'sucker', 'reptile', 'dragon', 'serpent' or 'vampire'. It is also linked to Sumeria itself and the legend of the Dragon Queen Tiamet. As De Vere points out in *The Dragon Legacy*,

"The vampire descends from the supernatural Dragon Royalty of Sumeria back to the Ubaid (Scythian) Overlords of what was to become known as Transylvania and Greater Scythia".

Through the Dragon and Grail bloodlines of the ancient Middle or near East, carried by the Scythians around Europe via Troy, Transylvania and Gaul, came the figures of Gog and Magog. So how did these giants come to be so central to the City of London's mythical narrative?

Twin Giants

The earliest account of giants being linked to the City seems to be when the London giants, one male, one female, were paraded at civic sessions in 1415.

In 1522 they both became male and were called Hercules and Samson. In 1554, two giant figures, described as Corineas and Gogmagog, were included as part of a reception for Philip of Spain on his marriage to Mary.

In 1598 a German visitor to London, Paul Hentzner, commented on the Guildhall by saying "Here are to be seen the statues of two giants said to have assisted the English when the Romans made war upon them: Corineas of Britain and Gogmagog of Albion".

In 1661 an election pamphlet was circulated which prompted comments including the suggestion that the circular be "put into the mouths of the giants in the Guildhall, 'Colebrand and Brandmore'".

Five years on brings us to the Great Fire of London, in which the Corineas and Gogmagog figures were seemingly destroyed. In his *New View of London* (1708) E. Hatton writes that the Guildhall was rebuilt in 1669 and the giant figures replaced with "Two new figures of gigantic magnitude" that would "be as before". However it remains unclear as to exactly when these replacements were installed. According to Jordan's pamphlet on the Lord Mayor's Show, two giant figures were employed as part of the procession in 1672 and were then to be given pride of place in the Guildhall immediately afterwards.

Writing in his book *Legendary London*, Lewis Spence suggests that these figures might have been of a temporary nature, however this apparent interim state did not prevent the Lord Mayor from having to enter into a special covenant to ensure that the huge figures would not suffer any damage.

In 1815 the Shakespearean critic Francis Douce referred to Gog and Magog, suggesting that they were present in the Guildhall in 1669, but were not replaced immediately after the Great Fire of 1666, but it was during this period after the Great Fire that the names Gog and Magog were first used as separate identities.

These figures were believed to have been constructed out of wickerwork and pasteboard. The use of wicker here is interesting because its etymology relates to Wicca, Wicking and Viking, while in ancient Russian (Scythian) the Vihkr means whirlwind or vortex.

The word Wicca is derived from the Saxon willow (wicker) which means to bend or yield, in this case to the whirlwind or vortex. Thus the Wica (Witch) yields his or her spirit to that of the daemon and then in doing so assumes the role of trance-seer, a notion and practice which formed an essential part of the Scythian culture.

However, it wasn't long before the giant wicker figures of Gog and Magog fell into disrepair. They were replaced in 1708 at the hands of Captain Richard Saunders, one of the leading carvers of his day, who was able to bring his skills to bear in creating two much sturdier replacements.

In the *New View of London*, Hatton tells us that the city's hackney coachmen were regularly heard to swear "by Gog and Magog". London apprentices were in awe of their names being uttered, another indication perhaps that they had been accorded near deity status within the City and the surrounding area. Further theories postulate that Gog and Magog may have represented twin gods of London, whose own seats of power were the two hills on either side of the Walbrook. This idea gains further credence in view of a similar set of twin hills in Cambridge which are known as the Gogmagog hills. In his book *Gogmagog, The Buried Gods,* the dowser T.C. Lethbridge wrote about his excavations on Wandlebury Hill, near Cambridge, where he uncovered hidden turf carvings of the two Gods.

This provides strong echoes of the Caucasus Mountains in Scythia where Gog is named after a mountain or hill range. Once again the backdrop of Scythian history and culture seems to provide answers to some mysteries surrounding the origins of Gog and Magog, but as we shall see this extends to that other City phenomenon, the dragon.

Flying Serpents in Dragon City

If one takes a stroll along the Victoria Embankment it soon becomes apparent that the City of London is full of dragons. These mythical creatures appear as the main motif on the City's coat of arms and mark several boundaries and bridges of the City, not least the pair of rampant dragons found at the southern end of London Bridge, which thousands of commuters pass daily as they ebb and flow out of the City's commercial heart. More dragons are also found perched atop numerous landmarks and churches in the area. If London is a dragon city, the winged serpents that adorn its urban terrain may act as some sort of talismanic protector for the dealings undertaken in the City itself, thus defining the area which remains one of world's foremost financial centres.

Stories of dragons, griffins and serpents are deeply embedded in the culture and folklore of many of the world's ancient civilisations from China, India, the Middle East, to the Americas and Mexico. One country in particular can boast a greater degree of dragon lore than most – England. Native New Zealander Marc Alexander, a former Fleet Street journalist with a passion for English folklore and legend has chronicled over seventy English towns and villages that harbour local dragon traditions. In England, part of the dragon mythos involved the belief that the dragon was a gatherer and protector of treasure, a notion that perhaps owes its origins to early Mediterranean Europe, where serpents often appeared as guardians of temples and sacred spaces.

In European culture dragons can be sub-divided into two clear groups; those with and those without wings. The former variety are considered to be dragons in the proper sense, since the dragon is, by definition, a winged serpent, which has great symbolic significance. In England there are well over 300 barrows or earth mounds which were used as burial chambers for the ancient chieftains of the Neolithic period. These revered leaders were usually entombed along with hordes of treasure, and it could well be the case that stories of mighty dragons guarding the treasure these barrows held were circulated in their locality to deter would be grave robbers. In the case of the City of London the dragon is the guardian of the wealth of the Realm, including the Commonwealth countries and various dominions. Either way, there is the ever-present symbolism of the winged serpent cast as custodian of commerce and personal gain.

But, of course, there is far more to the hidden history and symbolism of the dragon than merely the safe-keeper, as in ancient Egypt, where the dragon performed the function of transporting the dead Pharaoh towards the stars.

The earliest accounts of serpent worship arriving on British shores came in the form of the Tuatha de Dannan, the 'People of the Serpent Goddess Dana' or Danae, who later became assimilated into Diana.

These were a unit of the ancient sea voyaging Mediterranean Danaans who had deserted their homelands in Asia Minor and the Aegean Sea, forming part of a series of migratory expeditions into Northern Europe that spanned several centuries. One of these waves of occupiers had allegedly come from Troy and was led by none other than Brutus. The Tuatha de Dannaan soon became synonymous with the Druids whom they instructed in the magical arts. Initiation into the Druidic Order was originally a clandestine matter, performed in subterranean tunnels and underground chambers within solitary locations where earth energies combined to create the serpent force, such as stone circles, 'places of the dragon' and burial mounds. The timing of these initiations usually coincided with the important festivals of the 'sacred wheel' of Britain, comprising of the solstice, equinox and cross quarter day festivals of the old pagan calendar.

The Druids were answerable for introducing new gods into Celtic worship. In this respect their role was very much the catalyst for introducing religion to the Celts without being part of this religion themselves. Thus the Celtic peoples allowed the Druids to orchestrate their religious ceremonies and while they had their own Kings and Chieftains, above these were the Scythian Kings and above the Scythians were the Elven Druids, the Priest-Kings representative of the purest Eurasian bloodline.

In a similar vein to the Egyptian priests of the legendary Djedhi, the Druids received knowledge on how the summon and control the dragon power that had been handed down to them from their predecessors the Tuatha de Dannaan. They used the pentagram as a symbol of the five-fold body of the dragon, whose power they would attempt to raise and direct into the earth's energy grid in Britain.

There is an age old theory in Britain that lines of energy connecting various sites called leys were actively used by the early Druids who believed that they were real paths and places of the dragon. It was thought in the first instance that these dragon paths had been used by the ancient Celts as trade routes, as they ran in direct lines straight over hills, not around them, as one might expect. Some have suggested that the Romans laid their roads down over some of these original paths, whereas the belief persists that beneath was part of a geodetic network used by the ancients, based on subtle forms of energy – a grid that formed part of the ancient capital. This may in some cases explain why the Roman roads are so straight.

In Saxon times Englishmen replaced London and moved their capital to Winchester. Medieval travellers going from London to the ancient Roman settlement of Silchester (near Basingstoke) which heads towards Winchester, named the road the 'Devil's Highway' as its design and engineering they considered to be beyond the capabilities of mere mortals. Perhaps calling it the 'Dragons Highway' may have been more appropriate, especially if there was a more secret dragon path beneath the road.

Among other things, stone circles have always been associated with dragon paths and the Druidic tradition. These were the Temples of Keridwen, a Druidic goddess who rules over Samhain (the Oct 31st pagan festival) as Crone or Dark Mother. She is a serpent goddess and also the Moon goddess, a shape shifter who is sometimes equated with Diana or indeed Hekate. British versions of the goddess found in figurines from this period have been identified as Rhiannon, Arianrhod and Danu. The ley lines, dragon paths, barrows, burial mounds and stone circles were all considered to be places of the dragon.

As for the mythical creature itself there are certain facets which are common to the appearance and qualities of the dragon. Firstly, for the most part, they tended to be depicted as giant reptiles, serpents or lizards with the capability of flight, and in some cultures they are equipped with feathery wings. Some of the legends portray the dragon as a serpent, supported by either two or four legs. The dragon's prime attribute was to project fire – which the dragon sometimes exercised in its own defence, burning up its victims in the process.

Dragons were the garners of gems and precious jewels, and the guardians of priceless artefacts belonging to treasure troves. Some dragons were the couriers of a large jewel coloured red or white which was said to show their longevity. Dragons possessed the key to a lengthy existence and they were said to be the fountainhead of arcane knowledge and magic.

Many ancient cultures revered the dragon as an iconic godhead figure along with many kings of ancient civilisation who claimed reified status. None more so than the rulers of Sumer, Mesopotamia and ancient Babylon, which was the birthplace of the dragon line. But as we shall now see – this has much deeper implications then merely a mythical creature who appears in stories and fairy-tales.

The Depth of the Dragon Line

The area that was once ancient Mesopotamia forms the right horn of a sickle-shaped area of land in the Middle East. Called the 'Fertile Crescent' on account of its crescent moon shape, the area also includes the lands of Canaan and Egypt on the left horn which extends down to the timeworn city of Thebes. It is here, particularly on the eastern side that the earliest tales and legends of dragons are to be found. In southern Mesopotamia which came to be known as Sumer, ancient inscribed tablets were discovered which tell of flying serpents and dragons – the same winged variety that were later appropriated as the markers for the City of London.

The Sumerians had several names for these flying serpent gods, 'Anumma' or 'Annunaki' being the most popular. Following the founding of a dragon worshiping culture in Mesopotamia, a hierarchical priesthood was formed which created a coalition with a group of magicians called the Aishipu, who along with the Priest Kings became self-installed representatives of the Primal Dragon, which they believed, gave them direct access to the considerable dragon power.

One of these legendary Priest Kings was Tammuz, the nature god and serpent deity of Mesopotamia. Tammuz is the earliest known archetype on whom the talismanic figure of St George is based. According to authors Tim Wallace-Murphy and Marilyn Hopkins in their book *Rosslyn – Guardian Of The Secrets of the Holy Grail*, they say that "most modern authorities now believe that Tammuz and St George are the same person portrayed in a varying mythological guise".

In this respect it is interesting to note that the dragons who mark the entrance to the City of London financial sector are depicted with one claw holding a shield containing a red cross on a white background, the symbol of the Sun in the ancient Phoenician culture. The same red cross on a white background was adopted by the Knights Templar, whose original headquarters were situated on the site that is now Holborn underground station. The site of the later headquarters was near Thames embankment, "Barran Novi Templi", or Temple Bar, where Fleet Street conjoins with the Strand.

The image of the red cross on the white background is most familiar today, as any British sports fan knows, as the emblem of St George, patron saint of England, as well as being used as the logo of the Red Cross, the humanitarian aid organisation. But St George is now seen as the mythological counterpart of Tammuz, who as the nature god and dragon deity, is also equated with the Green Man symbolism that has associations with certain degrees of Freemasonry.

The figure of King Nimrod of Babylon is revered in the Ancient and Accepted Scottish Rite as the creator of Freemasonry, thousands of years before its official founding. Masonic legend has it that Nimrod oversaw the massive mobilisation of labour in the inception and building of the Tower of Babel, and it is Tammuz who by repute is the offspring of the Queen Semiramis and Nimrod. Their trinity is represented by the Fleur-de-lys symbol adopted by France, which also figures prominently on the British Royal Crown where it is interspersed with crosses of the Knights Templar.

In fact, according to genealogist and bestselling author Sir Laurence Gardner, the child of Nimrod was Boethos, also known as Hoetep-Sekhemwy, who founded 2nd Dynasty in Egypt. This new dynasty (circa 2890 BC) saw the Nimrod lineage being introduced and subsequently installed into the Pharaonic line. The grandson of Nimrod was King Raneb, the second Pharaoh of the 2nd Dynasty. It was Raneb who established the 'Goat of Mendes' worship in Egypt, although the cult was found to be in existence much earlier in Apis. Commenting about this in *Genesis of the Grail Kings* Sir Laurence says "This is especially relevant because in both the Grail and the Dragon traditions (which are fundamentally one and the same), the Goat of Mendes has always been directly associated with Nimrod's grandfather Ham. Mendes was a city just northwest of Avaris in the Egyptian delta and the sacred goat (often called Khem, Chem or Ham) was the zodiacal goat of Capricorn. In accordance with the Dragon Court Tradition, Ham was the designated Archon of the Tenth Age of Capricorn and in this respect his symbol was an inverted pentagram".

In the Court of the Dragon Kings
The Dragon Court to which Laurence Gardener refers was founded by an Egyptian priest who bore the title Ankh-fn-Khonsu (circa 2170 BC), whom the notorious 20th Century occultist Aleister Crowley called the 'Priest of the Princes'. Ankh-fn-Khonsu's seat of power was at Thebes on the left horn of the Fertile Crescent.

The Royal Dragon Court was later endorsed as a Pharaonic investiture by Queen Sobeknefru, as the 12th Dynasty Dragon Queen of Egypt.

From here more Dragon Queens (the carriers of the Dragon blood) were inaugurated into the lineage which developed and permeated into other Royal Houses of Europe and Scythia. But the Dragon line actually began in ancient Mesopotamia and Sumer where the Sumerians split with some going North and becoming the Scythians in one subdivision, whilst the other descended into Ancient Egypt to find Pharaonic recognition in the Court of Queen Sobeknefru. It then became transported to Phoenicia before being taken back to the Scythians through marital unions.

The Tuatha de Danaan, the Trojans, the Fir Bolg, accompanied by their Arch Druid consorts then became the next recipients of the Dragon heritage along with the Elven dynasty of Pen-Dragons.

The parallel Dragon lines from Ham, Japhet and Tubal-Cain survived and re-invented themselves as Royal Houses of Scythia and Anatolia, who have their own marital links with the Egyptian princesses and Dragons. It was from this pedigree that the first British Pen-Dragon (Pen-Draco Insularis), Cymbeline of the House of Camu-lot became King circa 10 AD. The Celtic Pen-Dragons were not chosen on a succession of descent basis, they had been carefully selected from a diversified consortium of monarchical Dragon families by a council of Druidic elders who made the final judgement. The last of the Pendragons was Calwaladr of Gwynedd who died in 664 AD. With him went the Dragon influence, as Britain succumbed to the Germanic Anglo-Saxon invaders who brought the worship of their own deities with them. Notably this new worship focused on Woden, the Germanic equivalent of the Norse Odin. While the days of the old Dragon kings appeared to be gone, their dynastic descendents maintained the essence of the Dragon Court which continued in influential European and Middle Eastern circles. In 1408 the Imperial Royal Dragon Court and Order was formally reconstituted by Sigsmund Von Luxemborg, King of Hungary.

Today, the Imperial and Dragon Court as it is known, continues as a select brotherhood, drawn from a small elite boasting royal ancestry who controversially claim a lineage back through the Elven and Plantagenet affiliated line of Anjou and further still, back through the Anjou line to the Royal Houses of both the Trojans and Scythians and ultimately to the near eastern lands incorporating Israel, Egypt, ancient Phoenicia and Sumer.

The inner temple custodians of this occult fraternity are the Vere Grand Masters who reside in Southern England and elsewhere in Europe.

In a recent interview with former Sovereign Grand Master Prince Nicholas de Vere von Drakenburg it was disclosed that from the age of seven onwards, his father told him their ancestry was 'steeped in Royal blood, and most significantly what is termed Royal Witchcraft'. According to De Vere, Royal Witchcraft is a "a major ancient draconian, druidic facet continuing within the later history of the Dragon tradition and within the Vere family".

In fact the Veres were once the now defunct Earls of Oxford, five of whom were ceremonially admitted into the Order of the Garter at St George's Chapel in Windsor Castle. Some authorities, notably the leading Egyptologist Dr Margaret Murray have advanced the theory that the Order of the Garter was a Christianised veneer for continuing the Old Religion as part of the traditional Royal Witchcraft that De Vere has unwittingly mentioned. We shall return to this in some detail later on.

The Vere family also maintain that they have more genes in their blood than 'ordinary' people. This admission is backed up by the claim that the so-called Dragon genes have been identified in research conducted at both

London and Oxford Universities that give two types of gene that go to make up a 'contemporary Dragon'.

The Insignia of the Imperial and Royal Dragon Court and Order shows a red cross situated above a dragon in the circular Orobouros serpent shape.

The dragons that mark the entrance to the City of London use the same symbolic imagery, but in reverse, as it the dragon who is above in the red cross.

This then is the secret history of the dragon, its symbolism and role as the City of London's talismanic guardian, its position as an object of veneration by ancient cultures and its place as a standard bearer for paths of unseen energies.

But as we shall now see, the City of London harbours many more secrets of a preternatural nature, manifold in character, that play a significant part in the arcane lineage of London.

CHAPTER THREE
Secrets of the City

Torment in the Tower

William the Bastard, Duke of Normandy, was a pagan who followed in the family's religious tradition. His father's nickname was "Robert the Devil" which is often interpreted in an allegorical manner, but according to author Michael Harrison in his highly acclaimed book *The Roots of Witchcraft* it should be taken – as was originally intended – in a strictly literal sense. The Normans were quite openly followers of the Old Religion, which according to Harrison, attracted William and his followers to England in the first place: England was considerably more pagan than their native France, which was in the process of falling under the subordination of the Roman Church.

William the Bastard, that pagan devil, soon became William the Conqueror, great King of England, architect and builder of the Tower of London, which was constructed largely from stone brought over from Caen, France.

William also imported a Norman expert, Gundulf, to design the White Tower, the oldest and most significant of the many buildings that constitute the Tower. It was built on the ancient Bryn Gwyn or White Mound that forms part of an important ley line, according to John Wilcock in his *Guide to Occult Britain*. It is here, underneath the White Mound that the decapitated head of Arch Druid of Britain, Bendigain Fran, better known as Bran the Blessed, is buried together with the body of Brutus, London's legendary patriarch.

In the Welsh *Mabinogion*, a 14th Century compendium of legends, Bran is described as a King of Britain, "exalted with the Crown of London". In common with Welsh mythical figure Kerridwen, Bran possessed a magical cauldron of regeneration, which he eventually gave up to King Matholwch of Ireland.

The *Mabinogian* describes how Bran, or more specifically his head, came to be buried under the White Tower. While on an expedition abroad, he sustained a war wound at the hands of his enemy Caswallawn, who succeeded in piercing Bran's ankle with a poisoned spear. Bran, sensing that his end was nigh and that his early demise would bring about a state of ruin within his kingdom, commanded his loyal accomplices to cut off his head, which was transported to Harlech by seven of his most trusted companions. In the legend, his head had remained alive, in a magical sense, as a vessel for occult powers.

After a further move to a separate location, Bran's head was eventually conveyed to its final resting place beneath the White Hill of London, where the White Tower would later be built. Bran's head was still believed to have possessed magical capabilities, so it was buried facing towards the continent in order to ward off potential invaders and to ensure the fertility and well-being of London and the British Isles.

The cult practice keeping severed heads as sources of mystical power was certainly no innovation, having begun with the Scythians before becoming appropriated into Druidic tradition, even finding parallels with the story of the head of John the Baptist and the skulls of numerous Saints still kept in reliquaries around the world today. The Druids appropriated the practice into Celtic religious praxis, and much later we find the venerated Baphomet head idol of the Templars.

As for Bran he was also known as Bendigeid Fran, or 'Blessed Raven'. In Celtic lore the raven is looked upon as an oracular bird that still inhabits the area of the White Mound. The legend foretells that London and the Monarchy will perish if the Ravens ever leave the Tower. This omen of impending doom is apparently taken very seriously by the Monarchy, who keep a cage full of them next to the White Tower. Churchill too heeded the warning during the Second World War, when their numbers suddenly thinned. He had the ravens restocked immediately and placed under special protection.

John Wilcock comments "They stand spookily on the grass outside the Tower, rarely moving and apparently showing no indication to fly away." Perhaps this is because their wings are regularly clipped by the Yeoman Ravenmaster who feeds and cares for them.

A second raven stock is kept at another venue, ready to replenish the winged incumbents of the Tower should any disaster befall them.

The Tower was many things: a fortress, a royal place, an incarceration unit for the high-but-not-so-mighty in society and those treasonable persons who allegedly posed a threat to the State. But it was also home to the Royal Mint as well as the treasury for the Crown Jewels and, until 1834, the original London Zoo. The Tower is a location that has developed its own particular ambience down the centuries. John Wilcock speaks for many when he describes it as "a prehistoric site rich in legend, bloodshed, imprisonment, ritual sacrifice and legendary hauntings". One particular, lesser-known case had just about everything that warrants a story to be termed 'sensational', something that the current press are always eager to exploit, only in this instance it was all true.

Lady Frances Howard, daughter of Thomas Howard, the First Duke of Suffolk, was born on 31st May 1590 into a highly privileged background.

It was fairly common during this period in history for young people from such salubrious families to have their future marriages planned for them while they were still juveniles. Such was the case with the Duke of Suffolk and his daughter and so, at the age of fifteen, Frances was betrothed to the young Earl of Essex in January 1606.

The marriage took place immediately but the Earl left soon after the nuptials to continue his education abroad, while Frances travelled to London to live with her mother. But her mother was unable to exert any manner of control over the headstrong, petulant and self-seeking Frances. She became mistress to the Prince of Wales, and when she was sixteen she was introduced to Robert Carr, Viscount of Rochester, who would later become the Earl of Somerset. He was the King's confidante and favourite, some would say virtual ruler, since none could gain access to James I except through Robert Carr. Robert and Frances were equally attracted to each other, and became lovers. Like Frances, Robert was subservient to no one, but he was nonetheless under the guidance of Sir Thomas Overbury. Overbury enjoyed a relationship with Carr which bore many similarities to that which existed between Carr and the King. In fact Overbury was so much in the confidence of Robert Carr that the secret papers of the King, all of which passed through the hands of Robert, also found their way into Overbury's.

With Overbury being secretly privy to the King's secret correspondence, he began to imagine himself to be in an exalted position, describing himself as the "greatest man in Britain". In *Brief Lives* the Oxford writer John Aubrey commented "Twas a great question who was the proudest, Sir (Walter) Raleigh or Sir Thomas Overbury, but the difference that was, was judged on Sir Thomas's side".

As Frances' relationship with Robert intensified, potential disaster loomed. Frances' husband, the Earl of Essex, having completed his foreign education, returned home in 1609 with a view to consummating his marriage.

Essex was a withdrawn, sombre individual who stood in complete contrast to his wife's more forthcoming, vivacious circle of friends. He had had very little experience with women at all, consequently his vain attempts to cement his marriage were reduced to virtual buffoonery on his part as Lady Essex completely rejected her husband's clumsy advances.

A few year previously, when still in her early teens, Frances had been introduced to a Mrs Thornborough, the wife of the Bishop of Bristol. Thornborough's influence on Frances lead her to develop a keen interest in astrology, palmistry, potions and poisons, which she procured from her supplier Simon Forman, based in the London borough of Lambeth. By the time of her husband's unwelcome return, Frances had found a new confidante in the court dressmaker Anne Turner, wife of George Turner of the Royal College of Physicians. Being herself a keen amateur Alchemist, Turner was secretly known as court purveyor of potions, cures and poisons.

Forman, the supplier of the pair's alchemical preparations, was considered a dangerous quack by what passed for a medical establishment at that time, but what his physician peers may not have known, although they may well have suspected as much, was that Forman was also a sorcerer magician of some standing. Frances visited him for a private audience after being introduced by Turner and according to J. Buffery in his book *London Witchcraft*, Frances soon became the sorceror's apprentice, paying regular visits to Forman's home. Here, surrounded by magical sigils and flickering candlelight, the eager young Alchemist Frances was initiated by Forman into the tradition of the grimoires.

As her visits became more regular, the relationship between student and master deepened, with Frances becoming Forman's 'sworn daughter', writing to him as "father" and signing herself as "your affectionate loving daughter Frances Essex". This is significant, for in the so-called Royal or high society Witchcraft, secret knowledge was most often handed down from parent to child.

During one of her visits to Forman's house, the doctor supplied Frances with two concoctions. One of these, a present for her, was to be administered to Lord Essex who was becoming a real problem, and the other to arouse Robert Carr into keeping apace with his impetuous lover.

Soon after this exchange, in a sudden fateful twist, the doctor died. Fearing that the dead man's Lambeth home would yield up many secrets regarding Forman's necromantic dabblings, possibly implicating both Frances and the court dressmaker in the process, the pair swiftly resolved to remove any incriminating evidence from the house.

Undeterred by her near outing as a sorceress, Frances proceeded to bring a lawsuit for nullity of marriage against Essex, leaving her free to marry Robert Carr, provided the divorce from Essex was upheld. However, for all her scheming, Lady Essex had not planned on the reaction of Robert's mentor, Sir Thomas Overbury. At first Overbury had encouraged Carr's relationship with Frances on the basis that such an illicit liaison would help his own progress in high society. Being someone's beau was one thing, but full union in marriage was another altogether more legal commitment, that would potentially rob Overbury of his considerable influence over Robert, not to mention putting an end to his inside knowledge of the King's personal business.

Overbury used all the influence at his disposal to undermine the connection between Lady Essex and Robert, the soon to be Earl of Somerset, even resorting to blackmail, which proved a bad move on Overbury's part. All this succeeded in achieving was to incur Robert's anger and the unremitting wrath of Frances.

Meanwhile, Frances had begun to patronise yet another provider of potions, one Mary Woods, without quite realising that Woods was on the make for all she could get. After one visit to Frances' house, she left with an amount of cash and a diamond ring. She was arrested for theft at the behest of Lady Essex, but maintained that the money and the ring were part of a deal in exchange for poison drugs which were to be administered to Lord Essex. Owing to Essex's high position, the whole affair was covered up and Mary Woods completely disappeared from the scene.

Frances now enlisted the help of her great uncle, Lord Henry Howard, whom A. L. Rowse describes in his book *The Tower of London* as being "clever and reptilian". At Frances' request, Howard instigated his great niece's divorce proceedings, with part of the plan involving the distancing of Overbury until the divorce was completed. Since Overbury possessed evidence against Lady Essex which would annul the nullity suit, Lord Howard devised a plot to keep Overbury quiet, once and for all.

Robert Carr had prevailed upon the King to offer Overbury the choice of two postings, which Overbury promptly rebuffed at Robert's instigation. In those days, such a reaction to a proposal made by the King himself was seen as a matter of contempt, and on 26 April 1613, he found himself imprisoned in the Tower. Stage one of Lord Howard's scheme now complete, it was his grand niece's turn to drive the final nail into Overbury's coffin.

Mrs. Turner, the court dressmaker and erstwhile supplier of Frances' alchemical preparations, had found a new and far more predominant collaborator in a certain Doctor Franklin, who like his predecessor Forman was also a magician, albeit of a darker, distinctly Satanic, bent.

Frances and Mrs. Turner hatched a devious plot to poison Overbury while he languished in the Tower. Overbury's attendant and the Tower's Lieutenant were cunningly replaced with more pliable characters, leaving Overbury completely at the mercy of his foes.

The slow poisoning of Overbury began with heavily laced delicacies sent by Frances and Mrs. Turner. When Overbury first fell ill, his condition was to put down to the food in the Tower but as his health worsened, the doctor was sent for.

Lady Frances Howard had ensured that the Lieutenant of the Tower, Sir Gervase Helwes, had been properly prepared, so that when an enema containing mercury sublimate was rectally administered by the doctor, no query was raised by any of the officials in attendance. Unbeknownst to Overbury, Frances and Mrs. Turner had bribed the doctor's boy assistant to add a fatal dose of mercury to the solution. Later that night Overbury died in agony.

Job done – as far as the scheming Howards were concerned.

The marriage of Essex was annulled, leaving Frances free to marry Robert Carr. Even by the standards expected of such ceremonies within the English Court, the wedding was a lavish affair. Despite the Crown being three quarters of a million pounds in debt, King James still found the funds to foot the entire bill, even going so far as to lavish £10,000 worth of jewels upon the young bride on her happy day.

No expense was spared for the new Earl and Countess of Somerset. Frances was given away by Lord Henry Howard in the chapel and the whole occasion was a stunning success for the Howard family.

In June 1614 Lord Henry died. Although it was Frances and Mrs. Turner who were the perpetrators of Overbury's homicide, It was Lord Henry who masterminded the ensnaring of Overbury in the Tower. But the murderesses had bribed and coerced too many people for their plot to remain a secret for long. The demonic Dr. Franklin, being so taken with his part in supplying the fateful poison to Mrs. Turner, began to brag about it quite openly. While in Holland, the boy assistant to Overbury's medic recounted the full story of the deadly mercury enema to an English agent, who promptly informed the Secretary of State, Sir Ralph Winwood, himself a sworn enemy of the Howard family.

The authorities closed in. The Earl and Countess of Somerset were confined to their home in the first instance while investigators searched Mrs. Turner's premises, where they uncovered a multitude of artefacts associated with the practice of witchcraft. Wax figurines and other effigies used to influence or cause harm to individuals whom they represented, were found. While is true to say that those who use such methods of sympathetic magic believe they can equally be used for the purpose of healing, Mrs. Turner was no 'white' witch in today's sense of the word. Scrolls containing various ritual workings, along with some pieces of human skin were also discovered. When Mrs. Turner's private papers were searched through, letters from Frances were found and examined.

On the strength of this evidence of occult foul play, the Earl and Countess of Somerset were taken to the Tower and charged with murder. Frances pleaded guilty and was sentenced to death. The court observers noted that she took the sentence calmly and retired quietly from the court.

Robert pleaded not guilty and therefore had to face the Crown prosecution team in the guise of the formidable figures of the Attorney General, Edward Coke and Sir Francis Bacon, the Grand Master of the London Rosicrucians and a prominent member of the secret society network. With this pair ranged against him, there was only ever one likely outcome and so, Robert was found guilty and sentenced to be executed. Crowds gathered on Tower Hill expecting to see the sentences carried out.

In all, thirteen people were tried and the lesser conspirators were executed. But the ringleaders were inexplicably pardoned, much to the bewilderment of the Tower Hill mob.

In the case of Robert Carr, King James had no intention of letting his former favourite go to the gallows, and to this end Bacon wrote letters to King mooting alternatives.

Summing up this trial in her highly acclaimed book *The Divine King in England* Dr. Margaret Murray writes "Bacon's letters and the whole conduct of the trial show that the accusation and investigation were aimed at Somerset only". Frances was pregnant with child and female prisoners in this condition were not usually executed. Bacon wrote to the King suggesting that the Somersets should remain in the Tower, which they did for a further six years, before being released in early 1622. During their stay, they were able to reside in comparative luxury. Frances was allowed to move her bedroom furniture in, along with chairs and other soft furnishings, with three maids to wait upon her.

Several persons implicated in the matter were also involved in highly questionable occult and pharmaceutical practices. The most prominent of these was, of course, the Countess, who not only planned and perpetrated Overbury's murder, but was also a practitioner of the black arts, perhaps even a Satanist by popular definition. Yet she was allowed to get away with it all.

But perhaps some kind of karma did rebound upon her. She led a miserable life after being released, racked by ill health and finally dying of cancer while still quite young, some ten years after release from the Tower.

The White Tower also has its fair share of previous incumbents who are said to haunt the establishment. Guy Fawkes can occasionally be heard wailing vociferously. The phantom forms of Sir Walter Raleigh, Lady Jane Grey and Anne Boleynn, have all apparently been seen in the White Tower. The English poet and dramatist John Ford (1586-1640) wrote a publication called *Sir Thomas Overbury's Ghost*, to add further to the spectral list.

This prehistoric place that began life as an underground observatory situated down a 150 foot well, had become "the most perfect medieval fortress in Britain". As well as the Crown Jewels that are still housed there, the White Tower is home to a weapons museum, founded by Henry VIII.

But not far from here, there is another early underground site, one that remained hidden for 2000 years, that is until it was surprisingly unearthed just over half a century ago.

The Underground Temple

In September 1954, in the closing hours of a planned archaeological excavation by the Roman and Medieval London Excavation Council, a startling discovery was made at a Bucklesbury housing redevelopment site, that was to set in motion an unparalleled series of events that would go down into the annals of post-war London folklore.

The dig team led by Professor W. F. Grimes had unearthed a head of the Roman god Mithras. The two thousand year-old carved head was fashioned from fine grained saccharoidal marble, probably taken from Carrara in Italy, and had been deliberately buried in a shallow pit. In a strange coincidence on the very day of the find, 18th September 1954, the *Telegraph* printed a short article about the unearthed temple declaring that London was about to lose "the remains of the only Roman Temple found within its precincts". In this *Telegraph* interview, Professor Grimes said that a number relics relating to several eastern cults were reported found at the site.

The following day the *Sunday Times* published a photograph of the head stating that it was of Mithras, drawing public attention to the fact that the temple was about to disappear beneath the foundations of a modern office block. The next day was very much watershed day as bulldozers were primed to move in for site demolition.

The *Times* feared that it was too late to halt this process, so in a final attempt, they ran an article along with an editorial that pulled absolutely no punches in its phraseology, mirroring a growing public outcry. Entitled *A Temple for Destruction* it contained lines like "bulldozed out of existence" stating that the temple will be "destroyed almost before it had been seen" and that other "civilised nations would be aghast at this act of British barbarism".

These days, government departments are often quite rightly accused of being completely out of touch in ignoring similar pleas for the conservation of historically significant sites, particularly when the lure of capital investment and property development is the main driving force. But not so Churchill's administration in 1954.

Following daily front page exposure in the nationals, the government intervened and the Cabinet reached a decision to accept an offer made by the owner of the redevelopment site to transfer the remains of the Mithraic temple, known as a Mithraeum, to an open site at ground level adjoining Queen Victoria Street. This resolution seemed to please everyone, but it did not please Professor Grimes, who afterwards lamented that the reconstruction was virtually meaningless, since it was not situated on the original site. What did remain intact, however, were the various artefacts besides the Mithraic head that were uncovered at the ancient site.

Mithras was a primeval Indo-Iranian deity venerated in Persia around

2000 BC, though the deity's exact origins were, in all likelihood, connected to the earlier Indian Vedic worship of a deity named Mithra.

Later, during the Sassanian period in Persia, which spanned circa 224-651 AD, Mithras was cast in some religious quarters as the mediator between the forces of light, as represented by the Zoroastrian deity Ahura Mazda, and the forces of Darkness in the form of Ahriman. In this respect Mithras operated in the grey areas between the other two gods. In Britain his birth can be viewed in stone at Housesteads near Hexham on Hadrian's Wall. Here Mithras is seen at the centre of the twelve signs of the zodiac which encircle him.

To the Romans, Mithras was a Sun deity in the form of the unconquerable Sun god, Sol Invictus. But more diversely Mithras was also invoked with the Moon and stars along with the Sun, and his presence was said by devotees to linger from the middle of the night, through the following day until the setting Sun in the evening.

Early astrologers, astronomers and mystics considered there to be seven heavenly bodies; those which were visible to the human eye before the invention of lenses and telescopes. The seven planets (the Sun, the Moon, Mercury, Venus, Mars, Jupiter and Saturn) all play a significant role in the full Mithraic mysteries, which consisted of a graded initiatory system corresponding to the seven planets, that were performed in caves or dedicated underground temples. The London site was originally a cave by the River Walbrook which became a temple of Mithras before its removal and reconstruction in Queen Victoria Street.

There is also a Royal link here with the Tower ravens. The first degree of the Mithraic rite was known as the Corax, which means 'raven'. Acolytes admitted into this degree often wore a raven head mask and wings. Ravens were seen as the Sun's messengers and in the early times it was the Sun gods who endowed the right to the divine Kingship. Thus the raven symbolised the close affinity between God and King, which could possibly account for the great interest shown by the British Monarchy in the ravens of Tower legend. But ravens are also seen as harbingers of destruction and in the first degree of the Mithraic mysteries, the neophyte was ritually murdered by the Pater Patrum (Father Priest) in order to be spiritually reborn. This symbolic death mirrored the ancient Persian practice of 'sky burial', in which the corpses of the deceased were placed on funerary towers, to be consumed by ravens.

After being ritually reborn, the initiate would be given a mantra to repeat as part of his rebirthing process. Astrologically, the Corax degree fell under the jurisdiction of the planetary god Mercury, a statue of whom was discovered in the ruins of the London mithraeum. The statue represented the god as a figure seated upon a rock, accompanied by a ram and a tortoise.

Mercury is also symbolised in the Corax degree by the sign of the Caduceus, a magical staff surrounded by a pair of entwined serpents representing the powers of good and evil, binding and loosening, healing and poisoning. The image is often topped by wings or the horns of plenty as symbols of commercial success. Besides Hermes/Mercury, the caduceus wand is also associated with the Phoenician Baal, the Egyptian Isis, and the Babylonian Ishtar, all of whom have been represented carrying it. In her book *Man and The Sun*, Jacquetta Hawkes sums up the cult of Mithras by saying "Initiation from grade to grade was accompanied by rites that might try courage and endurance and were sometimes barbarous". The final degree, that of the Pater (Father) was ruled by Saturn. After the initiate had passed through various trials of fortitude – he was given the 'Crown of Mithras'.

In the Roman rendition, Mithras is born out of a rock and first appears holding a dagger and torch. There are analogies with Hekate here and Mithras is also shown riding a horse, armed with a bow and arrow, accompanied by a dog, lion and snake. He is hunting a stag, the horn of which is represented by a crescent or sickle moon.

Hekate is one of the leaders of the 'wild hunt', which is one of the occult's oldest legends. Statues of Hekate have also been discovered at some Mithraic temples, and indeed a statue of a goddess in the form of an exotic roundel which showed the female figure riding a horse accompanied by a hound, was discovered at the London temple site. The goddess is surrounded by Danubian riders and before them is a table or altar containing a fish. Could this mysterious iconic figurine possibly be a depiction of the dark goddess with a form of a wild hunt? Both Hekate and Mithras hold lit torches and can therefore be seen as "illuminated ones". Boundaries, crossroads, keys and serpents also feature in the symbolism of both deities.

Fish meals and sacrifice were sanctified in the rituals of all the underworld gods and Moon goddesses. The fish is also a symbol for the Babylonian deities of Tammuz and his consort Ishtar along with King Nimrod. The fish headdress of the Babylonian Dragon Priesthood later became the mitre of the Christian Bishops. Mitre is Greek for Mithra, or Mithras.

In his definitive book *The Mysteries of Mithras: The Pagan Belief That Shaped the Christian World*, Payan Nabarz PhD presents compelling evidence to support the claim made in the subtitle. To give just some examples: Mithras was born of a virgin on December 25, his followers referred to themselves as brothers, saw wine as sacrificial blood and viewed Sundays as hallowed. Nabarz believes that the adoption of facets from one religion into the other resulted "in an unhappy marriage of the worst aspects of the two", with respect to Christianity and Mithraism. Indeed, the site upon which the Vatican now stands was once a Mithraic temple.

With the ongoing spread of Christianity as the new norm, Mithraism was forced underground towards the end of the 4th Century AD and a new grade, Chryfii (hidden one) was introduced.

Thus the remnants of Mithraism became a secret society and continued to exist, in part, in this form. The London mithraeum also acquired some new religious tenants who were far from Christians or indeed followers of Mithras. Statues of a Bacchic group and a broken torso were also discovered at the site which archaeologists dated to approximately the 4th Century AD, the same time that the Mithras worship declined and went further underground. According to Nicholas de Vere, Bacchus/Dionysius was a god of the blood and death cults of the Mediterranean region, though the origins of Bacchus may well be Egyptian.

Bacchanalian rites were frenzied and often culminated with the consumption of the deity, or at least his substitute, by the initiates. It was very much a 'do what thou wilt' cult. That phrase became synonymous with a certain Aleister Crowley who spent his last years in London and Hastings and was the head of the O.T.O. (Ordo Templi Orientis) from 1922 onwards. We shall be looking at this secret fraternity in more detail later. The seventh degree of the original, pre-Crowley O.T.O. graded system is dedicated to Mithras entitled 'Mystischer Templar' or 'Grand Councillor of the Mystical Templars'. The introductory degree above Prufing (Probationer) was the 'Minerval', which implies a connection to the Roman goddess of wisdom, art and war, Minerva. A bust of Minerva was also discovered at the London Mithraic site. The largest rite in Freemasonry is the Ancient and Accepted Scottish Rite which contains 33 degrees in all, the 24th of which involves the enactment of the inner (Solar) mysteries of Bel, Mithras and Tammuz. However, London was also the venue of a more modern macabre discovery which was also linked to fraud, Freemasonry and the Vatican.

The Hanged Banker

During the early morning journey to work of the 18th June 1982, a *Daily Express* postal clerk made an unforgettably gruesome discovery. The body of a man known as 'God's banker' was hanging by the neck from a three foot length of orange rope, suspended from scaffolding beneath Blackfriars Bridge, London.

In life, the hanged man's name was Roberto Calvi and until his untimely demise he had been chairman of the Italian Banco Ambrosiano. On the last day of trading in May 1982, this Milan-based financial establishment had found itself under the scrutiny of the Bank of Italy. They had become alerted to the probability of financial irregularities of a massive nature surrounding a $1.4 billion loan by Banco Ambrosiano's subsidiaries to the

Institute for Religious Work or IOR. This was a financial institution often wrongly referred to as the 'Vatican Bank'. In actuality the IOR belongs not to the Vatican city state but to the Pope alone. Calvi's bank assisted in the formation of foreign shell companies, ten of which were in Panama, that were under the control of the Papal bank. Banco Ambrosiano then loaned these shells $1.3 billion while the Papal bank contributed monies of its own.

The shareholders of Calvi's bank began to learn of impending problems when stock began to fall. Eleven days later, the chairman Calvi fled, firstly to Austria, then England, using a fake passport, taking sanctuary in a Chelsea Cloisters apartment on 15th June.

Since 1977, Calvi had been a member of P2, Italy's most powerful Masonic lodge, which had nonetheless been dissavowed and suspended the previous year by the Grand Orient of Italy who, having been instrumental in its founding in 1966, now wanted no further involvement in its affairs.

Two days after Calvi's arrival in England, his secretary, Graziella Corrocher, who kept the outlawed P2 lodge's books and papers, fell to her death from a fourth floor window, leaving behind a dubious suicide note which read "May Calvi be cursed for the damage he had caused the bank and its employees". The following day it was the dark suited 62-year-old Calvi's corpse that marked another apparent suicide – or so everyone was led to believe.

However, rumours soon began to circulate that Calvi had been the victim of a ritualised murder involving Masonic symbolism, carried out by unknown persons who feared he was about to disclose certain secrets concerning P2's involvement with the Papal bank, Banco Ambrosiano and much more.

The noose around Calvi's neck was said to be symbolic of the 'cable tow' used in the Entered Apprentice initiation ceremony of the Craft (the first three degrees of conventional Freemasonry). The symbolic penalty for the betrayal of any of the brotherhood's secrets involves having one's tongue removed and buried at low water mark where the tide ebbs and flows, twice in twenty-four hours. Calvi's body was, of course, discovered where the tide ebbs and flows. His pockets were filled with blocks of coarse masonry which may have been placed there to ensure quick and complete strangulation, but this is also a part of Masonic symbolism too. Coarse masonry is symbolic of the tyro or Rough Ashlar representing the 'uncultivated mind', whereas the Perfect Ashlar (a smooth block or cube) personifies a man who has been 'cultivated' within the ranks of Freemasonry before he is fitted to take place in society.

In Masonic ritual the Rough Ashlar is always placed in the south, at the edge of the pavement in front of the Junior Warden. The Perfect Ashlar is also placed at the edge of the pavement before the Senior Warden. According to the ritual it should be suspended from a tripod or derrick by a rope secured to a winch. A derrick is a section of structured framework just like the scaffolding that Calvi's body was suspended from by a rope. The location of Blackfriars Bridge is the South East, SE1.

According to the author Stephen Knight the Italian logo of the P2 lodge was the figure of a Black Friar and P2 members were purported to wear black cassocks when performing their rituals. But Knight's research has proved to be a sticking point as far as Masonic historian author John J. Robinson is concerned. In his book *Born in Blood*, Robinson says that he was unable to prove that the Black Friar motif had been used in Italian Freemasonry, although there is one Italian lodge that calls itself Frati Nere (Black Brothers). One can only speculate that Knight was referring specifically to the outlawed P2 lodge in regard to the Black Friar emblem, as opposed to general Italian Freemasonry.

In London, Blackfriars was at one time the location of a friary church administrated by a Dominican Order called 'Blackfriars' due to the black habits they wore. It was this group that developed the use of pulpits, which is a motif present in the Blackfriars Bridge stonework. The bridge is situated close to the area which takes its name from the Knights Templar, "Barram Novi Templi" or Temple Bar, the point where Fleet Street joins up with the Strand, was the gate of the then new order's precincts, which reached from Aldwych up the Strand along a sizable part of Fleet Street and down to Victoria Embankment and the Thames, where they had their own wharf. The Temple itself contains their original round church plus a number of graves. Blackfriars Bridge is also situated within a mile of London's Freemasons Hall in Great Queen Street.

Strong rumours continued to circulate around the various investigative circles that Calvi's hands had been tied up behind his back, which if so, brought murder on board as the probable cause of death. But the banker's involvement with P2, an abbreviated form of the lodge's full name Propaganda Due, provided the suspicion that his death was neither accidental nor suicidal, despite a City of London inquest verdict of pronouncing the latter. A second inquest in June 1983 recorded an open verdict, though murder was still mooted as the most likely cause of death.

The leading player in the P2 set-up was its self-imposed Venerable Grand Master, Lucio Gelli. He was a fascist businessman who had fought for Franco in the Spanish civil war, and on the Eastern front for Nazi Germany in the World War II. After the war he was forced into exile and fled to Argentina, and became economic advisor to President Peron. Over a period of years, Gelli was able to build up a network of international contacts that enabled him to exercise much power and influence through his P2 lodge. Its membership was drawn from the highest echelons of society including politicians, judges and the chiefs of the armed forces.

After its disengagement from the Grand Orient of Italy, P2 became a law into itself, apparently answerable to no one – a secret society within a secret society. P2 was so expertly run by Gelli that not even its own members knew exactly who else belonged to it. P2 had branches overseas, mainly on the American continent and in Argentina where one of its members was the Argentine Naval Commander, Admiral Emilio Massera. This man was part of the military junta that instigated the invasion of the Falkland Islands in 1982, and whose ships mostly never left their docks in Argentina once the British fleet had began the campaign to successfully re-take the Islands. Gelli had been primarily involved in supplying Exocet missiles to the junta prior to the Falklands invasion through Calvi's Argentinian arm of Banco Ambosiano de America del Sud, which was based in Buenos Aires. In David Yallop's best-selling book *In God's Name*, Gelli is described as "the Puppet Master with a few thousand strings from which to select" – strings that went right to the heart of the Vatican and other places of power. For example, Gelli recruited the leading financial consultant to the Vatican, Michele Sindona, into P2, and it was he who brought in Calvi. But Sindona, who was Sicilian by birth, had many more unholy connections in the form of the Gambino family and their Sicilian cousins the Inzerillos, who were right at the heart of the Sicilian Mafia. Sindona was known as 'The Shark', and his chief talent was as a laundryman.

Another key figure in these murky matters was Archbishop Paul Marcinkus, who hailed from Cicero, Illinois – an old friend and former bodyguard of Pope John Paul II. Up until 1989, Marcinkus ran the Papal bank and was also instrumental in setting up the P2 lodge along with Gelli. But Marcinkus was no ordinary Archbishop. Despite being a major player in both the Vatican and P2, his real loyalty lay with probably the most powerful and elite secret society in the world – the Knights of Malta. This 900 year-old organisation is today said to act as an intelligence broker between the CIA and the Vatican. Marcinkus is cited by David Yallop as being behind the death of Pope John Paul I, who died suddenly and inexplicably in his sleep, supposedly of natural causes, just 30 days after his appointment in September 1978. He had begun an anti-corruption campaign and was set to launch investigations into the Vatican's links with the P2 lodge and its other associates. For P2, the liberal Pope's death could not have been more timely, enabling the Vatican's P2 collaborators to continue their activities without enquiry. The replacement, Pope John Paul II, Marcinkus' friend, chose to leave them alone, thus no further investigations proceeded. This left Calvi and Marcinkus free to provide a laundering service for currency which had come from Latin American drug cartels, who were apparently controlled by the CIA.

Marcinkus was also a director of Calvi's bank. Shortly before his death, Calvi was in the process of conducting delicate negotiations with the secretive Catholic fundamentalist organisation, Opus Dei, who had approached him with an offer to bail out the bank. This was in spite of the fact that Calvi had already lost an estimated $50 million of their money! Opus Dei was, of course, featured in Dan Brown's best selling novel *The Da Vinci Code* whose plot also involved a church-employed assassin.

Calvi was up to his neck in the financial mire and affected parties thought that he was about to spill the beans and open up the whole P2 scandal – something that would have rocked the Vatican right down to its Mithraic foundations. It could simply not afford to let that happen, neither could the powerful Knights of Malta, P2 itself or the Mafia. It was in the collective interests of all these groups that Calvi be rendered a corpse.

When Calvi's body was first spotted under Blackfriars Bridge, City of London Police concluded that it was suicide and that there was nothing to suggest an untoward demise. Twenty years on, however, Detective Superintendent Trevor Smith's review of the case found a minimum of twenty serious errors in the investigative process. Det. Supt. Smith said that the postmortem was cursory and not the type that he would have expected in such a case of suspicious death. In his opinion the suicide verdict was rushed through. Scotland Yard finally agreed to re-open the case. When Calvi's body had been returned to Italy, it suddenly disappeared and was missing for a further twenty years. Then just as mysteriously as it had previously vanished, Calvi's remains were rediscovered at Milan's Institute for Forensic Medicine. This prompted a new enquiry to be launched, which concluded that Calvi had probably been murdered prior to being strung up and hung from Blackfriars Bridge to make it look like suicide, thus finally affirming the suspicions of many.

The stage was set for a new phase in the investigation, which as it progressed, brought in five prime suspects who were eventually charged with Calvi's murder. The accused were Giuseppe "Pippo" Calo, a Mafia boss and money launderer, currently serving several life terms in jail. He was a major loser when Calvi's bank went bust and millions in laundered money went with it. The others charged with conspiring to kill Calvi were Flavio Carboni, a former P2 lodge member and business partner of Calvi with Mafia connections, his Austrian girlfriend Manuela Kleinszig, his bodyguard Silvano Vittor and finally Ernesto Diotavelli, a senior Roman underworld figure and friend of Carboni.

The trial took place in Italy but the prosecution was in trouble before the start. They were unable to extradite Kleinszig from Austria and had to acknowledge that there was insufficient evidence against her anyway. Worse was to come. The prosecution had to recommend that she be cleared of all charges, but on hearing the rest of the evidence against the other accused, the jury decided that they should all be cleared of Calvi's murder, a verdict which took the jury ten days of deliberation to reach.

The investigation and subsequent trial had cost millions and its outcome was a devastating blow for the Italian authorities, who had been working closely with the City of London Police all throughout the proceedings.

But that hadn't stopped the trial from ending in virtual farce. The original City of London inquiry had failed to link Calvi's death to Scotland Yard's investigation into the murder of Segio Vaccari, another key suspect in the murder case. Vaccari, described as a playboy and shadowy underworld figure was stabbed to death in a frenzied attack at his luxury flat in Holland Park, West London, just three months after Calvi's corpse was first discovered. His cleaner found him collapsed on a sofa having been stabbed seven times in the heart.

Vaccari was said to have been part of a three-man death squad who had lured Calvi on to a small boat on the Thames where he was strangled. Detectives believed that Vaccari was silenced because he had threatened to reveal the perpetrators of Calvi's murder.

A witness at the Calvi murder trial in Italy said that Calvi was silenced by Vaccari in order to prevent him from disclosing secrets involving the Mafia and Banco Ambrosiano's links with politicians, the Vatican and Freemasonry. Calvi's briefcase that he was carrying immediately before his death has never been found. It was believed at the time that the documents it contained amounted to 'political dynamite'. The Court at the murder trial in Italy heard that immediately following Calvi's alleged execution, one of the defendants, Carboni, who had accompanied Calvi to London, removed the papers from Calvi's briefcase before taking them to an unnamed business associate who had just landed on a private jet from Geneva, Switzerland.

Calvi had once advised that everyone should read *The Godfather* because "Then you will understand the ways of the world". In his life and quite possibly in death too, it was certainly his world.

The whole Calvi saga reads like a plot straight out of the worlds of Ian Fleming or Dan Brown, a real-life 007 meets *The Da Vinci Code*. While the evidence suggests that responsibility for Calvi's murder lay at the hands of the Mafia, it cannot be gainsaid that whoever was behind the murder knew enough about Masonic ritual and symbolism to impart that the contravening of oaths of obedience and silence will provoke the ultimate penalty upon the transgressor.

In this respect we need to consider not only the P2 fraternity but also the Knights of Malta, who have the penultimate degree in the elitist York Rite of Freemasonry named after them. Their origins date from Medieval times but they are still a major influence on the global stage. In the early 1930s, John J. Raskob, one of thirteen founding members of the American Order of the Knights of Malta hatched a coup against President Franklin D. Roosevelt which was blown by one of its own initiates, Marine Major General Smedly Butler. The Order of the Knights of Malta is also known as the Knights of St. John of Jerusalem and Knights of Rhodes. Their prime loyalty symbolically is to the Pope as the head of the Vatican State. In this guise they essentially form the military arm of the Vatican and each Knight is pledged to pursue its advocated policies both socially and politically, on penalty of death. They are sworn to total subservience to the head of the Order in a blood oath rite that is taken in grim fortitude. Their headquarters are in Rome and like the Vatican, the Knights of Malta are also acknowledged by many countries as a sovereign state in themselves. Their Priory of England was first founded in 1144 at Clerkenwell and the 16th Century a prioral palace and gatehouse known as St. John's Gate was built there. This became the headquarters of the Sovereign Order of Saint John of Jerusalem, the protestant branch of the Knights of Malta. The St. John's area in London lies less than a mile to the north of Blackfriars Bridge.

Whoever was responsible for strangling Roberto Calvi on the Thames before stringing his body up under Blackfriars Bridge knew enough about Masonic oaths and symbolism to make it appear to be some sort of ritual retribution for the imminent betrayal of secrets.

The opaque depths of the Calvi murder may never be fully penetrated, but the City of London might have yet more secrets of its own to throw up in the case of hanging banker at Blackfriars.

The Patriarchal Citadels
Mention 'The Crown' and most people will immediately think of the Monarchy in connection with such principle bodies as the 'Crown Prosecution Service'. However when the term 'The Crown' is used in connection along with anything apart from the jewels, it is not referring to the person of the monarch, or even the Royal Family, but to a committee of approximately thirteen men of significant influence, who preside over an independent sovereign state which is simply called 'The City'.

This body is headed by the Lord Mayor (not the Mayor of London) who is elected for one year (by the quasi-Masonic Livery Companies) and is usually a Freemason. As an indication of the power, symbolic and actual, vested in the Lord Mayor, it is a fact that when the incumbent monarch wishes to enter the City, they have to formally request Mayoral authority to do so, and in a symbolic gesture they must bow to the Lord Mayor, upon meeting with him at Temple Bar, the old seat of power of the Knights Templar.

This is because 'The City' is subject to neither Parliamentary nor Sovereign rule, but in acknowledgement of allegiance, the Lord Mayor hands over his ceremonial sword to the reigning sovereign at their rendezvous point. He must carry his sword of office with him when carrying out official duties, and many of the old churches within the City have special brackets for the Lord Mayor to hang his sword when he visits.

Another City body is the Crown Agents. As their name suggests, they are a Crown Agency working for the Monarch. The British Government act for them as debt guarantors which is just as well, as the Crown Agency had to be bailed out by the Bank of England during the 1970s to the cost of hundreds of millions of pounds, which was paid by the taxpayer.

In 1996 the Crown Agents were privatised and renamed 'Crown Agents for Overseas Government and Administration Ltd'. The company acts as a holding concern for a number of other companies. As Crown Agents, they previously managed the personal capital of the Sultan of Brunei for many years. In turn, the Sultan has financed numerous private endeavours for the Royal Family, along with their distant cousin, George Bush. The Sultan is believed to be a funder of unsanctioned UK and US Intelligence activities, whatever that may constitute.

The City, the Crown and the Corporation all amount to the same thing. The annual pageantry of the Lord Mayor's Show commemorates the last link to the City's medieval grandeur for all Londoners to enjoy, yet the vast majority of the people of London have no say in the election of the Lord Mayor or his Sheriffs, for that is a right reserved solely for the City Liverymen.

The Livery is one of the largest but little known institutions of the City. This powerful network comprising 108 'Companies' which employ some 23,000 liverymen, is quite unique, both in its infrastructure and history. The network of City Livery companies provides us with one of the earliest examples to be found anywhere of a Masonic guild operating as a craft, trade or profession. The oldest of the Livery Companies is the Weavers, which was founded in 1155. Originally they consisted of trade members only, but the Livery Companies often admitted members who had no connection with their specific trade. Entry to the Livery could be achieved through one of three different routes.

Firstly patrimony (a son born after his father had become a Liveryman), secondly through apprenticeship and finally through a redemption process which involved a straight payment for entitlement of entry. By the 1300s upper class gentry were being admitted as Liverymen, a policy which led to King Edward III becoming a member, following the private funding of his exploits by the Liverymen with the knowledge that they would receive no repayment of their money. Edward III was also the founder of the Order of the Garter, whose ceremonies are held in St. George's Chapel at Windsor.

Liverymen were often associated with religious and other esoteric fraternities. The established Guilds of the Livery were also became known as the 'Misteries', a word which had a double meaning here because the Italian word for trade is 'mestiere' which became corrupted into 'misterie' in English and was misspelt as such. Every year the Liverymen meet in the Guildhall, Brutus' seat of power, in order to elect two Aldermen who have both served as Sheriffs, one of whom will be appointed Lord Mayor by the Court of the Aldermen. The Liverymens' electoral gathering in the Guildhall always takes place on the same day each year, 29th September – Michaelmas day.

The cult of St. Michael was at its height in Britain during the 5th and 6th Centuries when Michael became a unifying factor in the realm of the pagan gods, taking on their role and becoming the guardian of the old mystic shrines and the magical power of the Dragon. The Guildhall also has its own guardians in the form of Gog and Magog whom we have already explored in Chapter two. The Guildhall is also the venue for the 'Silent Change', the ceremonial transfer of the sword and mace to the new Lord Mayor. This ritualised passing on of the artefacts of authority from the outgoing to the incoming Lord Mayor is always carried out in total silence, hence 'Silent Change'.

During the 1350s, after an outbreak of the Black Death, the government of the City was wrested from the various councils and handed over to City Livery Companies. The purge of the Knights Templar several years earlier had been pursued far more ferociously in France than in England, thus, from behind the scenes, the remaining Templars of London were able to retain a good deal of influence in the City's affairs, with the main focus of power apparently being held within the Mason's Guild. These Guilds adopted their own pricing, income and working conditions policies and exercised thorough management over the quality of their members' wares. Failure to meet their required standards was met with harsh punishment which was inflicted upon the offending employees. In return for operating this strict code of practice, the Guilds received monopoly powers and members became known as Liverymen on account of their distinguishing uniforms. They were ruled over by a Master and two Wardens, designations that were later adopted by Freemasonry in their lodge rituals.

The Livery Companies have a pecking order in rank headed by the Great Twelve which reads as follows:

The Worshipful Company of Mercers (General Merchants)
The Worshipful Company of Grocers
The Worshipful Company of Fishmongers
The Worshipful Company of Goldsmiths
The Worshipful Company of Merchant Taylors
The Worshipful Company of Skinners (Fur Traders)
The Worshipful Company of Haberdashers
The Worshipful Company of Salters
The Worshipful Company of Ironmongers
The Worshipful Company of Vintners (Wine Merchants)
The Worshipful Company of Clothworkers

The Merchant Taylors and the Skinners both share in the alternating positions of sixth and seventh in order of precedence, owing to a ruling made in 1484 by the Lord Mayor after a violent dispute between the two Worshipful Companies. The Mayor decreed that one Company should be in the sixth place one year and the seventh the next, a curious arrangement that is still in existence today.

The names of several well-known dignitaries may also be found within some of the Livery Companies, which are as follows:

Engineers (94): Duke of Edinburgh
Airline Pilots and Navigators Guild (81): Duke of Edinburgh, Prince Andrew
Merchant Taylors (6 or 7), Queen Mother
Glovers (62), Margaret Thatcher
Grocers (2), Sir Edward Heath
Butchers (24), Queen Mother, Lord Vestey (Lord Prior of the Order of St John of Jerusalem, the Protestant arm of the Knights of Malta)
Salters (9), Duke of Kent (Grand Master of English Freemasonry)
Clothworkers (12), Sir Peter Gadsden (a former Grand Master at the United Grand Lodge)

One of the early Grand Lodge Masters and also a Liveryman was the Duke of Wharton. He was also a member of the 'Monks of Medmenham', which is popularly, but erroneously, known as the 'Hellfire Club'. This elite club of aristocrats and politicians, which would meet to conduct semi-pagan or Satanic rituals, was led by Sir Francis Dashwood, the British Chancellor of the Exchequer at the time. The rites which allegedly included feasting, fornication and other bacchanalian delights, took place at Dashwood's Medmenham Abbey in Buckinghamshire and also in a cave complex dug especially for the purpose beneath his West Wycombe estate.

The 108 Livery Companies are divided into two sections, the 'Old' and the 'Modern' – any Company formed before 1926 falls into the former grouping. The Worshipful Company of Parish Clerks is somewhat paradoxical because it is a City Livery company with no Livery. The Parish Clerks were minor clerics in Holy Orders, and as such they have no place in order of precedence because this positional charter only applies to the Liveried Companies. Nonetheless, the Master, Wardens, Assistants and Brethren of the Parish Clerks of London and the Liberties there of the City and the Suburbs of London and the Liberties there of the City of Westminster; the borough of Southwark and the fifteen Out-Parishes adjacent, count amongst the oldest of the City companies. The later Royal Charters that were granted by Charles I, in February 1635/6 and February 1638/9 are stored in the Guildhall Library.

Another of the Livery Companies, the Goldsmiths, play host to and undertake the Trial of Pyx. This ceremony was first introduced in 1282 and involves an examination by a jury consisting purely of Freemen of the Goldsmiths Company and is presided over by the Queen's Remembrancer, a judicial post of some antiquity, who swears in the jury accordingly, following the procedures dictated by the Treasury.

The Trial involves the jury making a thorough evaluation of the gold, silver and cupronickel coins struck by the Royal Mint to ensure that they are of the correct weight, diameter and composition as decreed by law.

The Queen's Remembrancer also plays a central role in the 'Quit Rents' Ceremony, which like the Trial of the Pyx, also dates back some 800 years. This strange rite is always held in October at the Law Courts in the Strand next to Temple Bar. Here the City Solicitor demonstrates to a convened group that he cannot cut through a faggot of wood with a billhook, which he later manages to cut with an axe or sharp knife. This ritual can be dated back to when a blunt billhook and a sharp hatchet were paid as rent for holdings at the Moors, Shropshire. In modern times the City of London, in the persons of the City Solicitor and the Comptroller pays a 'quit rent' to the Queen's Remembrancer. A second quit rent is paid at the blacksmith's forge next to the Knights Templar jousting ground in the parish of St. Clement Danes. On this occasion the quit rent amounts to six horseshoes accompanied by sixty-one nails.

The City Solicitor counts the nails on a chequer cloth, which is apparently where the word 'exchequer' derives from. This also has Masonic overtones as the floor of the Freemason's Lodge is always chequered in design. The faggot of wood that the City Solicitor tries to cut with a billhook is, in fact, a rod of Druidic hazel, the same width as the Remembrancer's forefinger. Hazel is the traditional wood used to make a magician's wand, based upon the belief that if cut from the tree at sunrise using a knife which had had blood spilled upon it, the hazel wand will harness the raw solar energy which the magician will attempt to utilise. This belief dates back to pagan and Biblical times when Mercury's caduceus staff was made from hazel, as indeed were the rods of Moses and Aaron. In Roman times the rod of hazel was seen as a badge of authority.

Another ceremony rooted in biblical times is 'The Royal Maundy' which has its origin in Christ's washing of his disciples' feet the day before Good Friday. The British Royal Family took up the custom and added the issuing of money and gifts to the needy which they undertake every year on Maundy Thursday in Westminster Abbey. The Royal Family's part in the ritual began in the 12th Century when Henry I's good Queen Maud washed and kissed the feet of the poor at Westminster.

However in a dark parody of the Maundy Ceremony the Lodge brethen of the Ancient and Accepted Scottish Rite of Freemasonry don black hooded cloaks and while mournful organ music plays in the background each dark robed member takes it in turn to snuff out a burning candle, thus commemorating and dramatising the death of Jesus without ever mentioning his name, as he is not seen by them as being inspired or divine. This is the Maundy Thursday Ritual, of the Chapter of Rose Croix, when the Lodge is left in total darkness (Florida USA version).

There are more Freemasons per capita in the City of London financial sector than anywhere else in the world. The Bank of England even has its own Masonic Lodge (No. 263) as does Lloyds in the form of the Black Horse of Lombard Street Lodge (No. 4155). Lombard Street takes its name from the northern Italian region of Lombardy. This is significant because in the Lombard kingdom, an early system had been put in place that recognised the skills of the architects of the time, all of whom were drawn from the upper class.

The population of the Lombardy region was split into three distinct classes. The free men, effectively the semi-free, were protected by their feudal masters and the serfs, who were totally under the heel of their superiors. In 643 an edict was made law that allowed the Master Masons, called Magistri Comancini, (Masters of Como) to draw up their own contracts and salaries, a decree that was only accorded to the upper class free men of the town of Como. Thus the free men were grouped into a corporation similar to that of a collegium. The edict relating to the Magistri Comancini enabled these elitist professional groups to survive and prosper through having the sanction of a complete monopoly, protected by the corporation, which was to last several centuries in the Lombardy region. This was undoubtedly one of the places where the seeds that were sown would later emerge and be assimilated into Freemasonic infrastructure. In their groundbreaking book *The Dark Gods*, co-authors Anthony Roberts and Geoff Glibertson say, "In the Middle Ages, an island on Lake Como bore the headquarters of a secret, magical society of adepts, known as the Comacine Masters. They all wore black and are hailed by many Masonic historians as being among the five founding groups of a codified, esoteric Freemasonry. The Comacine Masters are dealt with in Frederick Armitage's *A Short Masonic History* (2 vols, H.Weare, 1909-11)."

Much earlier in its history, the Lombardy area had been invaded by Phoenicians who married into the existing Venetian nobility and usurped their titles for themselves, either by purchasing or simply taking them. By the late 12th Century they had become known throughout all of Europe as the 'Black Nobility', establishing a power base for a while, in Amsterdam. One of their descendants was called William of Orange. In 1688 the Prince of Orange landed on the beach at Britain in much the same area that Brutus had centuries before, prior to sailing along and up the river Dart to make eventual landfall at Totnes. As the husband of Queen Mary, the Prince of Orange had manoeuvred himself into becoming William III, King of England. He was said to have also been a student of esoteric practices, and had conducted experiments involving alchemy – interests that were shared by his personal physician, Johann Schweitzer, who also went by the name of Helvetius.

In 1694 William of Orange signed the charter for the Bank of England, thus ensuring that the City of London became a centre for world finance, a position it still holds today.

In the financial district opposite St. Paul's Cathedral there is another reminder of London's mystical links with the past, in the form of a Black Sun motif adorning a building that was initially built to house the offices of the *Financial Times*. The design appears right at the entrance to the building and consists of a Black Sun containing the face of Winston Churchill encircled by a zodiacal wheel showing the twelve signs. The origins of the symbol of the Black Sun, or 'Nigri Solis', can be traced back to the ancient Babylonian religion where there is an inscribed reference to the "Black Sun shining within us". In ancient Egypt, the designation of the hidden Sun was Mon, the secret counterpart to the Sun god, Amon Ra. The hidden sun was known to the initiates as the Black Sun, a source of esoteric illumination and power.

After the secret knowledge of the Black Sun had gone underground with the coming of Christianity, The Black Sun symbolism, or fragments of it, were used by some of the esoteric secret society groups before resurfacing in the 20th century in a perverse form, with its use by Himmler and the Nazi elite. It is worth noting that the Nazi swastika is a reversed version of the original symbol, which usually signified the Sun, that had been in use throughout many cultures for thousands of years. That the Nazi swastika was reversed could point to its hidden meaning being similar to a negative, or 'Black' Sun.

The esoteric meaning of the Black Sun stems from the teaching that there are two suns; one is etheric or invisible and made of pure philosophical gold, the other is black and visible. The Black Sun is the only one perceived by the uninitiated. But the Black Sun is not the only arcane symbol that may be related to the current city financial and business institutions. In early times there were two types of law, the Law of the Land related to people who lived on the land and their culture; and the Law of the Water. This was also the law of the high seas, a higher law that has precedence over the land, which later became Maritime Admiralty Law.

Cash 'flow', of course, alludes to the movement of water, and the 'bank' is the firm (or sliding) foundation which prevents the water from flowing out. All ships are denominated as female and the Captain of a merchant vessel has to provide a Certificate of Manifest for every item on board. When it is delivering a package, the item is shipped to you. Birth and delivery are both obviously connected with the female, or more specifically with the womb, and it was the womb of the goddess that was worshiped by the ancients. When a vessel is in port it is said to have docked or to be in *dock*, Birth and Death certificates represent the opposite ends of the wheel of life span and these have to be signed by the doc-tor.

On the 10th April 1606, King James I completed the charter for the Virginia Company. This and some additional updates established some relevant edicts. The Virginia Company had two main branches, The London Company and the New England Company in the American colonies. The Company owned most of the land that now constitutes the USA and the Caribbean Islands. The controlling members of the company were known as the 'Treasurer and Company Adventurers and Planters of the City of London' and the charters and rights of the company were to be passed to their descendants on a continuous basis.

The Criminal Courts operating on Company lands were to be administrated under Admiralty Law, the law of the sea, while the civil courts were to be governed by Common Law, the law of the land.

The official US Webster Dictionary version of the Admiralty Law reads as follows: "In the US such jurisdiction being vested in the federal district court and in England in the probate, divorce and Admiralty division of the High Court of Justice". All of which brings us back to British Admiralty Law as the overriding authority, administered from High Court in Temple Bar and controlled by the Crown. When the USA became independent, the Virginia Company merely changed its name to the United States of America. In a corporate merger with the New World Country, or rather, Corporation. The lands of the Virginia Company were originally leased to the colonies under a Deed of Trust, but ownership remained with the British Crown in the City of London. The Crown ordered that if the Native Americans refused to accept the Christian doctrine, the religion would be enforced upon them, thus the way was paved for the cultural destruction of the native population of North America. The churches were divided into denominations and they too were administered under Admiralty Law.

Originally, Admiralty Law was said in principle to have been based on the Code of Hammurabi, King of Babylon c 1792-50 BC and the first of the Amourite dynasty that would go on to become the Pharoanic Hyksos of Egypt. Hammurabi established the highest Laws of Justice in honour of his predecessors Bel/Marduk and Enki/Ea, the Serpent Cult rulers.

Many cultures have a pagan past and in Britain churches were built on old pagan sites in order that "they should be converted from the dowership of demons to the true God" as Pope Gregory told St. Augustine. This turned out to be quite a lengthy process, starting in 500 AD and lasting about 600 years. The pagan magical practices still exerted a strong influence over the worshipers. The network of sites was so constructed that each monument could be used as a centre for ritual and magic, and in this respect, the City of London was no exception.

One of the oldest churches within the City boundary is the Priory Church of St. Bartholomew 'The Great', known more simply as Great St Barts, which was founded in 1123 by the Augustinian Rahere. In 1133 Henry I granted the Prior and its Canons the right to hold St. Bartholomew's Fair.

Whilst in Italy, Rahere had had a dream of being elevated to "high place" by a winged beast and addressed by St. Bartholomew who commanded him to erect a tabernacle of the Lamb in the suburb of London at Smithfield. When Rahere came to England he requested a meeting with Henry I in order to explain his missionary vision and the King duly accorded him the land which comprised "a very small cemetery" upon which Great St. Barts was eventually built. The church's most infamous incumbent was Benjamin Franklin, who worked in the printer's office, housed in part of the Lady Chapel during 1725. Numerous City Livery Companies have close ties with the church. It was also the location for some scenes from the movie *Four Weddings and a Funeral*, starring Hugh Grant and Andie McDowell.

In Broad Street Ward in the City is the Church of All Hallows London Wall also known as All Hallows by the Wall, or near London Wall, on account of the fact that it was also built with its vestry on a bastion of the Roman city wall in the early part of the 12th Century. In 1474 a cell for reclusive anchorites and similar eccentrics was constructed next to the chancel wall that was later occupied by Simon the Anker who lived there for 20 years.

During that time he was also able to write *The Fruyte of Redempcyon* which was also published by Wynkyn de Worde in 1514.

Another City church prefixed with the title 'All Hallows' is Barking (by the Tower) in Byward Street. In 675 AD Eorconweald, the Bishop of London, inaugurated an Abbey there and endowed it with the land beneath the church. In early times it was referred to All Hallows Barking and St. Mary's.

Later excavations revealed a buried undercroft and arch, built with Roman materials, along with a sandstone cross dating from Saxon times inscribed with the word(s) "Werhere". Writing in his *London, the Biography*, Peter Ackroyd describes this as "strangely evocative of We Are Here", which conjures up all sorts of ideas as to who was originally responsible for the inscription.

Richard I built a Lady Chapel north of the church and there is a legend that his heart was buried in it.

St. Andrew Undershaft in Leadenhall St, achieved its name in the 15th Century due to an extra large maypole that was annually erected next to the church. But on the so called Evil May Day of 1517 the City apprentices rioted. One man was hanged and 300 were arrested. The maypole was then housed under the caves of properties in Shaft Alley before being reviled by the curate of St. Katharine Cree who declared it to be a "heathen idol". It was cut into segments and burnt.

John Stow, London's first historian, was buried at St. Andrew Undershaft in 1605. The Merchant Taylor's City Livery Company replaced a marble monument to him in 1905 that had been previously placed in the church by his wife 300 years before.

Every year the Lord Mayor attends a memorial service at the church and places a new quill into the hand of Stow in a ritualistic gesture to the historian. The old quill is then presented to the child winner of the best essay on London along with a copy of Stow's book. Apart from this special commemoration, the church is no longer in use for religious services.

The secrets of the City are numerous and still possess the capacity to amaze and surprise, both in their extent and nature. At its heart is the financial district that is seemingly intertwined with the secret society network and aspects of occult symbolism.

The current financial crisis can probably be attributed to the speculative malpractices of the few having such a detrimental effect on the many, with some insiders benefiting from stock market fluctuations whilst those responsible depart with sexed up pensions! But is this really all just coincidence or does something else lie concealed at the bottom of the credit crunch cesspit?

The whole scenario has echoes of a secret society or occult fraternity infrastructure with a select group in possession of secret knowledge that is deliberately witheld from the profane, on penalty of retribution upon anyone who does divulge secrets to the uninitiated.

This is somewhat similar to the plight of a financial advisor to a leading bank who advises his managers that they are overlending to speculative bodies, threatens to inform the Chief Executive, turns up for the next morning only to find that his desk has been cleared for him and he no longer has a job. This has actually recently happened, consequently more and more people are now beginning to wonder if the current crisis is being manipulated in some manner.

The secrets of the City may yet throw up more revelations of an astonishing nature. One such story involves the secret history of Parliament, which is situated in its own environs just to the West of the City and was once a Druidic Temple.

CHAPTER FOUR
The Staff and the Sickle

The Seat of Law

The Palace of Westminster, better known as the Houses of Parliament, was built, along with Westminster Abbey, on a large patch of land known as Thorney Island. Westminster Boys' school and the headquarters of MI5 also share the same eyot in the Thames, which is now indistinguishable from the shore, covered as it is with the concrete and roads of modern London. As the name suggests, this area was once overrun with briar and thorn bushes, surrounded by a network of ditches whose precise boundaries have never been fully established. This unwelcoming appendage was pinioned by the Thames and two rivulets of the River Tyburn at either side that flowed into the main river. Its northern shoreline could be forded at low tide. Perhaps unsurprisingly, a Viking charter issued in the 8th Century AD by King Offa, described it as a 'terrible place', but apparently this depiction had little to do with the brambles and more to do with holy terror. London historians of occult matters have implied that the island was once the site of a pagan temple dedicated to 'Apollo', who they claim was probably a Celtic or Gaelic god, most probably Grannus, dedicated to water cults, sun and light, in a similar vein to his Mediterranean counterpart.

However there may be an earlier, more Middle Eastern connection with Thorney Island. Thorny enclosures are particularly associated with Neith, the extremely ancient Goddess of Saia in the western delta of Egypt, the mother of all deities who is identified with Isis, Hathor and the birth of sun god. Neith is also a personification of Water, as in primeval chaos, but in her earliest incarnation she is identified by her oldest symbols of the arrow and shield. She was a hunting goddess and thus equated with Artemis, Diana and Hecate.

In Egypt, thorns of acacia are an emblem of Neith, representing the horns of the crescent moon, symbolism that is likewise associated with Hecate and which was adopted by countries of the northern Mediterranean.

Then there are the Christian connections made in Biblical verses in which the Lord appears unto Moses in the midst of a burning bush. The crown of thorns that was placed on the head of the Christ before the crucifixion was said in one tradition to be made from acacia, which had the twin purpose of both mocking and using the sacred Hebrew wood of the Tabernacle.

But it is with the Egyptian goddess Neith that the symbolism of the thorny enclosure has its oldest associations. Her festival date, along with that of primary Egyptian deity Isis, falls on the 24th of June and is commemorated at the Burning of the Lamps of Sais.

This was old midsummer when Jupiter, the old oak god, who gave his name to the month of June, was sacrificially burnt alive, or in this instance, a substitute victim would be selected for this purpose. St John the Baptist is also commemorated on the 24th June, he being largely remembered for losing his head and therefore a prime candidate for taking the central symbolic role in the Christianised version of the 'oak king' customs. Conversely, the midsummer's festival was fixed to that of the pagan solstice, falling on 22nd June, the previous day being a Druidic festival also. The oak bearing mistletoe was another important Druidic element in worship. One of the main Druid centres in London was Tothill fields, which encompasses Thorney Island, close to both Parliament and Westminster Abbey. But this was once a Druidic circle with a Druid college nearby. Here, some historians of occult religions have claimed that the Druids sacrificed to, and worshipped, the Celtic god Teutates.

Many of the Celtic deities had triple facets and there were three main gods who required offerings. Again, certain accounts, mostly Roman, recall that prisoners of war were often burnt alive in huge wicker cages as famously portrayed in the film *The Wicker Man*, in order to fulfil the requirements of Taranis, the thunder god, whilst Esus the Lord and Master preferred his victims to be strung up on a sacred tree. For Teutates however, water was the method of sacrifice in the form of sacred wells, lakes and rivers. The River Walbrook (near the Bank of England) although now under concrete and unseen to modern man has yielded at least forty-eight skulls thought to have belonged to ritually sacrificed individuals. The name Teutates is derived from the Celtic word 'teuta' which means tribe, therefore Teutates was 'god of the tribe', a god of the people.

Other derived variations of teuta become tenta, touata and tuath, from which we arrive at Tuatha De Danaan, the tribe of the serpent goddess – known variously as Dana, Danae, Danu, etc. These were a nautical branch of the ancient migrant Mediterranean Danaans who deserted their colonies in the Aegean and Asia Minor territories in order to pilot a series of ventures in northern Europe.

One of these expeditions was supposedly led by Brutus, London's semi-mythical founder. In his book *Return of the Serpents of Wisdom*, author and accomplished Grail genealogist Mark Amaru Pinkman accredits Brutus and his Danaan Trojan companions with according Britain with its original name – Albion.

In his book Pinkman says that Britain's old title 'Albion' came from the name of Albina, the eldest daughter of Prince Danaus, who led a Danaan migration to Greece from their original homeland in Panapolis, Egypt. According to classical scholar Robert Graves, Albina became the 'White' or 'Barley' Goddess, the white sow equated with Cerridwen, the goddess of the Druids. Graves tells us that the White Hill, or White Tower inside the Tower of London complex actually preserves the memory of Albina in its title. A form of the name Albina was given to the River Elbe which translates to Albina in Latin. Elbe in turn is linked to the Germanic word Elvin and Elf-woman. In Celtic countries the letter 'V' from Elvin was substituted for the softer sounding 'Ph' or 'F' thus becoming 'Elfin' and only when pluralized as 'Elves' did it return to its orginal form.

Another name for Elves is of course 'Fairie(s)' which for the most part immediately conjures up visions of the small, fleet-footed females, personified in 'fairy tales'. Yet there is far more to the 'fairie' concept than this, which involves the Albi prefix among other things.

Fairies are linked to stone circles, ancient burial mounds and prehistoric monuments. Fairie is a description of the condition of being bewitched or enchanted, and the name itself is also connected to the legends of demons and witches.

The Celts had their own fairie faith that centred on the belief in a spiritual realm inhabited by supernatural beings that had existed in the British Isles from prehistoric times.

In early Celtic society some members of the monarchy were said to harbour the fairie blood or the fate of the Grail bloodline. The Celtic Princesses were sometimes called 'Elf maidens' and their bloodstock known as the 'Elven bloodline', which emanated from the town of Albi in the Languedoc region of Southern France. This bloodline became known as the 'albi-gene' from which the French Cathar sect of Albigensians took their name, which meant 'of the Elven blood'. The Albigensian Cross, which is also the Egyptian Ankh, was used by the Inner Temple officiates of the Imperial and Royal Dragon Court, which today is presided over by the Vere Grand Masters who live in Southern England and Europe.

This particular line descended through the Tuatha de Danaan, also variously known as the Dragon Kings of Anu and the Egyptian Cult of the Dragon. Its adherents claim that this is a continuation of a very ancient bloodline that became part of the pre-church British Elven institution.

The main influx of the Danaan emigration was focused upon Ireland during the 15th Century BC when the Danaan leaders were accompanied by three Arch-Druids and two Arch-Druidessess.

The links between the Danaans and the Druids were summed up in the words of one Irish manuscript which stated,

"All who are adepts in Druidical and magical arts are the descendants of the Tuatha de Danaan". This being the case it is well worth mentioning here that in the book *Gods of the Celts*, by leading Celtic authority Miranda Green, she states that Teutates, who it is said was worshipped by the Druidic circle in Tothill fields on Thorney Island, actually refers to a description of a tribe rather than a godhead figure. Teutates or Tuath then could be an anglicised form of the Tuatha de Danaan.

According to some sources these people of the serpent goddess who eventually became the Druids in Britain and Ireland had their origins in the Middle East, Turkey to be precise. We know that there were Danaan colonies at Panopolis, Egypt and Byblos in Phoenicia. Another author Michael Mott notes an interesting clue, in his work *Caverns, Cauldrons and Concealed Creatures*. Mott observes the likeness between the word 'Tuatha' and the Egyptian 'Tuat' meaning 'underworld gateway', through which the Pharaohs were said to pass on their journey to the next life.

The genetic origin of the Tuatha de Danaan is said by some writers to lead to the tribe of Dan from the Old Testament, seizing on both the fact that Dan is phonetically similar to Danaan, and that Dan is described as a 'serpent' in the Bible. Most tantalising of all the theories perhaps, and certainly the earliest reference to the origins of the Tuatha de Danaan, is that they were said to have developed the practices of Tantra in old Sumeria. Here they were known as the legendary 'Tuatha d'Anu (tribe of Anu) or in Gaelic lands, 'daouine sidhe' meaning people of powers. The Sanskrit word 'siddhe' means the same thing, describing the type of mystical powers that advanced yogis and fakirs are said to possess.

The daoine sidhe were of the Dragon/Elven line and wielders of the serpent power. It was they who branched off from the ancient Babylonian community and went north, re-inventing themselves in the process as Scythians, whom we have already discussed in earlier chapters. The Tuatha de Danaan, then, were the Dragon Kings of Anu and the legendary Babylonian 'Great Father of the Sky and Earth', also known as 'The Lord of the Rings'. A Dragon in the tribal sense was an Overlord/Archdruid of blood descent from the Eleven/ Dragon bloodline. One etymology of Druid is 'Druidhe' meaning 'Kings above Kings'. This is best illustrated in a passage from the *Texts of the Tain*, an ancient Irish work, which reads 'The men of Ulster must not speak before the King, the King must not speak before his Druid'.

In Britain and Ireland the Druids became the real power behind the throne, in a consultancy capacity. The Druid colleges such as the one found at Thorney Island in London generally prevailed over everything else in the ancient community. Here, the Druid elders would both educate and indoctrinate the future tribal kings of Britain and Ireland. These Druid colleges were said to be held in capital cities or similar places of importance. The fact that there was also a Druid Circle located on the Westminster/ Parliament site, marks the location as a ritual centre of some significance in the early community.

There were seven main functions of the Druids according to Gerald Waite who wrote *Ritual and Religion in Iron Age Britain*. The two most important functions were religious doctrine and civil justice or law making. If this is so, then Thorney Island and Tothill Fields were obviously a location where some of the first laws were made and religious rites enacted, echoing the function of the place today, since Parliament is a place of law-making and Westminster Abbey one of the most important places of worship in the country – where indeed Kings and Queens are crowned.

Order of the Serpent

Another area of London boasting a Druidic history is Parliament Hill, which can be accessed via the road of the same name that runs alongside Hampstead Heath mainline railway station.

Parliament Hill also has its own marker stone, which proclaims the long-given right of free speech. It was also, so the story goes, on Parliament Hill that Dick Whittington heard the sound of Bow Bells calling him back to London. In actuality, Whittington was a Liveryman, being a member of the Mercers Guild. This Guild is the leading Livery in order of rank and precedence.

During Druidic times, Parliament Hill was also known as Landrin (Lake City), one of many names from which London could be derived (See Appendix). Areas of land surrounded or bordered by water were important to the Druids because such locations were thought to be hosted by powerful energies and spirits. Ley hunters insist that such power centres form part of an energy grid, since they are situated on ley lines such as the one that connects Parliament Hill, Penton Reservoir and the White Tower (See Appendix).

If we take into account that the largest of London's lost rivers, the Fleet, once rose by two heads on Hampstead Heath, each separated by Parliament Hill, we can see why the Druids felt that this was an important location for them. The Fleet was known as the 'River of Wells'. Today you can trace the railway cut at Farringdon, passing the Clerks Well, Sadlers' Wells and others, all the way up to Angel in Islington. In the other direction, going towards the Thames, the Fleet runs close to St Andrew's Church, Holborn, before joining the Thames at a point that was once called the London Fen. This is the area called Temple, once owned by the Knights Templar. The other side of the Fleet/Thames conjunction is where legendary Brutus was said to have created the first city of London.

In fact looking at a map showing London's lost rivers, one is struck by the number of extinct waterways, appearing like offshoots from a vein that once flowed in the Thames artery. Names remain: Tyburn, Fleet and Walbrook as mentioned before, the Lea, Peck, Neckinger, Westbourne, and the Celtic sounding Effra in South London, and several others beside.

The Druids assembled in their enclosures upon these old London sites but were well aware of the potential psychic power that could be harnessed in these places. In order to unlock, unleash and utilise such perceived energy it is perhaps not surprising that the Druids did not commit their ritual methods to writing. Instead, the commitment was accomplished by memory alone. This was a process that took near to twenty years to master and complete.

Such systematic vetting and evaluation was quite severe in practice. Candidates for admittance into the Druidic orders had to show their bloodline genealogy before acceptance was granted. Incidentally this system of entrée is also used by the powerful Knights of Malta, whose would-be neophytes have to be able to trace their bloodline ancestry back 300 years before they are allowed into the Order. It is noteworthy that the Knights of Malta were once known as the Knights of Rhodes, on account of their occupation of that island. Interestingly, so too did the Telchines, a branch of the Danaan.

In Britain, the Druidic neophyte's advancement through the mystery school induction involved the mastery of three basic degrees: Bard, Ovate and finally, Druid. In the first degree a new acolyte would don a green robe (the colour attributed to learning) for the purposes of instruction into the ways of Druidism. One of these functions involved the special role of 'diviner', in which the Ovate admitting would learn the interpretation of auguries and omens. For example, such an interpretation would be formed by bones being thrown in the air, with a meaning drawn from their position upon landing. Similar methods are used by shamen in Africa. The Ovate would be expected to become aware of, and be able to harness, the subtle energies about him, for healing and other purposes.

Bards were storytellers, poets and musicians. In an age where storytelling was very important and ritualised part of community life, Bards carried important elements of tradition with them such as the secrets of the Ogham tree alphabet. Finally, after many years of study a candidate would be elevated to Druid status, in order to study philosophy, astronomy, mathematics and all the secrets of nature, or mastery of the serpent powers. The origin of the name Druid is hotly disputed among etymologists but the Priesthood sometimes called themselves 'Naddredd, Gaelic for 'sorcerer' or 'serpent'. Thus the serpent power practitioners of the British Dragon culture were therefore called Naddredd or Adders, the higher ranking initiates of the Druid Order became known as the Druid Adders and these members still had to embrace a further seven degrees of adepthood to master before they become an Arch Druid, the supreme rank of Druidry. After they had ascended to each degree, the initiates were given a different coloured sash to tie around their white gowns of Druidic office, along with a 'Gleniniau Naddredd', which is more commonly called the 'Serpents Egg'. This symbol, made from a blue-green glass bead set in gold, was hung round their necks by a leather thong. The cosmic serpent's egg was symbolic of the most powerful of the Druid Adders who would display seven serpents on their chest to signify their elevated rank.

There were correlations with other cults, notably Mithraism, which (as explored earlier) also had seven degrees of initiation. Seven was the magical number that governed ceremonies and occult mysteries, linking alchemy and astrology into a greater oneness.

Another significant number is thirteen, which we shall explore in greater detail in the next chapter.

The early Druidic group comprised of thirteen people, as did the later witches' coven, giving rise to much discussion amongst occult historians about possible links between the two cults. The proposition that both the Druids and Witches were sustaining a secret tradition that was much older than that of the Celtic civilisation is commented upon by Rosicrucian author Lewis Spence, when he writes

"Although we do not hear a great deal about it in British history, there is no doubt that Witchcraft, as a more or less secret cult, persisted in Britain throughout the ages, but I do not believe it to be part of Druidism or the Secret Tradition. Rather it was a debased remnant of the still older Iberian magic which to some extent Druidism embraced, but which it also superseded and perhaps tried to weed out."

The Druids also embraced the ancient name for Britain, Albion, which later became the Lodge name of the Ancient Order of Druids, a modern organisation that is said to be steeped in original Druid tradition.

On the 15th August 1908, the Albion Lodge held a rather special investiture at Blenheim Palace, Oxfordshire. The newly appointed President of the Board of Trade, a certain Winston Churchill hosted his own inauguration into the Druidic Albion Lodge at Blenheim.

The Druid revivalists have also coined the Alba/Albi prefix when naming the equinoxes and solstices. The Winter Solstice is called Alban Arthurian, meaning light of Arthur, Summer Solstice – Alban Herwin or Hefan, Spring Equinox Alban Eiler and Autumn Equinox Alban Elved – whether this is really based on ancient tradition or not is a moot point.

Bile's Gate, the Sanctified Thames and Boudicca's Mound

One of the most important festivals within the old pagan calendar, or 'Wheel of the Year' is the fire-festival, Beltane. Etymologists generally agree that the word takes its name from Celtic meaning 'bright fire', or 'shining one'. Beltane also takes its name from a Celtic version of the Middle Eastern Baal/Marduk and Latinised Belinus or Bel, who was known as the 'Bright One' – a god of light and fire. Although not strictly a Sun deity, Bel does have some solar attributes.

In Freemasonry, Baal or Belo is represented by the 'Blazing' or 'Eastern' star, symbolised by the inverted pentagram, an emblem of the Dog Star Sirius. This version of the pentagram is distinguished by the head of the 'Goat of Mendes' or 'Baphomet' that it contains, which the Knights Templar were accused of venerating when they were first arrested in France on Friday October 13th 1307, signalling a purge at the behest of the Pope and the French King, which spread into other countries, including England.

For the supposed beneficiaries of the Templar knowledge, the Freemasons, the Blazing Star is said to be central to all Masonic undertaking, since Sirius is the first star to rise in the east in the Egyptian latitudes.

In Europe, there are many places named after Bel or Bile. London, for example, has Bile's Gate or Billingsgate, one-time site of the famous fish market. Here the skulls of the deceased were taken through the entrance of the gated city, probably dedicated to Belinus 'the Brilliant', for him, or his Celtic equivalent Bile, to transport via the Thames to the otherworld, although there are other etymologies for this site. The authors offer another etymology later on much closer to the Brutus history.

The early Celts also venerated the cult of the head, as did the Templars. Freemasonic ritual also places significant symbolic importance on the human skull.

The river Thames has a significant part to play in esoteric and ritual matters. In England, the Druids' venerated rivers that flowed from west to east, as the Thames does, which makes the Thorney Island and Tothill Fields sites of still greater mystical relevance.

Tothill Fields was the venue of the ancient 'Troy Game', that originated circa 600 AD, conducted between knights on horseback every Sunday during Lent. Its origins are obscure but it is supposed to have been played by the Romans and its name strongly suggests a connection with Brutus. There are allusions to the Troy Game in Virgil who describes the customs of the Trojans and the martial nature of the proceedings. To quote Sir Thomas Mallory "So it befell in the month of May, Queen Guinevere called upon her Knights of the Table Round; and she gave them warning that early upon the morrow she would ride on Maying into the woods and fields beside

Westminster. And I warn you that there be none of you but that he be well-horsed and ye be clothed in green, either in silk, outher in cloth, and I shall bring with me ten ladies and every Knight shall have a lady behind him…"

This Troy Game obviously served to enliven the leisure time of the elite, nonetheless it did have a slightly more serious and mystical aspect to it.

On Tothill Fields, in the identification with the original Knights of the Round Table and by the enactment of the Troy Game, the Trojan remnants of London's early history can clearly be felt.

It was to the Thames that Brutus came, accompanied by his entourage of Danaans, Druids and other Trojan exiles, in order to found Troia Nova (New Troy). On Thames at Little Wittenham, an altar to Jupiter, 'Optimus Maximus', the Roman sky-god, was found, but the Trojan cultural link was still evident in other fields along the Thames. For example, beneath the site of Billingsgate, an excavation uncovered a Greek rhyton (a vessel often used to pour libations) dating from the 2nd Century BC, along with a miniature water pitcher from the 6th Century BC.

A little upriver from the bridge at Staines, the Thames watermen conducted their own ritual in the form of a rite of endowment, enacted around an alternative version of the 'London Stone' that is still referred to by the same name today. This stone was erected in 1280 as a City of London marker. Here the watermen would conduct a ritual procession around the stone, bumping or knocking into any sheriffs or aldermen from the Livery or Masons' Guilds who happened to be present. This was in reverence of the Thames equable character, displayed by the watermen in the ceremony.

The practice of magicians and diviners to gather by the Thames bank is carried on, albeit in tradition more than intent. The Thames was used for prophecy, with the churning river playing its part in the rituals undertaken. If a Thames fisherman happened to catch a monkfish it was promptly nailed to the boat's mast as a talisman, in the belief it would ward off bad luck. There was also a superstition amongst the watermen that someone in the Priesthood should never be permitted to board their craft. In eulogy to King Herring the fish's skeleton was returned to the river after consumption of the flesh.

If anyone ought to be accorded the title 'Magus of the Thames' it should be Dr John Dee, the Elizabethan sage, Rosicrucian Grand Master and personal astrologer to Queen Elizabeth I. Dee was on of the most accomplished men of his era, being a proto-scientist, alchemist, mathematician, Kabbalist, astronomer as well as astrologer, navigator and occultist. An expert on ciphers, he acted as a spy for the English crown, taking the moniker '007', representative of the hand shielding the eyes. Centuries later, the author Ian Fleming, himself no stranger to the occult, took Dee's spy name and gave it to his own fictional spy creation, James Bond.

Dee, probably the greatest mind of the English Renaissance period also coined the term 'British Empire' and was instrumental in staking British, over Spanish, claim to Canada and the Americas.

Dee's residence at Mortlake, London, housed both his laboratory and the most substantial personal library in England at the time. It was here at his house on the banks of the Thames that Dee first had his visions of the spirit Uriel.

With respect to Dee's learned recommendations that Britain had legitimate right to claim Canada and the North Americas, he cited a rare piece of research very much on the lines of what we have ascertained above, namely that Brutus' forebears had married in to King Arthur's retinue via a Welsh character named Madog ab Owain Gwynedd, who supposedly discovered the Americas some three centuries before Columbus. Recent books on Rosslyn's famous Templar chapel (built Pre-Columbus) have confirmed that carvings found inside the church represent plants that could only have come from the Americas, such as maize, although officially they were not discovered and introduced to Britain at that time. Although this solid incontestable proof exists in stone, conventional historians remain unable to offer any explanation whatsoever as to why these exist. Dee obviously knew of these secret alternative histories. He associated with a group of initiates close to him whilst at the Royal Court; this group were at one time called 'The School of the Night' which included a member of the De Vere family – Edward. Again this confirms the very subtle but pervasive Elven influence that extended across time from Brutus to Elizabethan England with the inclusion of prominent Royal stewards being chosen from the Elven/Dragon lineage. We shall return to Dr Dee in some detail later, when discussing the Windsor Royal Covens.

The river Thames' important role in the rituals of London's inhabitants has seen it being used as a repository for sacred artefacts for many thousands of years. The flint and animal bones that have been discovered in the river point to practice of considerable antiquity.

At around the time of Brutus' fabled arrival on British shores, local inhabitants constructed a primitive bridge across the river, in the area now known as Vauxhall. This may have acted as a pathway to enable votive offerings to be made while invoking gods over the water. Various Iron Age artefacts have been found at Brentford and Battersea, along fairly short stretches of the Thames. For example, at a Battersea site, cauldrons, axes, and an iron scabbard containing the image of two dragons were found. Another scabbard, also featuring a dragon figure, was discovered further to the west of the Thames at Hammersmith. At London Bridge an Apollo figurine minus its legs was found, as were a lamp with the head of a ram and a human mask at a site in Greenwich.

To the east of Blackfriars Bridge, many insignia made from pewter were discovered, including the wheel of St Catherine, identified with Proserpine, Persephone and Kore, as Queen of the Shades, ruler of the souls of the dead and one of the wheel goddesses of the underworld.

Weapons that appear to have been ritually chipped have also been found in the Thames, as indeed have numerous 'witch bottles'. These rather curious objects appear to have become popular during the 1500s. These bottles typically contain assortments of diminutive artefacts, including half-burnt coals, nails and pieces of torn cloth. The witch bottle or 'bellamine' was a protective spell that was created to ward off malevolent witchcraft and they have been found in the Thames at St Paul's Pier Wharf, Stepney, Westminster, Chiswick, Gravesend and Lambeth. This practice of using witch-bottles was at its height during the 16th and 17th Centuries as citizens tried to protect themselves from Witchcraft by placing the charms within the foundations of buildings.

Nonetheless, it is heads, or rather, skulls, that are found in great abundance in the Thames. At London Bridge they were placed in the river over a lengthy period spanning many hundreds of years. During Medieval times London Bridge was the only man-made crossing point – it seems the custom of displaying the heads of criminals and traitors on spikes, as a warning to the city's inhabitants that the same fate might befall them should they turn to crime, continued the practice to some degree.

The head of the legendary giant, Bran, was transported down the Thames to its final resting place at Tower Hill, as a talisman against future invasion.

The Roman Belinus is cast as the skull's transporter. The archaeologist, psychic researcher and dowser T.C. Lethbridge has some interesting views on Belinus. Lethbridge asserted that the gods Belinus, Lucifer, Apollo and Gog are all closely related.

He says that Gog and Magog are British deities representative of male and female energies. Gog, he believes, was a rendition of Ogmios, another 'bright one', a Celtic version of Hercules who invented the sacred Ogham alphabet of the Druids. Ogmios also had Sun god attributes.

The Ogham alphabet contained 20 letters in all, each one being known by the name of a different tree, in line with Druidic concepts. The letters were generally carved into wood or stone but Druids could, rather amusingly, communicate the letters by stroking their noses in certain ways as well. Later, under Roman influence, Ogham became structured on Latin. The Ogham alphabet was particularly important when the Druids began to write down some of the knowledge that they had successfully passed down the centuries from generation to generation, in a purely oral form.

Lethbridge advanced a theory that that Magog was actually a moon goddess, a view supported by Lewis Spence who equates Magog with Ceridwen – the Druidic goddess.

In ancient times the British Druids were held in reverence, with Gaulish admittants coming to these shores for advanced instruction in developing their Druidic knowledge and abilities, with Belinus, the cult of the head and the Thames each having a role in this. Gruesome finds made last century seemingly support the view that the Druids used human sacrifices in their rites. As mentioned earlier, forty-eight human skulls, all of young adult males, were found at Walbrook, not far from the site of Mithraic temple.

All of these heads appear to have had their flesh removed prior to being cast into the flowing river, thus bearing the hallmarks of some sort of ritual demise. A further ten skulls were found in the river Lea, one of the former Thames tributaries which runs between Hackney and West Ham, spilling into the Thames at the Leamouth.

One theory about the Walbrook heads posits that they were the unfortunate vestiges of Boudicca's last stand, said by some to have been fought in London. Verifiable historical details of this event are deficient by some degree, including the exact location of the battle. In his book, *Boudicea*, Lewis Spence (using the Latinised name for Boudicca) offers King's Cross as the most likely site, an opinion based on strategic considerations. He gives the exact location as the area once called Battle Bridge, now marked appropriately by Battle Bridge Road, which lies between King's Cross and St Pancras stations.

The specific whereabouts of the pagan Queen's tomb has remained a mystery for centuries, with several suggestions from different historians. Of particular interest is the site upon which now stands platform 10 of King's Cross station. However, situated nearby and to the northwest of King's Cross is Parliament Hill, upon which lies an ancient embankment known as 'Boadicea's Mound', that was found to be empty on excavation. It is believed by others that Boudicca's body was cremated, but again evidence to support this remains scant. Parliament Hill was said to be the location for Boudicca's last encampment with her army, prior to hurtling down to Battle Bridge, now King's Cross, to face her Roman opponents. This alleged battle took place in August 61 AD, where, in an enclosed area of land, her chariots could not jockey for position as they needed to do in order to be fully effective against the Romans. According to some sources it was this last bloodcurdling charge down the hill to Battle Bridge that cost the lives of some 90,000 participants in the epic battle that ensued.

The Roman historian Dion Cassisus (150-235 AD) recounts Boudicca, Queen and Druidess as wearing a 'great twisted golden necklace', when she rode into battle. This amulet had tremendous mystical importance because it was said that Boudicca had worn it as part of a ritual to invoke the terrible goddess Andraste, after having unshackled the sacred hare, prior to her last battle. Boudicca was believed by many to be a Priestess of Andraste, the British goddess of war whose name means victory, not unlike Boudicca's own, which means triumph.

But Boudicca and her army were totally annihilated, apparently deserted by her talismanic goddess. Boudicca retreated finally, in order to administer poison to herself, which had been specially prepared for her in the event of defeat at the hands of the Romans who she despised. The poison was made by her Chief Druid – Synwedydd.

Modern Druid Ross Nichols, Chief of the Order of Bards, Ovates and Druids said of Boudicca "she fought for her old right of a matrilineal succession against the usurping and tyrannous Romans."

Thus Boudicca, Queen of the Iceni was seen as an ancient feminist trailblazer. Such was the ferocity of Boudicca's campaign against the Romans that Emperor Nero even considered withdrawing from the island altogether. Since that time, many people have seized on Boudicca's image for various reasons: romantic, political and nationalistic, but it remains clear that she is very firmly woven into the elements of Druidism. It is believed by some scholars that by aligning herself to these aspects she was able to gather such a massive army of followers over which she exerted unbending control. But Boudicca was neither the first nor the last royal figure to be aware of the powers of the occult.

CHAPTER FIVE
London's Lost Symbol

The Group of Thirteen

The word 'coven' is popularly associated with gatherings of witches, but as a collective term, it actually has much broader connotations. The word first appeared in the English language in the early 1300s as a name for a group of thirteen persons, with a designated leader, who are bound by oath to a specific objective.

In its religious form, the group of thirteen would consist of twelve people, or disciples, chosen by a Master or 'God Incarnate' to whom their loyalty was betrothed. Again this does not necessarily mean witch covens as we have previously mentioned, the number thirteen was also used in conjunction with the Druidic covens of the first millennia BC.

In her book *The Divine King of England*, Dr Margaret Murray refers to what she terms the 'Royal covens' which she says consisted of the King and his councillors, the former being regarded as the Master or God Incarnate. According to Dr Murray, Royal coven members could also become High Priests of covens containing personnel of a less substantial rank, who in turn could also be leaders themselves of different covens of a lesser standing, each declining in the pecking order, right down to the level of the rural village coven.

Dr Murray further comments "Such a system gave the King, as Grandmaster of all covens, immense political stature and power, as long as all the members of the Royal coven were loyal; but it gave equal power to any ambitious member who was not true to his oath."

It should also be stressed that the number thirteen is not a matter of completion in itself, but more of a group comprising one and twelve, as far as the formation of the coven was concerned.

London historian John Stow comments on a secular grant of land made during the reign of King Edgar 959-979 AD; he says "Edgar some time King of England granted unto thirteen knights a portion of ground without walles of the City of London, left void in the East part of the same city, together with a gilde which he named Knighten Gilde, that is now Portsoken Ward". Port Soken Street currently sits north of Tower Hill.

On the 1st August 1129, King Henry I held a great council of clergy at

London, which comprised thirteen in number, with himself as its head, followed by two Archbishops and ten Bishops. The exact purpose of this royally instigated conclave was for the King to persuade the Bishops to award him sole authority concerning the forbidding of "priests to have concubines", but then for him to receive "large sums of money from the Priests for licence to live as before" according to Henry of Huntingdon.

Dr Murray claims it is no accident that our ancient cathedrals should also exhibit the number thirteen. She says "even here the essence of the pagan number is preserved and each coven of Bishoprics with their respective cathedrals shows the pagan formation of one and twelve, the Archbishopric set over twelve Bishoprics".

She also points out that there were thirteen cathedrals that formed the so-called Old Foundation and these were served by the secular clergy and not affected by the reformation of Henry VIII. The list of cathedrals includes London in the Old Foundation.

In 1318 the Barons had become deeply unnerved over Edwards II's continued acquiescence to the plans of the Despencers, Hugh le Despencer, Earl of Winchester along with his son Hugh the younger. The Barons held a meeting and together, they decided that the country should be run by a ruling council comprising twelve members under the King acting as chief, making thirteen in all. But Edward was having none of it and quickly gathered together his forces to range against Roger de Mortimer, the 8th Baron of Wigmore and 1st Earl of March.

Mortimer was forced into capitulation and duly sent to the Tower, from where he escaped two years later, fleeing to France. The collaborators were rounded up. Stow declared "There were taken in the field Thomas, Earle of Lancaster with Lords, Knights and other to the number of sixty-five" Sir Andrew Herkeley sentenced nineteen of the captives to death and imprisonment for seventy-two, forming a grand total of ninety-one in all.

As Dr Murray readily emphasises, the numbers of sixty-five and ninety-one are mentioned in both separate accounts, these are of course, she tells us, multiples of thirteen.

The final council held in Edward's reign shows the coven committee in its complete formation – in this instance, three Bishops, three Earls, two Abbots, two Barons, two Justices and a Speaker of Parliament, Sir Walter Trussell. This group of thirteen was the parliamentary committee which had been consigned to command and collect the King's official statement of abdication.

From here it was all downhill as Edward's fortunes took a macabre turn for the worse. His chief adversary Roger de Mortimer had been at large in France and by 1326, Mortimer had become lover to Edward's Queen,

Isabella, who was the daughter of Philip IV, the French King. Mortimer and the Queen crossed the English Channel and made a challenge for the throne of England. Edward soon found himself without adequate forces to defend London from Mortimer and Isabella. Edward then went on the run. He was finally captured at Neath on 16th November 1326. Four days later he handed over the Great Seal of Kingship to the coven committee of thirteen. Edward was now at the mercy of Mortimer and the Queen who showed him none whatsoever. They placed him in the custody of Sir Thomas Gurney and Sir John Maltravers, who were apparently induced by Isabella to treat Edward with as much severity as they could muster. However, this ill treatment did not cause his death, therefore a more lethal method had to be devised, which was to be executed in secrecy. Edward was moved about from one location to another in order that his followers would be confused as to his whereabouts and therefore thwarted from mounting a rescue attempt.

Finally Edward was taken to Berkeley Castle under custodianship of Lord Thomas Berkeley who was answerable to Queen Isabella. The facts surrounding the King's demise are unclear but one tale of his death relates the following curious account. Edward II was afflicted by haemorrhoids, a condition not entirely unrelated to his own sexual proclivities. A visitor in the semblance of a Cunning Man arrived at the castle, claiming to have a wonderful cure for the King's painful ailment. Edward was persuaded to lie on a bed on his stomach, while a specially lubricated bull's horn was inserted into his rectum. Into the bull's horn was poured a specially prepared elixir containing pain reliving properties, or so the King was assured. But the poor Edward had failed to reckon with the malicious hand of Isabella, as the Cunning Man quickly convened with his collaborators, who thrust another mattress on top of the King pinning him down. The remaining henchman brought a white-hot iron which was administered into the horn that by now had penetrated well into the lower bowel area of the King.

According to Dr Murray the significance of 'bowelling' forms part of the ritual salying of the 'Divine sacrificial victim', as it emphasises the power of fertility. The intestines and genitals of said victims were usually burnt in a dark memory of the ancient rite of incinerating the Divine Victim, followed by the scattering of their ashes.

If Dr Murray's suspicions are correct, Edward's cruel murder at the behest of Queen Isabella (who was known as the She-Wolf in France) bore all the hallmarks of a particular type of ritual killing that had been practised since Norman times. Many of today's Witches believe that the famous New Forest coven to which Gerald Gardner is said to have belonged may have survived since Norman times and been responsible for the death of King Rufus in a ritual killing. It may be that Queen Isabella was very likely a sorceress, as

Edward was not too unsympathetic towards the Old religion.

In 1324 an influential Anglo-Irish aristocrat by the name of Dame Alice Kyteler found herself at the centre of Ireland's first major witch trial. Found guilty of Witchcraft, heresy and sacrificing to demons, Dame Alice managed to escape her accusers and together with her daughter, she fled to England. Her maid Petronella was not so lucky and was burned at the stake, refusing right to the end to receive Christian rites and conversion.

Dame Alice arrived in London and placed herself under the protection of Edward II who subsequently decreed that all charges against her be dropped. Resident in Edward's household at one time was a Spanish Kabbalist of high standing called Raymond Lully (1235-1315/16 AD) Lully was also known as 'Dr Illuminatus', the first mention of the term 'Illuminati' in connection with the occult.

As for the number thirteen and its uses in royal and ecclesiastical circles, one of its last surviving functions is still evident in the legal system – at the heart of trial by jury, being twelve members of the jury, overseen and directed by a Judge on behalf of the Crown.

This number turns up again and again – a prime example of the coven of thirteen was evident at the coronation of Richard III, the shortest reigning monarch in English history. When the new King rode in procession along the streets of London to Westminster, he was accompanied by a group of knights and noblemen. Thirteen of these, headed by his own son, followed immediately behind him, their names documented accordingly:-

Edward, Prince of Wales
The Duke of Norfolk
The Duke of Buckingham
The Duke of Suffolk
The Earl of Northumberland
The Earl of Arundel
The Earl of Kent
The Earl of Surrey
The Earl of Wiltshire
The Earl of Huntingdon
The Earl of Nottingham
The Earl of Warwick
The Earl of Lincoln

Behind this procession there followed a substantial company consisting of Lords and Knights. These were also named in the royal records, but the first thirteen or Royal Coven were recorded separately. According to Dr Murray, the Plantagenets, the Tudors and the Stuarts all maintained the coven grouping in their assemblies and committees.

On an even more esoteric note, there were originally said to have been thirteen astrological signs, as opposed to the twelve in common use by astrologers today and this may well have an unexpected link – with the City of London.

The Secret Sign of the Dragon

This particular story begins in France and involves the surfacing of secret documents that once belonged to the fabled Prieure du Notre Dame du Sion, or the Prieure de Sion – a secret society that was central to the investigations as revealed in the bestseller *The Holy Blood and The Holy Grail*, by Michael Baigent, Richard Leigh and Henry Lincoln. However, the precise nature of all the documents were not disclosed, such were the complexities they contained.

These papers formed a privately published work called *Le Serpent Rouge* (The Red Serpent) which has a strange, mystifying and extremely controversial history.

At 7am on the morning of March 6th 1967, the body of a certain Louis St Maxent was found hanged. Just two hours later, the corpse of one Gaston De Koker was also discovered hanged. The following day, March 7th, saw the body of Pierre Fegre, also hanged, this time at 6.20am.

All three of the deceased individuals were jointly named as co-authors of *Le Serpent Rouge* (which had been deposited at the National Library). The deposit slip read February 15th 1967, but this was found to have been forged in order to mask the real date of the deposit, March 20th 1967, some thirteen days after the deaths of the alleged authors.

But then the tale begins to get even more curious, as apparently the three co-authors weren't actually the authors at all. Seemingly their names were deliberately used as substitutes in order to cover up the real identity of the bona fide author or authors.

What was so special about the contents of *Le Serpent Rouge* that someone felt that they had to go to such extraordinary lengths in order to conceal their provenance? At least one documentary maker has suggested that the documents were an elaborate hoax perpetrated by a Frenchman named Pierre Plantard. Others are convinced they are genuine, particularly as they display knowledge of genuine esoteric enigmas known to few people outside of secret societies.

Le Serpent Rouge discloses bloodline genealogies of the Merovingians, two maps of France showing the early Merovingian period along with a ground plan of St Sulpice, the Roman Catholic centre for occult studies located in Paris, which was once the site of burial for the Merovingian kings, and where a temple dedicated to Isis once stood.

Perhaps the most significant section of *Le Serpent Rouge* was thirteen page document comprised of poetic pieces related to each of the signs of the zodiac – but with a difference – one additional sign of the zodiac was included, Ophiuchus, sometimes referred to as Serpentarius, which is sandwiched between Scorpio and Sagittarius.

Some astrologers, along with historians of esoterica and the occult, now believe that there were originally thirteen signs that formed the ancient zodiac. Ophiuchus is measured when the sun enters the constellation, which is in the second half of Scorpio, generally speaking. It is known as the 13th sign, the hidden House of the Dragon. As we have pointed out in Chapter two, the City of London's motif is the dragon, or flying serpent, and the point at which the City meets the Temple is marked by a pair of reptilian beasts bearing the red cross on a white background of the Knights Templar. This is Temple Bar where the Lord Mayor of London meets the Monarch and where the latter must ask permission to enter the City precincts. Here the British Monarch is subordinate to the Crown Temple – a committee of approximately 12-14 men including the Lord Mayor, who is almost always a Freemason and serves the Crown Committee for one year. It is worth reiterating that the Crown Temple run the City as an independent state which has its own police force which is not answerable to either the reigning Monarch, nor the rule of Parliament.

Besides its City of London connection – the inclusion of the dragon, or winged serpent, as the thirteenth astrological sign can also be calculated on the basis of the Moon phase cycles. The twelve traditional astrological signs are of course Sun signs. The traditional Sun sign astrology is calculated by the sun entering each constellation. There being 360 degrees in the zodiacal wheel, 360 divided by 30 degrees gives rise to twelve – the twelve signs of the zodiac. These twelve Sun signs also correspond with the twelve calendar months of the year, along with their duration of 28-31 days, though the astrological signs begin in the latter part of the calendar month. On the other hand, if we take the number of weeks in a year, 52 and divide these by the duration of a complete Moon cycle, four, we arrive at the number 13. There are therefore 13 Lunar months in a year – with each Lunar month being 28 days in length. The system being described in the Prieure de Sion documents is therefore a completely alternative astrological system, as it uses Moon phases instead of the Sun's position, as in the more conventional variants. This carefully guarded secret astrology, the preserve of secret societies, is based upon the female menstrual cycle of the Goddess which, of course, is pivotal to Lunar worship and Witchcraft in general.

Le Serpent Rouge contains several references to the Goddess in the form of Isis, also referred to as the 'Queen' (of heaven) who became identified with the Biblical 'Magdalene'. In the House of the Dragon/Serpent, for example, which falls at No.11 in their system, the text begins, 'Cursing the profaners in their ashes and those who live in their tracks, leaving the Abyss where I was plunged in finishing the gesture of horror: Here is proof that I knew the secret of the Seal of Solomon, that of this Queen I have visited the hidden residences'.

The angel of the Abyss is Abbaddon, the sacred word of the Masonic 'Knight of the East and West', which is the 17th degree in the Ancient and Accepted Scottish Rite of Freemasonry. The ritual ceremony of the degree reveals that the name Abaddon originated in Palestine and was brought to the West by the Knights, eleven of whom were bound by oaths of secrecy undertaken by a special council.

The designation of Isis as Queen can be traced back to Nimrod's consort Queen Semiranmis, and probably before that to the Dragon Queens of Ancient Babylon. Yet, the most profound revelation contained within this section of prose is the writer's claim to know the secret Seal of Solomon. This is the six-pointed star, or so-called 'Star of David', formed by interlocking two equilateral triangles, which appears on the current Israeli flag. Yet this is not a symbol representing Judaism, but of the extreme politico-religious movement of Zionism and others of a more occult nature. The hexagram appears on the national emblem against the express wishes of many Jews, who claim it is against traditional values, even the Holy Torah itself. The first Israeli Parliament and the foundation of the state of Israel itself was funded by the Rothschild dynasty, whose family crest was adopted by the nation into the bargain – it is of course, the Seal of Solomon.

This symbol can be found across the globe, in the ruins of ancient temples and cathedrals alike. In its old Phoenician/Canaan aspect it represents Saturn – the god whose name gives us Saturday. He also has many names and guises – Chronos, Baal, Molech, Rex Mundi and the actual figure of King Nimrod of Babylon, who was celebrated during the festival of Saturnalia in the run up to what we now celebrate as Christmas (Dec 17-23 in ancient Rome). In one period during its existence, Rome was even referred to as 'the City of Saturn'.

Yet, Saturn has chiefly one designation – as King or Lord of the World, and in this respect his most important alias is El, the supreme father of many gods. It is from this word El that we get the modern words such as: elite, elected, elevated and elemental. The colour associated with Saturn is black, along with the symbol of the square, which is features heavily in Masonic symbolism. When a university student graduates they wear the square black 'mortar board' and black gown, to indicate that they have joined the scholarly elite. Similarly, Court officials wear black Saturnine robes of office, as of course, do Priests. Saturn also has legal aspects, as it measures and restricts individuals to enforce laws. The Judge, also robed in black, sits at the 'bench' which is Old High German word for bank, while the prisoner or defendant appears in the dock – both vestiges of the ancient Admiralty Law – the law of the sea – the higher law.

Some of the most prominent symbols within the higher echelons of the Western Establishment have their roots in the ancient emblematic links with Saturn. Saturn, being closely associated with the classical element of Earth, is the God of banking. The name of Saturn is associated with the half goat, half man 'Satyrs', who inhabited Arcadia in Greek mythology. The ancient Middle Eastern picture of the Biblical character of Cain is said to be the same sort of hybrid human. This is hardly surprising as Cain was said to have come from the loins of Saturn, under one of his many guises, Enki/Samael, probably on account of both being considered deities or lords of the earthly world. Enki is an ancient Sumerian deity, while the name Samael refers to his role as Serpent/Dragon.

According to Sir Laurence Gardner in *Genesis of the Grail Kings* and De Vere's *The Dragon Legacy*, Cain was the product of an experiment between Enki/Samael and his daughter Eve. Upon reaching adulthood, it is said that Cain was mated with Lilith Luluva, the pure bloodline daughter of Lilith the Beautiful, Dragon Queen of the Anunnaki, from whom the legend of Lilith is said to have sprung.

There are Eastern parallels with the name Cain and that of 'Khan', meaning King. This could be on account of Cain's father Saturn's designation as King of the World. Returning to the Bible, tantalising clues exist concerning Cain and his descendents.

The writer Ignatius Donnelly says "The race of Cain lived and multiplied far away from the land of Seth, in other words, far way from the land destroyed by the Deluge." He continues "The Bible does not tell us that the race of Cain perished in the Deluge...Cain went from the presence of Jehovah: he did not call on his name. The people that were destroyed were the sons of Jehova who died in the flood, not the race of Cain, as had been stipulated by the Hebrew chroniclers, the descendents of Adam, or so they would claim."

According to De Vere, Cain was first rightful human King who carried the divine Royal blood of his father, Enki/Samael or Saturn – the King of the World. In the Jewish legends Cain and his descendents lived in a place called 'Arka', a subterranean world from which the Greek Arcadia is derived. In her seminal work on the Grail legends entitled *The Merovingian Mythos, and the Mystery of Rennes Le Chateau,* Tracey. R. Twyman postulates that Cain and his people could have actually lived in the so called Holy Mountain, the Cave of Treasures or New World in order to see out the flood. This has some resonance with the passage in the Bible about Cain being away from the presence of God perhaps? Twyman's definitive study further suggests that one legend depicts the Grail as being a stone within a mountain. She claims besides Cain his father Saturn would also be buried there. Twyman also maintains that the six-pointed star – the Seal of Solomon – represents the mountain, with the upwards pointing triangle denoting the mountain, or tower of Babel, and the inverted triangle denoting the direction downwards into the mountain leading to the Centre of the Earth and the Grail stone. Twyman advances that an alchemical sigil consisting of a six-pointed star with an inner sun at its hub, supports the mountain/Seal of Solomon link. It is an obscure theory based on many years of research. Returning to the Saturn/Cain bloodline we can now generally recap on the above to state that the bloodline descended along the following lines throughout history: through Babylon via King Nimrod to the Egyptian Pharaonic Hyksos and then into the Davidic line of Israel, before branching off into both the Tuatha de Danaan and Trojan bloodstock. Later, this link would encompass the Houses of the Merovingian Kings mentioned in the Rennes Le Château mystery, Angevin and the Plantagenets, including the House of Tudor. This brings the bloodline very close historically to our own times and its meandering course leads enticingly, once more, towards modern London.

Besides Saturn the hexagram/Seal of Solomon is also a symbol of Molech and Astoreth. The symbol is sometimes referred to as the Star of David but is anything but, and never did have anything to do with David, but was used by his son Solomon who is said to have had star altars dedicated to Astoreth and Saturn. This last connection with Saturn is important to both Mithraism and Druidism which are of substantial significance to early London. The Saturnine and Cain influence are both linked with the number 13. As we have established, there are 13 lunar cycles in a solar year, because the moon moves itself a geometric distance of 13 degrees every day across the sky. There exists a calendar which does actually reflect this system. It is known as the 'Fixed Lunar Calendar' which comprises 13 months, accounting to the precise number of days calculated – which in this instance is 364, but it has never been used in the major countries of the world, probably on account of the fact that it does not reflect the number of days in an average year, which is, of course, numbered at 365. Nevertheless the 364 day Lunar Calendar has been covertly observed by the secret societies, most notably the Prieure de Sion, the Knights Templar and the Essenes, whose usage is based on the Book of Enoch (Enoch, the great-grandfather of Noah), in which the angels foretell of the coming Deluge and instruct Enoch to count the days in the year which amount to 364.

The number 13 is also connected to the Knights Templar. By 1126 there were 13 of them, but their membership, rather than being formed in 1118, looks like having been in existence as early as 1111, the year when they were actually founded by the Ordre de Sion, at least according to the Prieure de Sion documents.

The Templars are mostly associated with the number 13 through their persecution at the hands of French King Philippe the Fair, who issued secret sealed instructions to his wardens to be opened at first light on the morning of Friday 13th October 1307. He decreed that all Templars were to be seized immediately along with their assets, held incommunicado and prosecuted, all except those in residence in Bezu and Rennes Le Chateau, the closest to the Ordre de Sion, who were obviously in some position that rendered them beyond the hand of the French Inquisition. Some contend that this special privilege was granted because they possessed special knowledge that protected them in some way.

What was this secret intelligence? Could it have had anything to do with the contents of the *Le Serpent Rouge* and the bizarre cover-up conducted by the supposed author using the names of the apparent suicide victims in 1967? The link here is the involvement of the Ordre/Prieure de Sion. Detractors have laid claims, as mentioned earlier, that Pierre Plantard conducted this as a joke and much has been made by the author Dan Brown about the Rennes le Chateau link with the survival of Jesus and his apparent bloodline, but could there be an altogether different explanation – another level of mystery?

Perhaps the most telling clue came in the discovery and interpretation of one famous Baphomet head that the accused Templars allegedly worshiped. This was unearthed during a raid on a the Templar preceptory in Paris in the form of a silver gilded female head, inside which were two skull bones wrapped in a white linen cloth, surrounded by another cloth, coloured red. Also attached to the package was a label which said simply "Caput (head) 58M". The latter part of the caption is the most intriguing as numerologically the numbers five and eight add up to a total 13 whilst the letter M being the 13th letter of the alphabet is written in the form of M, the astrological sign for Virgo. But why was this head female?

The Egyptian Virgin Birth
The astrological sign of Virgo is symbolically linked to both the Biblical figure of Mary Magdalene and the ancient Egyptian goddess Isis. Isis gave birth to her son, the god Horus, on 25th December, despite being a virgin herself. Horus was said to have performed miracles, been in possession of

special esoteric and spiritual knowledge, had a group of twelve followers, making 13 in all, and to have died and been resurrected over a three day period. If all of this is beginning to sound strangely familiar, it is probably because the Horus legend, which predates that of Jesus by many centuries, was appropriated by early Jewish scribes who made use of legends originating from Egypt, Sumeria and elsewhere, in their own compilations. This view on the true origins of Jewish and Christian myth is now supported by several leading Egyptologists and other alternative historians. There is also much astrological symbolism involved in this particular belief system. The 12 disciples or followers represent the 12 astrological signs in the conventional system with the godhead figure as the Sun or 13th heavenly body. This is also based on the Sun's lowest trajectory in the northern hemisphere which occurs on 22nd December when the Sun effectively 'dies' for a three day period before being resurrected or born again on 25th December each year.

This astro-religious combination emphasises the Sun god adulation, whereas the 28 day system uses the lunar cycles with Ophiuchus – the Serpent Holder as the thirteenth component in the lunar astrocalendar system. Ophiuchus is also identified with the son of Apollo – Asclepius – a healer in Greek myth. Every reader will be familiar with the magical staff with the serpent coiled around it, used almost universally as a symbol for medical organisations and is currently the emblem of the World Health Organisation. This staff and serpent belong to the legend of Asclepius.

The staff of Asclepius metamorphosed into both the Caduceus of the Roman god Mercury and the rod of the Greek Hermes – these deities are closely linked to the Egyptian Thoth – god of magic, language, writing, geometry, science and medicine. This magical staff is said to represent both positive and negative energies personified by the twin serpents that encircle the staff in the Caduceus version.

On a more stellar note, later Rosicrucians during the Renaissance period believed that an exploding supernova which occurred in the Serpentarius (Ophiuchus) constellation during 1604 heralded the coming of a new age. They interpreted the appearance of new stars in Serpentarius and Cygnus constellations symbolically, and thought the representative Serpent and Swan as being 'a portent of some convulsive change in the order of the world'.

The legend of Ophiuchus helped to create the Ophites, a secret Gnostic sect which was founded in Syria and spread to Egypt and other countries in the ancient Mediterranean. Ophite is Greek for serpent.

The Ophites traced their ancestry to ancient Sumeria and the figure of Seth (Sat-naal) the Guardian of the Holy Mountain, the descendents of the legendary Annunaki Gods of Sumeria. Pivotal to the Ophite belief system was their conviction that Sophia, personified as Goddess of Wisdom, was the Serpent Goddess, the Black Mistress. But the Ophites were not the only secret sect to adopt Sophia. According to Dr Hugh Schonfield, one of the decoders of the Dead Sea Scrolls, if one translates the Templar word 'Baphomet' into Hebrew and apply the Hebrew 'Atbash' cipher, it immediately converts into Sophia. Summarising his report Dr Schonfield comments "There would seem to be little doubt that the beautiful woman's head of the Templars represents Sophia in her female and Isis aspect."

Writing in her book *Sophia, Goddess of Wisdom* Caitlin Matthews says, "This school of dark night spirituality is found in most traditions that venerate the Black Goddess, not because she is sinister or evil but because she is the power-house from whence our spirituality is fuelled. It is a way of unknowing, of darkness and uncertainty. Yet the experience which is obtained by this path is one of illumination, when the sun shines at midnight. This is the kindling of Sophia, who is the transcendent pole of the Black Goddess, though finding the connection between the two sometimes takes a long time because of our dualistic conditioning."

But the Templars apparently wasted no time in making such a link, keeping this heretical knowledge to themselves while operating under the veneer of Christianity. Caitlin Matthews also observes that "the dragon energy of the Black Goddess recurs in the myth of St George and the Dragon. This story is often taken to mean the overthrow of both the earth and of women, but its subtext is more subtle than that. The dragon of the Black Goddess is transformed into the maiden Sophia..." The author also identifies this process with the Grail Cycle.

In summary what this leaves us with is the apparent dualistic veneration of Baphomet by the Templars. On the one hand the Dark Goddess in the form of Sophia, the serpent or Dragon Queen, and on the other, the bearded male figure that alternate Templars conceded was their relic of adoration. This figurine also has a place in the mystical Kabbala and is identified as 'Chokmah', also meaning wisdom.

However Ophiuchus is also cast as a bearded figure with even closer connections to the Dragon/Serpent symbolism.

The Christianised version of Isis/Sophia is the Magdalene. M is the thirteenth letter of the alphabet, then in addition there are the two 5+8 numerical markings also found on the unearthed Templar relic referred to earlier in this chapter. Dragons, Templars and the No.13 all come together in London.

The astrological House of the Dragon known as the 13th sign helps to reveal the inner meaning of the talismanic Dragon – London's obscure logo that entwines the serpent power of Isis/Sophia representing the feminine lunar cycle, with that of Ophiuchus, as the male counterpart.

The result amounts to complete power, whether it be on an occult basis, economic, political, or as an independent state operating discretely within the Sceptred Isle. The dragon is symbolic of this, both in power and protection, thus enabling and overseeing the City of London, so that all its affairs continue to function, with a little help from the daimons of the City – the lost symbols of London. ·

CHAPTER SIX
The Windsor Royal Coven

The Order of the Dragon Nobles
There are also links between occult symbolism, the dragon symbolism and the number thirteen in the founding and continuation down the centuries of the Most Noble Order of the Garter.

This story begins at a royal ball. Legend has it that Edward III was dancing with a Countess when her garter accidentally fell to the floor, leaving her in a state of confusion and shock. The King immediately recovered the dropped garter and while fastening it to his own leg, he uttered the phrase, "Honi soit qui mal y pense" meaning "Shame on him who thinks evil of it".

In her formative work *The God of the Witches*, Dr Margaret Murray writes "The confusion of the Countess was not from shock to her modesty – it took more than a dropped garter to shock a lady of the 14th Century – but the possession of that garter proved she was not only a member of the Old Religion but that she held the highest place in it. She was therefore in imminent danger from the Church which had already started on its career of persecution. The King's quickness and presence of mind in donning the garter might have saved the immediate situation, but the action does not explain his words nor the foundation of the commemorative Order".

In her *ABC of Witchcraft*, prominent English witch Doreen Valiente elaborated further on the subject of the King's reasoning. She says, "This incident gave him the idea to found the Order of the Garter, with twelve knights for the King and twelve for his son, The Black Prince, making two thirteens, or twenty-six knights in all. The number thirteen was given further significance by the King's regalia as Chief of the Order. His mantle was ornamented with figures of 168 garters, which with the actual garter on his leg, made 169 or 13 times 13".

Of the actual founding incident, Valiente writes, "The above incident of court life seems a very trivial one for this noble order to have been founded upon, unless it had some inner significance. But if the garter that the lady had dropped was a witch-garter then the whole episode assumes quite a different aspect".

De Vere explains further, "The Garter was a small buckled belt, worn by women around the top of the left thigh or just below the left knee on men.

Apart from being a menstrual badge and a semantic symbol of the womb and the Grail it was also a representation of the serpent eating its own tail". In other words the Garter was the alchemical symbol of the Oroborous serpent, which by devouring itself, becomes a Dragon.

De Vere tells us that the Garter was the 'witches belt', the Devils badge, a dynastic emblem of a race that had descended from Lillith and Cain. The Garter in its true guise, as an alchemical Oroborous serpent, is a still a symbolic part of the venerable Angevin Imperial and Royal Dragon Court of today. This is the line that went on to to produce the Plantagenet Kings of England and Royal Stewarts of Scotland. A salient historical novel called *The King is a Witch*, by Evelyn Eaton, is based upon the Platagenets' links to the Old Religion, with especial emphasis placed on Edward III. The French author, Jules Lemoine also singled out the significance of the Garter when worn by a female witch, as the director of the secret brotherhood. She wears the Garter as a mark of her dignity, and in reference to her high position within the coven. It was the fallen garter incident that inspired the King to first create the Order of the Garter, which he founded circa 1348 as a society, fellowship and college of knights. Twenty-six in all were appointed (two covens of thirteen) at the Order's inception, which was held at St George's Chapel in Windsor Castle.

According to researcher Stephen Brindle, the original beams of the great circular Round Table that had been at the formation of the Edward II ideal, based on the Arthurian legends, were still set in the castle fabric today. This was featured in the BBC television series *Britain's Best Buildings*, in an episode about Windsor Castle. The programme disclosed that St George's Chapel contained an intricate arrangement of circular geometrical configurations that delineate the construction of the building itself. All this originates from a single circle drawn inside the centre of St George's Chapel which depicts the image of the Vesica Piscis, the symbol of the Virgin. The BBC broadcast concluded that the whole building was created as a monument to the Virgin Mary, or more specifically, her genitalia. The programme went on to quote a contemporary account which says that the Order of the Garter "took its beginning from the female sex". Some intriguing graffiti was also unearthed inside St George's Chapel, in a section of the nave, believed to have been inscribed by the mason who built it. Portions of the grafitti were illegible, but what could be seen, read "made me for thy secret"; 'thy' is a direct reference to the Virgin Mary and 'secret' means here, 'The Order of the Garter'.

However, the signs of this cult of the female sexual orifice can be traced back further than the image of Christ and the Virgin Mary – to the pagan Goddess and the Old Religion. In his book *History of White Magic*, Gareth

Knight cites an example – "Feasts such as Purification of the Blessed Virgin Mary or Festival of Lights in February and the Physical Assumption of the Blessed Virgin Mary in August, go back to the Mysteries of Isis and coincide with major Pagan festivals". One only has to observe some churches and castles in Ireland, Scotland and a few rare examples in England too; in order to see 'Shelagh-na-nig' (folkloric wife of St Patrick) who is often depicted above doorways, with her legs splayed wide open, sometimes appearing with the most graphic depictions of the vulva and labia.

In his book *Occult Conspiracy* Michael Howard reveals a link between the Order of the Garter and the Rosicrucians. He says that "many famous men who were either Rosicrucians or Masons have over the centuries been knighted as members of the Order of the Garter, a privilege which can only be granted as a personal gift of the reigning Monarch." Edward III also had links with a band of knights who had been initiated into the Templar mysteries while in the Middle East. When they returned to England they inaugurated a Lodge and practised esoteric and occult rites within its sanctuary. De Vere comments "The Windsor Royal coven and many others, reputedly old hereditary family groups were the custodians of traditions which had, by their own admission, little or nothing in common with the modern Neopagan revivalist movement or its reconstructed rituals". In other words De Vere is describing an elitist form of witchcraft that claims to have, and be based on, a hereditary bloodline which is very different to the modern reinvented or reconstituted witchcraft founded by Gerald Gardner in the 40s and 50s.

According to De Vere, the Most Noble Order of the Garter is Britain's premier Order of Knighthood, having apparently been generated by the ancient Caledonian Dragon Court. The definition 'Knight' derives from the Saxon word 'cnecht', which means 'servant' or 'to serve someone or a group'. In its real guise, the Order of the Garter is an Angevin, Elvin bloodline institution, which remained alive in the form of the Plantagenet Kings who are, of course, descended from the Angevin dynasty.

Upon the death of Richard III, the last of the of the Plantagenets, the Sovereign inheritance of the Order of the Garter passed onto the House of Anjou and its descendants, or at least it should have, according to De Vere. He maintains that the modern Windsors had no hereditary right to the Order and therefore "no right to confer it on anyone else". De Vere cites the two examples of Margaret Thatcher and Emperor Hirohito of Japan as being totally unworthy recipients, according to the Order's true function as preserver of a distinct Royal bloodline.

At the other end of the spectrum are De Vere's lateral ancestors, the Earls of Oxford, five of whom were Order of the Garter admittants, the last of these being Aubrey de Vere in 1660, the 20th Earl, who was also the last Earl to be a Privy Council member.

As members of the Privy Council, the Earls were close confidantes to Royalty including the Stewarts and Plantagenets. One of the earlier Earls to be inducted into the Order of the Garter was the 11th Earl, Richard De Vere, who at the same time as being inaugurated into the Prince's Degree of the Order of the Garter also received a degree of Societas Draconis (Prince's Mulusine's Dragon Court).

This was the European reconstituted version of the old Egyptian Dragon Court undertaken by Sigismund in 1397 before being formalised by him in 1408. Sigismund was the son of the House of Luxembourg – a dynastic family that diversified their own geneaology in order to lay claim to the bloodline of Melusine and Anjou, the source of the Plantagenet Kings of England.

It seemed however that Sigismund von Luxembourg, King of Hungary, to accord him his full title, was a descendent of the Lusignan Dragon Kings of Jerusalem. Whatever the precise truth of Sigismund's lineage, both he and Earl Richard De Vere were both admitted into the Prince Degree of the Order of the Garter at St George's Chapel, Windsor in 1415. It could therefore be argued that the act of being ritually admitted into the Order of the Garter had cemented the two differing bloodlines present in the Order of the Dragon.

Nicholas De Vere goes on to comment, "The contemporary Dragon Court is furthermore a combination of what Aleister Crowley would term several 'currents', of which the major external one to the family proper was bestowed via the Black Country Covenant of the Baphometic Order of the Cubic Stone, who trace their origins back to the Knights Templars. This was given in recognition of my family's hereditary involvement in Royal witchcraft and the historical Dragon tradition. Other external currents derive from the Knighthood of the Plantagenet Clan Donnachaid, Dragon cousins to the House of Vere, and laterally from Dr John Dee's 'School of the Night', of which Edward de Vere, 17th Earl of Oxford was a prominent member."

For his part Sigismund, who had been crowned Holy Roman Emperor in 1411, decided to expand his 'current' or strand of the Dragon Order in 1431. A number of influential European nobles from a political and military background were initiated into Sigismund's version of the ancient Order of the Dragon. Of particular interest here was the inclusion of one Vlad II Dracul who was father of Vlad Tepes.

Vlad II was nicknamed Dracul, which means Devil or Dragon, while his son Vlad Tepes signed himself as 'Draculya' – 'the Devil's son', which later became 'Dracula' roughly translating as 'the son of him who had the Order of the Dragon' But it was the sister of Dracula who had some interesting

Royal descendants: Mary of Teck, Queen Mary mother of King George VI and grandmother to the current reigning monarch of the UK, HRH Queen Elizabeth II. And it is the reigning monarch, Queen Elizabeth II who is current head of the Order of the Garter. The royal ceremonial investitures into the Order usually take place in June which also has some significant connotations with the old pagan worship.

The Babylonian Dragon King Tammuz is honoured on June 23rd. The following day is the official midsummer's day or St John the Baptist's Day, when it is customary to ignite midsummer bonfires on high places to coincide with the Sun's highest point in its yearly cycle. The Solar King, Tammuz, who is also associated with Green Man worship, is seen by many as the earliest protype for St George. The venue of the Order of the Garter inductions is, as we have mentioned, St George's Chapel, with the Knights being admitted into the order at the June ceremony walking down St George's Hall into the Garter Chapel. When the Order of the Garter was first established in 1348 by the Plantagenet King Edward III, along with his son Edward, the Black Prince, it was originally known as the Order of St George. The complete ceremony originally lasted three days with the sovereign and knights meeting on the first for talks in a special room that was guarded by the Black Rod (an officer but not a Knight of the Order).

In true Masonic fashion, Garter Knights swear an oath to both befriend and defend one another, whatever the situation, for their entire lives. In other words, this elite brotherhood's first loyalty was to one another, to be co-bedfellows in adversity and conciliation. They are Queen Elizabeth's most trusted 'Privy Council'. MI6 agent John Coleman described the Order as the inner sanctum, the elite of the elite of Her Majesty's Most Venerable Order of St John of Jerusalem". The latter are the Protestant arm of the Knights of Malta.

Committee of 300

"Only 300 men, each of whom knows all others, govern the fate of Europe. They select their successors from their own entourage. These men have the means in their hands of putting an end to the form of State which they find unreasonable". This quote in the Weiner Press was taken from an article published in 1921. It was written by Walter Rathenau, the financial advisor to the Rothschilds.

In his book *The Conspirators' Hierarchy: The Committee of 300* (Second Edition), Dr John Coleman examines the links between this shadowy elite group and the Order of the Garter. Coleman claims that the information he provides in his work is both "factual, precise and backed up by impeccable intelligence sources". Some though have called into question his intelligence sources. Coleman counters these suggestions by saying "…do not fall into the trap set by the enemy that this material is disinformation". Coleman, a former intelligence analyst and political scientific officer says,

"The Committee of 300 has a major bureaucracy at its disposal made up of hundreds of thinktanks, and front organisations that run the whole gamut of private business and Government leaders [...] The Committee of 300, although in existence for more than 150 years, [...] was always given to issuing orders through other fronts, such as the Royal Institute for International Affairs. When it was decided that a super body would control European affairs, the RIIA was founded through the Tavistock Institute, which in turn created NATO. Dr Coleman goes on to classify the Committee of 300 as "the ultimate secret society made up of an untouchable ruling class, which includes the Queen of England, the Queen of the Netherlands, the Queen of Denmark and the royal families of Europe. These aristocrats decided, upon the death of Queen Victoria, that in order to gain world-wide control it would be necessary for its aristocratic members to 'go into business' with non-aristocratic, but extremely powerful leaders of corporate business on a global scale". Stalin referred to the secret global elite as "Dark Forces", a phrase recently used by the Queen herself, if we accept the word of Paul Burrell, one time Royal Butler to Princess Diana. Other world leaders have openly acknowledged such an elite at large in the world, with US President Eisenhower speaking of this secret cabal as "the military-industrial complex", while heads of world governments simply describe them as 'the Magicians'. Was there an occult connection involved here? Most people view the ceremony of the Order of the Garter with its somewhat peculiar pageantry as a quaint, if not harmless eccentricity undertaken by the Royals. Yet, it is the Order of the Garter which heads and controls the Committee of 300, Coleman maintains, although not every Knight of the Garter sits on the Committee of 300.

One only has to consider the enrolment of Japan's Emperor Hirohito into the Order of the Garter, a move that almost certainly spared him from execution as a war criminal, to realise the hidden power of the Order. Queen Elizabeth always kept a close bond with the late Hirohito and latterly his family. All European Royal Houses are said to have seats of the Committee of 300, also known as 'the Olympians'. Other Garter Knights included Earl Mountbatten of Burma.

The public are not admitted to the Garter ceremony, which takes place behind closed doors after the would-be knight is summoned to the special throne room at Windsor by the Garter King and Black Rod. Only the Sovereign along with a high ranking Church dignitary can be present during the induction when the ritual swearing of the oath takes place. The wording supposedly reads "You being chosen to be of the Honourable Company of the Most Noble Order of the Garter, shall promise and swear, by the Holy Evangelists, by you here touched, that wittingly or willingly you shall not break any Statutes of the said Order, or any article in them contained (except in such from which you have received a Dispensation from The Sovereign), the same being agreeable, and not repugnant to the Laws of Almighty God, and the laws of this realm …so God help you, and his Holy Word." The central symbol of the Order of the Garter is a form of the Merovingian cross, which is surrounded by the Garter, appearing as roundel. The design is laid down over the centre of an eight-pointed silver star to create the Garter Star. Since just before World War I, the Sovereign of the Order has worn this symbol on his left shoulder of the Garter Mantle or cloak. This is the same manner as the habit of the Templars, who wore a red eight-pointed cross on the shoulder of their white garments. Representations showing the garter sigil of the Cross of St George have played a central role in the City of London's exploits since the 1300s.

For some, the original Garter Knights were merely a reconstitution of the Knights Templar some thirty-five years after their official demise. Unofficially, the Order had continued to exist, albeit in a different guise that enabled them, or remnants of that Order, to become more influential in England and Scotland, with the monarch adopting their new mantle of leadership by founding the Order of the Garter. Perhaps it is no coincidence that the Garter Knights bore the canopy that protected Queen Elizabeth II at her coronation in 1953.

According to Dr Coleman, both Queen Elizabeth II and Prince Charles are descendants of Godfroi de Bouillon through Henry the Black of the Guelph line (Venetian Nobility). It was de Bouillon who originally founded the Prieure de Sion (then the Order of Sion) which some say was one with the Knights Templar before dividing into two separate, but nonetheless linked, Orders.

The Order of the Garter operates under a Christian veneer by conducting its rituals inside St George's Chapel. There are 24 Companion Knights and their respective leaders, thus making a grand total of 26 (2x13) in all. Originally the Order of the Garter was to have embraced 13 Priest Clergy. The Order's collar comprises of 256 (2x13) red roses. The Order of the Garter is also known as the 'Foundation', as it creates an inner sanctum of chiefs who ensure that certain agendas are carried out, whatever they may entail. The Order also holds sway over the College of Heraldry. This college comprises of 13 heralds itself whilst the Order of the Garter has global control over the aristocratic heraldry.

In conclusion the Order of the Garter is certainly connected to the Knights Templar if only by virtue of influence, but probably much more than that, as the Garter itself is seemingly pivotal to the Windsor Royal Coven also. As for the shadowy Committee of 300 which the Order of the Garter allegedly has control over, Dr Coleman remains the sole source for the existence of a secretive structure – although if one looks at it, the bonding of the aristocracy, big business and mystical societies for a common purpose, may not be as farfetched as it sounds. It may also be noted that Edward III, founder of the Order of the Garter, also gave great credence to the Brutus lineage, coining the term for his realm as Troylebastion (Bastion of Troy). Bloodlines and pedigree are paramount in these royal circles and it seems that belonging to the stock of Brutus amounts to the *creme de la creme* of blue blood.

Yet returning again to the saga of a secret coven within Royal circles there is another twist, in the form of yet another hereditary order, not one based in Windsor but on the South Coast of England, a coven that would be called upon to use its ancient knowledge in order to conduct its own psychic war – and on which the safety of the realm was said to depend.

Old Ernie, the Earl, and the Invasion Spell

During the Second World War, many covert British operations took place, involving disinformation and intelligence smokescreens, all specifically concocted with one aim in view – to confuse the Nazi enemy.

Much has been made of the German high command's obsession with the occult and their attempted utilisation of psychic forces in order to frighten and confuse their allied enemies. Churchill and friends on the other side of the English Channel were only too aware of the potential power of occult knowledge, and how it could be used by those adept in the dark arts. One of Churchill's most famous wartime statements was a reference to the Battle of Britain pilots and their ultimate victory over the Luftwaffe, when he said, "Never in the field of human conflict was so much owed by so many to so few". But among occultists, and in particular, in modern witch-lore, Churchill's quote becomes a secret acknowledgement of the British witches' role in the fight against the Nazis and their proposed invasion of Britain, codenamed Operation Sealion. A fictionalised account of how a small group of witches repelled a Nazi invasion is given in Katherine Kutz's novel *Lammas Night*, first published in 1983. In the novel, a high-ranking British Intelligence Officer, Sir John Graham, harbours a secret life as the high priest of a witch coven. A junior member of his staff, Michael, who is also a member of his occult circle, goes missing while on a secret mission to gather intelligence on Nazi occultists. A psychic conflict ensues between evil Nazi magicians and Graham's white magic coven.

The plot involves a Prince who is integral to the working of a spell by the white witches against the Nazis. It is significant that real life witch Doreen Valiente acted as consultant on *Lammas Night* for Kurtz and it is no accident that the fictional plot in this novel and the witch-lore of pagan King Rufus are almost parallel here. Rufus was killed in the New Forest during a hunting accident, being felled by a lone arrow.

But was Katherine Kurtz's novel with its royal reference also pointing towards a real-life connection in actual wartime events?

To set the scene for the true story of the famed New Forest Coven that the father of modern witchcraft, Gerald Gardner, was said to have been initiated into, we first need to look at a local amateur Rosicrucian theatre group known as the Crotona Fellowship operating in Christchurch, Dorset in south-west England around 1939. The head of the company was one Alex Sullivan, who hailed from Liverpool and who wrote plays based on the teachings of Co-Masonry (a branch of Theosophically inclined Freemasonry that admits both male and female members) that were performed to the public in a theatre built by its players. In the spirit of the old folk mystery plays, the concept was that both the actors and the audience would learn from the esoteric messages contained within each performance.

Within this entourage of players was a much smaller group of other actors who were only involved with the productions because of their background, which from the outside seemed quite ordinary, yet, as it turned out was anything but.

For this small, close-knit group of 'ordinary' folk, who were drawn from quite commonplace occupations such as dress makers and grinders, were actually the nucleus of the New Forest Coven – a group that had practised in that area since Norman times and at the time was said to be one of the few surviving genuine witch covens in England. The Crotona Fellowship members identified as being involved with the New Forest Coven were George Alexander Sullivan, Dorothy Clutterbuck, Veronica Keen, Peter Caddy (later founder of new age community Findhorn), Cyril and Elizabeth Barnes, Elizabeth and Catherine Oldmeadow (writer on folk and alternative medicine), Walter Forder, and elocution teacher Edith Woodford Grimes (known as Dafo, although this was not her witch name), and family members Suzie Mason, Rosetta Mason and 'old Ernie' Mason.

Perhaps unsurprisingly the members tended to keep themselves to themselves and it is only largely thanks to the researches of Philip Heselton, author of *Gerald Gardner and the Cauldron of Inspiration* that we are able to identify them at all.

Gerald Gardner, acknowledged by most modern Wiccans as the father of 'the Craft', claimed to have been initiated into the New Forest Coven through his involvement with the Crotona Fellowship. But the other members of the New Forest Coven later had cause to regret admitting Gardner to their fold, as his zeal prompted him to publicise the fact that he was a witch. In so doing, he broke the law of the land, since at the time the practice of witchcraft was illegal under English law, not to mention potentially scandalous in country life. Gardner's involvement caused disquiet among other coven members, leading to his gradual disengagement from their group.

According to Dafo the coven was directly linked by lineage to William Rufus (Norman King William II). If correct, with such a pedigree, it would have been highly unlikely that the coven would wish to emerge from the shadows to court publicity, particularly in wartime England. Especially so, in view of the the the ritual they were said to have conducted in the summer of 1940, with England poised on the brink of an expected Nazi invasion.

Philip Heselton sets the scene for this auspicious event. He writes, "As July progressed without sight of the invasion it became obvious that Lammas would be the perfect time to perform a ritual of a more elaborate nature. Astrologically, it was a highly significant time because it is was within a week of an exact Jupiter-Saturn conjunction, something which only happens every twenty years and which is a balance point in the mundane cycle when things can be both started and finished. That it occurred very close to a sensitive point on Hitler's own chart (his Venus-Mars conjunction) could only help any efforts which were being directed towards his decisions – making abilities and preferences for action".

The Lammas cross quarter day marked the old pagan festival of corn and fire. Lammas has many etymologies but one is Welsh Gaelic, simply meaning August 1st. The festival itself is known by its Irish name 'Lughnasadh' or 'Lugh. In County Kerry it is known as 'Dark Lugh Festival', a strong indication that it would have coincided with a particular moon phase. Lammas eve 1940 saw the moon in its last waning phase, traditionally a time for invoking the dark goddess Hekate, who is worshiped when the moon is a sickle in the sky. The sickle is used to reap the corn at this time of year and is, of course, one of the magical tools of the Druid.

A number of people who knew about, or who were involved in, the New Forest Coven's ritual to repel Hitler's forces, have firmly suggested that there was a 'willing sacrificial victim' that night, who gave their life in order to raise the witches' 'cone of power' above their circle. Once this was done the ritually generated energy could be directed and sent, while at its peak, towards the Nazi enemy. Such an occurrence is described in detail by Katherine Kurtz in *Lammas Night*. Another possibly more factual source can be found in the writings of Gerald Gardner, who recalls exactly how the spell was performed.

The witch clan who often danced naked through the night, covered their bodies with grease (probably goose grease, which is used by long-distance swimmers) in order to insulate themselves against the natural elements. The story goes that the 'willing victim' that fateful night chose not do so and therefore died of hypothermia as a result. At the point of expiration, the victim's life force was assimilated into the pool of energy that was being built up by the rest of the coven, together with the words "Go away: go away: cannot come", which was then projected into Hitler's mind, thus casting doubt as to the proposed invasion of Britain by the Fuhrer. Before we dismiss this as a wild notion, it must be borne in mind that those participants who took part in this rite did so with deadly seriousness, literally as a matter of life and death. If we are to give any credence to Gardner's own account, one or two coven members apparently died as a result of the intensity of the ritual conducted that night.

The last of the individuals involved in the New Forest Coven, one Susie Mason, died in late 1979, so none of this could be verified by any living person at the time of writing. But one person who has been able to shed some light on these events and the dark secrets of the New Forest Coven was author Philip Heselton, whom Jonathan Tapsell was able to meet in 2000 when archiving the Doreen Valiente witchcraft collection. Philip Heselton informed Jonathan that there was someone he should meet who would have quite a lot to say about 'Old Ernie' Mason's esoteric endeavours. His name was Bill Wakefield, a former air steward with a deep interest in astronomy who had worked with old Ernie as a telescope lens grinder. Jonathan and cameraman Simon Williams made contact with Bill Wakefield and visited him at his home in Southampton, after he had agreed to lift the lid on the mysterious life of his former employer. Strangely, one of Mr Wakefield's first comments to his visitors was "Old Ernie said you would come", while his wife looked on approvingly, offering tea and biscuits. In time, Mr Wakefield began to reminisce and to recall his time with Old Ernie, whom he described as one of the most learned men that he had ever encountered. He said Old Ernie possessed a depth of knowledge few men could match. As a Fellow of the Royal Astronomical Society, Old Ernie was given much credit for passing his knowledge on to Wakefield, who had built three of the largest telescopes in England.

Jonathan conducted two interviews with Bill, the first with just audio tape, the second on camera two weeks later. Bill said of Old Ernie "He always told me that Alex Sullivan from the Crotona Fellowship was a true magus. But the entire [Mason] family were mind-control people, they were witches," Bill added.

Jonathan asked Bill if he could elaborate further. Bill said that the Mason family were people with extra sensory powers. Old Ernie, he said, possessed the ability to materialise certain artefacts in front of witnesses. Bill continued on the subject of Old Ernie, "he was visited by lots of people, business people, rich folk, academics, and one I remember used to come in a chauffeur driven car. It was a Rolls Royce with a crest on the side. When these people came it was very hush-hush. Old Ernie just escorted them through the workshop up into his chamber. We used to hear chanting sometimes coming from the room but we never asked questions".

Bearing in mind the royal connection which was mentioned in Kurtz's novel and also alluded to in the private papers of English witch Doreen Valiente, Jonathan pressed Bill to elaborate further.

"The Rolls Royce was dark, black I think, it came from the Naval dockyards in Portsmouth and the guest was very important, he was 'the' most important visitor I think. The car was always driven by a woman who also visited Old Ernie. It was very hush-hush," Bill recalled. During the first interview Bill Wakefield had already thrown up some intriguing information, but there was more to come, as in the second interview filmed two weeks later, Bill was able to recall Old Ernie's mention of the rite used to repel Hitler. Bill stated that in fact two persons had died participating in the ritual to repel Hitler that night. The power raised was superior to that being raised by the Nazis in their black magic rites, which used the deaths of unwilling victims in order to raise occult energy.

In the intervening period between the interviews, Jonathan had also been put in touch with another witchcraft contact who was linked to the New Forest Coven by virtue of her personal friendship with the publicity-shy Dafo, whose real name was Edith Woodford Grimes. The reclusive contact was Eleanor 'Rae' Bone, known to some as the matriarch of British witchcraft. When Jonathan contacted her she was 90 years old and one of the last surviving witches connected with the New Forest Coven. As such she was able to expand on the mysterious royal connection. In a watershed revelation Eleanor Bone said she felt that one of the leading characters in the novel *Lammas Night* was based on occultist Dolores North who was otherwise known as Madeleine Mountleban, astrologer, occultist, tarot reader and personal psychic to Louis Lord Mountbatten ('Uncle Dickie' to Prince Charles), Knight of the Order of the Garter and an alleged member of the Committee of 300.

Dolores North was an occultist with many a high level connection. She formed part the magical group known as the Order of the Morning Star and was responsible for typing up Gerald Gardner's book *High Magic's Aid*, published in 1949 under his O.T.O. magickal name Scire.

During the war, Dolores North had served in the Women's Royal Naval Service. Her husband, Commander Bill North, was also a fellow Naval

Officer of Mountbatten's and acted as the Earl's agent at the family seat Broadlands, which is located just north-east of the New Forest. Dolores North's WRNS status was believed to be a cover, allowing her to act as Mountbatten's personal psychic and chauffeur. Eleanor Bone couldn't say definitely if the woman chauffeur seen by Wakefield was Dolores, nor that it was Mountbatten who was the 'important visitor' of Old Ernie, but her account did echo with both Katherine Kurtz's story gleaned in part from Doreen Valiente and, of course, the interviews given by Bill Wakefield.

There seemed to be two driving prerequisites at the heart of the New Forest Coven. Firstly, self-sacrifice at all levels was required of those who participated in the spell against Hitler. Rufus too, Eleanor Bone maintains, had allowed his life to be taken in an act of self-sacrifice in order to fulfil the second most important pivotal part of the New Forest Coven's function – the acquisition and controlled raising of power.

If the ritual to repel a Nazi invasion did indeed take place, as those linked to the group have suggested, it would have probably formed the climax of a series of rituals conducted at various points in the lead up to Lammas, at which time a life would be offered to the old gods. It is interesting to note that Rufus was killed on August 2nd, so it seems to link in with the claims of the New Forest Coven and explain its important connotations to their worship.

Old Ernie was quoted by his former employee Bill Wakefield as once saying "I am the guardian of the ancient oral tradition of the land", in regard to the preservation of the secret teachings but in an interesting rider, Bill revealed "only it wasn't knowledge he passed on, it was power". It soon became clear to Jonathan that the Mason family were certainly at the heart of the New Forest Coven and Old Ernie was undoubtedly the real leader of this secretive group.

But there was another individual who was also linked into the rituals of the New Forest Coven and who enjoyed close connections with the House of Windsor. He was Cecil Williamson, an influential neo-pagan witch. In 1938, one year before the outbreak of World War II, MI6 recruited Williamson to investigate the Nazis' involvement with the occult. Again echoing Kurtz's fictional account in the character of Michael, Williamson seems to fit the bill.

Williamson was born in Paignton, Devon in 1909, the son of a senior Naval officer. He first came across witchcraft as a young boy, in the year 1916. He was visiting his uncle, the local vicar, when he saw a woman who had been accused of witchcraft being openly beaten by villagers. The young Cecil, seeing the woman lying on the ground, instinctively shielded her from her attackers. The two went on to become firm friends. Later in 1921, Williamson was a boarder at Malvern College School, where he was bullied, but he was aided by a kindly woman who was in residence at the establishment. She taught the young boy to defend himself psychically by casting a spell upon the bully, who did later have an accident, breaking his leg whilst skiing. He never bullied Williamson again.

In the summer holidays Cecil regularly went to France to stay with his grandmother and her friend Mona Mackenzie, a deep-trance medium and spiritualist who gave Williamson instruction in divination.

When his college days were over, Williamson travelled to Rhodesia (now Zimbabwe) to work in the tobacco growing industry, where he was given further occult training. This time he studied African magic – his teacher being Zandora, his servant.

By 1930, having gained quite an insight into witchcraft and magic, Williamson returned home and moved to London, where he found work in the film industry as a production assistant. It was during this period of his life that he made the acquaintance of Dr Margret Murray, Egyptologist E.A. Wallis Budge, Montague Summers and Aleister Crowley.

His investigative occult work within MI6 was actually in a special section of the Foreign Office. The horror writer Dennis Wheatley, his wife and latterly Crowley were also in the same department. Wheatley also had a direct hotline to Churchill and was well aware that occult knowledge could have the potential to be used as a secret weapon, for good or ill. One of Williamson's successes was to enter some false prophecies in a book alleged to have been written by Nostradamus. Williamson ensured that this bogus work was dispatched to France where it would fall into the hands of leading Nazi, Rudolph Hess, who was well-known to be interested in occult matters. After reading the book in question, Hess flew to Scotland where he crashed and was captured. Additionally, Williamson may well have been involved the coordination of the New Forest Coven ritual to repel Hitler. In 1993, six years before his death, Williamson made disclosures in which he stated that the New Forest ceremony was a propaganda mission, news of which was intended to spook the Nazi high command, who very much believed in the power of such things.

The final postscript to this story was told by prominent English witch Patricia Crowther.

During preparations for Operation Sealion, the Nazi high Command met to discuss plans to invade England. During the meeting, Hitler suddenly and inexplicably fell asleep. On awaking, the Führer declared that he'd had a change of mind and Operation Sealion should continue, but only as a form of bluff in order for the real invasion of Russia to begin. Orthodox historians remain baffled as to why the Führer decided to take this course of action when he could have almost certainly have conquered an unprepared England at that time. It was almost if someone or a group of persons had put a spell on him.

The Stone of Scone

One artefact said to embrace mystical energies of a spellbinding nature was the 'Stone of Scone', more popularly known as the 'Stone of Destiny' and, to the Irish as 'Lia Fail'. The history of this mystical rock reads like an alternative Bible, enmeshed with Egyptian and Phoenician mysteries. The legend of the stone begins with it being described as 'Jacob's Pillow Stone'. Believed to have borne witness to Jacob's covenant with God, the stone became a singularly significant cult artefact for the early Israelites.

The stone itself was said to have been used as a 'Coronation Stone' at Solomon's Temple in Jerusalem. The Hebrews referred to it as the 'Stone of Majesty' and the 'Pillar of Witness', the theme here is one of a continuous constitution, whereby the stone should be placed wherever the throne of David continued, if not in Israel, then elsewhere. An understanding between God and Jeremiah stipulates that "David shall never lack a man to sit upon the throne of the House of Israel". The 'Witness Stone' was used in the coronation of the kings. When Jerusalem fell to the invading Babylonians, Jeremiah hid the 'Witness Stone', before taking it to Egypt along with the daughters of the last king of Judah, Zedekia and other refugees.

Part of the divine covenant also stated that Jeremiah was "to build and plant" so in order to fulfil these requirements he needed to move to Egypt which he did, taking the sacred stone, his scribe Baruch and the king's two daughters with him. They were Tephi or Tea Tephi, and Scota whose ancestor Princess Scota, was the daughter of the Egyptian Pharoah Smenkhare (Anchencares) circa 1361 BC. This was the bloodline juncture where the Dragon lines of Scythia and Egypt conjoined. Princess Scota Scythia had a child, Geadbeal Glas, the ancestor of the Scots Gauls.

The early Irish records refer to the "Coming of the Great Prophet" with "Brugh" his scribe, identified as a corruption of the name Baruch. Brugh and the King's daughter arrived circa 583 BC, bringing the Stone of Destiny with them.

Writing about this event Rev. Bertrand L. Comparet, A.B, J.D. (1901-83) says, "In one of our congregations is a woman whose family geneaology shows that one of their ancestors came to Ireland with Jeremiah, and that this ancestor's duty was that of the custodian of the Stone, Tea Tephi, the King's daughter, married Eochaidh the Heremon, or Chief King of Ireland".

The Stone of Destiny was kept at the capital, Tara, for 300 years, during which time all the kings of ancient Ireland were crowned upon it. In 350 BC the stone was sent over to Scotland for the coronation of King Fergus, a descendent of the Irish Milesian kings.

There it stayed for nearly 1600 years. As with their Hebrew and Irish antecedents, all Scottish kings were crowned upon the stone until 1297, when the English led by Edward I invaded Scotland, hijacking the Stone of Destiny in the process. The object was then brought back to England as a spoil of war and placed under the coronation chair at Westminster Abbey. Every King and Queen of the realm has been crowned upon it since.

In Genesis 49, Jacob speaks from his deathbed to his twelve sons, addressing each of them in turn and bestowing upon them the characteristics of each of the fabled 'twelve tribes of Israel'. He also speaks of Joseph, saying "From thence is the shepherd of the Stone of Israel". In other words, the sons of Joseph are the true custodians of the Stone of Destiny. Some Anglo-Jews and Zionists claim they are of the tribe of Ephraim – descendants of one of Joseph's sons. The tribe of Ephraim has become inextricably linked with England, so much so, that to have the very Witness Stone of Israel resting in London would have fulfilled both the prophecy and their mythic requirements. Of course there is no way of proving that Jacob's ladder stone, the seat of David, the Irish Stone of Destiny, are all one and the same and many different mythologies surround this revered object. Equally there is no way of disproving it either. The salient point here is that those involved with holding and housing it did – and perhaps still do – believe it to be of some mystical import, an object of perennial power that underpins the constitution itself.

This was certainly the case in Scotland, indeed the Scots created an exact replica in anticipation of Edward I's invasion, and by hiding the real stone of Scone foiled the English requisition. An article in the *Dundee Courier*, of April 1991 stated that the Stone of Scone remained in Scotland. It was exhibited at the Peoples' Palace in Glasgow during 1990 and viewed by half a million visitors. If the original stone had been copied and Edward I set up with the bogus replica, who would have engineered such a complex subterfuge and what would have been their reason for doing so? There is probably only one person capable of having orchestrated such a move – Robert the Bruce. This may explain why, as Robert I of Scotland, he never asked for the safe return of the stone, because he knew that the original was safely hidden away in his own Kingdom.

Even by 1996, British Prime Minister John Major felt that he needed to quell Scottish nationalist emotions by ordaining the Stone's return to Scottish soil. This duly happened on St Andrew's Day in 1996 when it was delivered to Edinburgh Castle. Thus Scotland could now claim to be in possession of two identical stones, one of which was the real Stone of Destiny. There are wider implications, as Adrian Gilbert points out in his book *New Jerusalem* (Bantam, 2002), he writes "Thus, whatever the truth may be concerning the legends surrounding the Stone of Scone, it cannot be denied that its return to Scotland has coincided with events that would not have been foreseen five years earlier. Where this leaves England is the unanswered question of our times. Will it, as many politicians seem to hope, abandon independence and enter into a deeper union with federalist Europe?".

The salient question has now been answered with the ratification of the Lisbon Treaty which renders England null and void as a sovereign country, with its counties sectioned off as zonal numbers on an EU grid. This state of affairs also begs the question: will Charles sit upon the Stone of Destiny for his future coronation? If he does not, Charles may risk being considered not truly King. If measured against his royal predecessors, what divine authority will he claim then? If he demands the stone, even temporarily, for his inauguration as King but then later returns the artefact to Scotland; by default he has already surrendered his Divine Kingship and mystical authority, leaving Charles to wear the Crown in name only. There may be an even more powerful force behind this decision but we shall arrive there presently. Suffice to say Charles may find himself between a rock and a hard place.

The Monarch's Magician

Over the years, the current reigning monarch, Elizabeth II, has ratified a number of treaties which have increasingly tethered the UK to the European Union, but her previous namesake Elizabeth I, whose forces defeated the Spanish Armada in 1588, was fiercely protective of her realm's independence from the largely Catholic countries of mainland Europe.

Elizabeth I employed her own court philosopher, who also acted as her personal astrologer; indeed it was he who determined the most auspicious date for her Coronation upon the Stone of Destiny. He was of course, Dr John Dee, founder and Grand Master of the Rosicrucian Order of England who, some say, founded it to offer an alternative to the Jesuits. Dee, one of the most brilliant minds of his age was a renowned scholar, steeped in esoteric and academic disciplines: astrology, alchemy, geography, navigation, geometry, maths, cryptology, the Qabalah and of course, magic

Shakespeare depicted him as both King Lear and Prospero, while authors Michael Baigent and Richard Leigh credit Dee with setting the stage for the emergence of Freemasonry. Conventional historians even admit that he was the driving force behind the concept of a 'British Empire'. Writing in his biography *John Dee: The World of the Elizabethan Magus*, French says of the Elizabethan mage, "He was one of the most celebrated and remarkable men of the Elizabethan age. Philosopher, mathematician, technologist, antiquarian, teacher and friend of powerful people, Dee was at the centre of some of the major developments of the English Renaissance, in fact, he inspired several developments through his writings and teachings. But Dee was a magician deeply immersed in the most extreme forms of occultism."

During the Elizabethan period, Dee's was the largest privately owned library in England, totalling over 4,000 volumes.

In magical terms, Dee's most important work was his protracted series of 'Enochian' evocations which he jointly conducted with his assistant Edward Kelly – an Irishman of somewhat dubious reputation, who possessed a gift for psychic vision.

Dee and Kelley held the conviction that the true art of magic would change the European political order and provide unparalleled occult powers to the magical operators. Prefiguring by several centuries the New Forest Coven's own anti-invasion spell, Dee is widely held to have put a hex on the Spanish Armada by conjuring the storm that changed the course of the planned invasion of the British Isles (something also ascribed to Sir Francis Drake in witch-lore). Together, Dee and his scribe Kelly deemed themselves summoners of angels, whose communications via a strange and complex system of Angelic language received by the process of 'scrying', foretold of a coming global empire ruled by the British Crown. For the shew-stone into which the angelic visions were conjured, Dee used a flat obsidian mirror of Mayan origin. The mirror is on permanent display at the British Museum, along with other of his magical implements, including the famous carved wax disk known as the 'Sigillum Dei Aemeth', which Dee used as a magical 'attractor' for the angelic entities with whom he claimed to be in communication.

Dee was accorded high office in Elizabeth's court. He was, as we have mentioned, the driving force behind the formation of the British Empire, staking the British claims on North America via Templar discoveries, not Spanish ones. Much of this advice he dispensed came, no doubt, through his angelic visitations. He also coined the word Britannia and generated a plan for the British navy using Euclidian geometry and charted the Northeast and Northwest passages.

Dee also believed in pursuing a secret modus operandi. In this respect he is seen as a role model for today's secret agents. He helped set up Britain's first intelligence network, taking full advantage of his encyclopedic knowledge of codes and ciphers. In fact his own secret signature when working for British intelligence was 007, which was later appropriated by Ian Fleming for his fictional secret agent James Bond. Fleming who was friendly with the infamous Aleister Crowley, served in the navy during World War II and rubbed shoulders with several people who would have been aware of the New Forest Coven and their secret rituals.

As the first British secret service agent, Dee travelled all over Europe gathering information that would be of use to the British throne, utilising the advanced espionage techniques he had studied in a work entitled *Steganography*, written by fellow occultist Johannes Trithemius.

While in Prague, Dee sold Emperor Rudolph an illustrated manuscript written in code, purported to be the work of Thames embankment resident, Roger Bacon, who had incurred the wrath of the Church with his unorthodox beliefs and opinions.

Like Dee, Bacon was a visionary, but from an earlier period in history (1214-92). His manuscript contained predictions about forthcoming technology and inventions such as the microscope, telescope, car and aeroplane. Bacon's theory that the Earth was round, not flat, pre-dated the Polish astronomical genius Copernicus by some 200 years. In 1912 the manuscript was purchased by an American book dealer Wilfred Voynich and is known today as the *Voynich Manuscript*. The American buyer sent his newly purchased manuscript to the best code breakers and other experts, who scrutinised the strange illustrated work but its contents and the cipher used to conceal them proved impossible to crack. It was duly declared the most mysterious code in the world. It was therefore with some amazement that the news of its final deciphering was met. A certain Professor Romaine Newbold contended he had performed this great feat and had managed to translate several sections of the mysterious manuscript.

One piece of text describing the nature of the constellations has proven to be correct. An illustration of the Andromeda nebula is also accurate, but it is from a perspective that cannot be viewed from our own planet. Something else that cannot be seen on our Earth are the numerous plant forms illustrated in the manuscript.

In predictive and esoteric terms this was absolute cutting edge stuff, completely beyond the scope of most practitioners of the time, even within the occult realm. How much did Dee, a master of ciphers and codes, know of its content? Certainly he was well endowed with gold from the Hapsburg occultist, Rudolph II in return for this remarkable manuscript.

Was Dee himself a black magician? He always denounced those who practiced the dark arts, yet in many respects, he seemed to cross this line himself now and again.

Christopher Marlowe wrote a play, *Dr Faustus*, allegedly about Dee, portraying someone who seeks worldly perfection by altering the kingdom of God. In the play, government is depicted as being completely corrupt and in cahoots with the secret society network. The play finishes with the line "whose deepness doth entice such forward wits, to practice more than heavenly power permits". This was dangerous dialogue on Marlowe's part, as his play was pointedly damning of the Renaissance movement and the government's role in society. It came as no surprise therefore, when Marlowe was murdered in 1593 at the age of twenty-nine by one Ingram Friger (who had connection with the underworld and spy networks) who was subsequently pardoned a month later by Queen Elizabeth I. After Marlowe's homicide, the Elizabethan administration released details about his private life the manner of his death, all of which were deliberately concocted to paint him in a bad light.

The authorities of the time denounced Marlowe as 'an atheist and blasphemer' who had died in a tavern during a brawl. Sadly even today this mistaken account is still repeated as fact. Marlowe's death actually took place in a private room in a respectable house in Deptford owned by one Eleanor Bull, possibly run as a safe house for agents of the time. Marlowe was a member of Dee's 'The School of Night', and an associate of Thomas Walsingham, a relative of Sir Francis Walsingham, co- founder of the British secret service along with Dee. The murderer having been identified as one Friger who was possibly aided and abetted by two men – one a low life agent known as Nicholas Skeres and the second a more respectable subject – the Queen's mail courier – Robert Poley. Straight away one can sense the hidden hand of spies, secret societies, not to mention the Queen's full support for those concerned in this murderous episode. Even this account could be a macabre charade engineered by Dee and his School of the Night compatriots in order to get Marlowe out of the country, as some also believe Marlowe to be the real author of the works of Shakespeare. If so he would have been in possession of too many secrets and it would have been dangerous for him to remain in England. One can only wonder on which side Dee's loyalties lay during all of this.

A little while later in British history the secret societies and more specifically, several leading lights within them, were to take a much wider role in events, as they sought to create nothing less than a 'New Jerusalem' in the wake of the Great Fire of London.

CHAPTER SEVEN
The New Jerusalem

The Great Fire

In 1666 the Fire of London destroyed most of the city. It broke out in Pudding Lane, at the Royal bakehouse of one Thomas Farriner. At that time, most buildings in London were constructed from timber and often erected one on top of another with overhanging projections, making the fire a catastrophe waiting to happen. The Great Fire raged for four days before it was finally extinguished, having laid waste to a once prosperous city. No fire in any other western European city has been so destructive. Miraculously only six people were reported to have lost their lives in the whole conflagration, which was exacerbated by the hot dry summer weather and a strong easterly wind. But this devastating event became decisive in shaping the future of London in two ways; firstly, it provided an opportunity to rebuild the city under central planning and secondly, it is said to have eradicated much of the vermin responsible for spreading the plague. Both events are said to have paved the way for London's emergence as Europe's premier capital, which it remains to this day.

In the aftermath of the Great Fire, King Charles expressly forbade the construction of any wooden buildings, should a similar event ever take place again. This royal command was later reinforced by the Rebuilding Act, passed by Parliament in February 1667. This piece of important legislation specified the width of roads, permissable types of buildings, their placements, and other measures designed to ensure that the city was made as resistant to large-scale fires as possible. Never again would accidental fire pose a threat to the well-being of London.

Soon after the fire, a group of Commissioners was formed to oversee the rebuilding works – among them were architects such as Sir Christopher Wren and Robert Pratt, Royal Official Hugh May, Royal Society member and Professor of geometry Robert Hooke, City Surveyor Peter Mills and carpenter/surveyor Edward Jerman. All of these luminaries were steeped in esoteric lore, being either freethinkers or members of secret societies. These men were some of the brightest minds of their day. Hooke feuded with Newton over physics and later proposed a wave of light theory, not to mention leaving us Hooke's law – that is, stretching is directly proportional to force. The Commissioners were greatly inspired by some of the classical cities of Europe and wished to do away with London's hotch-potch, labyrinthine sprawl of medieval streets. Their vision was to create a New Jerusalem, a spiritual city of sacred proportions.

The buildings that sprang up in the wake of the Great Fire transformed the ravaged capital, creating labour and a vibrant trade in much-needed building materials. A second Act of Parliament commissioned the construction of 52 new churches under the guidance of Sir Christopher, with the finest of them being the Baroque masterpiece St Paul's Cathedral. Dedicated to the Patron saint of London, the new cathedral was built on the site of the earlier edifice of the same name, which was itself built upon the site of the original Temple of Diana left by Brutus. Wren's vision for a new capital of orderly streets permanently constructed of stone, was not to be. His grand plan was curtailed and hamstrung by a number of factors related to the deeds on buildings and the ground on which they were built, which is why to this day, London is laid out according to its Medieval jumble rather than a clearly delineated street plan of classical splendour. However, in amongst the tangle of London's winding lanes and streets, Wren and his contemporaries did manage to transform London, as it were, a phoenix rising from the ashes.

In the design of St Paul's, Wren combined his interest in the classical civilisations of Greece and Rome with his love of astronomy. The Cathedral platform is made for stagazers. Then there are also the acoustic properties of his design, which can still be experienced in the 'Whispering Gallery' in the Cathedral's mighty dome. The gallery is so named owing to the fact that a visitor may whisper against its wall and the sound will travel across the dome to the opposite side of wall where the whisper may be heard by another person. It was also rumoured that Nicholas Hawksmoor, an inspired architect who aided Wren in the building works, constructed another room to experiment with odd acoustic properties. This second room is said to exist inside the cathedral but is now bound and locked. Here, it is said, a person may shout at the top of their voice into the ear of another, who will hear nothing at all. A curious story that is something of a myth shrouded by time, but we shall return to the mysterious Hawksmoor in some detail later.

In the massive rebuilding project, buildings such as the Guildhall, the Royal Exchange, Customs House and the mighty Doric column known as the Monument, which commemorates the supposed place where the Great Fire first took hold, all sprung up in a matter of years following 1666. It would seem that divine intervention had saved the ravaged city, suggesting that London itself had a unique destiny. Wren obviously felt that Brutus' original temple to the moon goddess Diana should be marked or even celebrated and that there was a spiritual providence overruling the temporal nature of the individual lives of London's residents. Wren had at least given city dwellers of the time, and future generations later on, a glimpse of the sacred and left a remarkable symbolic vision for a new city – with St Paul's Cathedral acting as the jewel in the crown.

The Royal Society

Just six years before the Great Fire, an outstanding association had been formed in the wake of a speech given by Sir Christopher Wren at Gresham College in Bishopsgate, where he was a professor of astronomy. In the wake of his celebrated oration, a number of dedicated people formed around him. This association of progressives and freethinkers would become the Royal Society. Within a week of this famous lecture, Robert Moray, an influential Mason with court connections, had word from the King that the Society had gained his seal of approval in the form of a Royal Charter. What is remarkable about the formation of the Royal Society is the seismic shift away the former secrecy of scientists (who were really alchemists and magicians) to a new idea that experiments ought to be conducted publicly and the results shared. The Royal Society wished to remove barriers to learning such as language and political divides, while promoting the idea of objective truth and reason.

The Royal Society's influence on the rebuilding of London and the coining of the term 'New Jerusalem', shows clearly that the Fellows of the Royal Society held spiritual beliefs that went far beyond mere architecture.

Adrian Gilbert's book *New Jerusalem: The Great Fire, Sir Christopher Wren and the Royal Society* explores the esoteric ideas that underpinned the formation of the Royal Society in some detail. Gilbert writes about the belief that the British races (Scottish, Manx, Irish, Welsh, Cornish – along with the ancient Britons) were descended from the lost tribe of Israel. A sacred bloodline mythos underscores, Gilbert writes, the very idea of the British empire and ruling elite, running very deep through some Celtic Royal Families, right into the British nation state itself. The Tudors were certainly keen to weave in ideas of hereditary connections through their Welsh/Trojan ancestors. Some of these elements may have influenced the Biblical-Masonic elements within the Royal Society who viewed themselves, as Britons, to be inheritors of a mystical lineage springing from ancient times, projecting that vision onto the environs of London. Guildhall for example, the newly commissioned Town Hall for London, came to symbolise the power and majesty of the New Jerusalem, guarded as we have already seen, by the two giants Gog and Magog.

The legacy of the Royal Society can be viewed on many fronts but it set into motion the spiritual dominion of the city, differentiating it from just another metropolis or one of the many walled citadels of Europe. London had a meaning and purpose, the Royal Society had ensured that this was fused together in the city's past, present and future in a cohesive recognisable form – destiny.

Visions of the New Jerusalem

> *"I wander thro' each charter'd street*
> *Near where the charter'd Thames does flow*
> *And mark in every face I meet*
> *Marks of weakness, marks of woe"*
> – William Blake

Nearly 100 years after this first wave of visionaries in the Royal Society had made their mark upon London and added a unique perspective to the mystical landscape of the city, the celebrated poet, artist and mystic William Blake was born. His birth in Broad Street (now called Broadwick Street) in Soho, saw him christened in St James, Piccadilly and later apprenticed to an engraver after finishing his schooling. Later in life he married and settled in Poland Street before moving to Lambeth. For a time he moved from the capital to take up residence in Felpham, West Sussex but then returned to London once more. His only residences to survive intact are in Felpham and South Molton Street.

Today he is considered one of the greatest British artists, a printmaker and a poet, but in his day few had time for his work and he lived a precarious existence. Few who encountered him valued or understood his works. Some even regarded him as mad. Comparing Blake with the likes of Wren and other members of the Royal Society, it is certain that he was not staid, respected or influential and at times he waded into the waters of revolutionary politics, satire, and the solid British tradition of liberty for the common man. But his entry into all of the above was rather like that of his peer Emmanuel Swedenborg, a gentle and refined process. Blake remains transcendental in every sense.

Blake's book *Jerusalem* is hailed as his greatest work and within it he rejects the modern philosophy of man, by inventing his own inner material worlds to inhabit. The great mills of the industrialists are labelled as Satanic and Blake drew his inspiration from sources such as the Bible, Druidry, Hebrew mysticism and, of course, the natural world. As a child Blake saw a vision of God and continued throughout his life to be inspired by these divine revelations which drove him to produce the most fantastic drawings, etchings and paintings. Blake's wife was loyal to his cause and they worked together to produce books of his engravings and poetry. Public recognition was, to say the least, scant, and life was hard for the couple, as Blake was an artist before being a businessman.

His famous poem later set to music gives us another insight into his inspiration, which may suggest his parallel with Sir Christopher Wren and the Royal Society.

"And did those feet in ancient time
Walk upon England's mountains green?
And was the Holy Lamb of God
On England's pleasant pastures seen?

And did Countenance Divine
Shine forth upon our clouded hills?
And was Jerusalem builded here
Among these dark Satanic mills?

Bring me bow of burning gold!
Bring me arrows of desire!
Bring me my spear! O clouds unfold!
Bring me my chariot of fire!

I will not cease from mental flight,
Nor shall my sword sleep in my hand
Till we have built Jerusalem
In England's green and pleasant land."

Immediately there is a suggestion that England's 'green and pleasant land' is somehow visited by the Lamb of God – an allusion to the tradition of Joseph Arimithea, or are there other traditions at work here? Once Blake's own interests are understood clearly it leads to the idea that there may be deeper meaning to his words that are awash with mystical, even holy reference points. Jerusalem may seem to point towards a place revered by Christians but there is a notion that this is just a thin veneer of old Royal Society beliefs behind the form and words. The blending of Christian symbolism with London's pagan origins paint a very different picture, a place of secret signs, sacred proportions, knowledge of the heavens, old Gods and Druidic groves. One suspects that the Churchmen of his age, who were of little or no interest to Blake, had no idea of his true inspiration.

The New Jerusalem was no longer a place just merely composed of stone – it had a found a voice, a true champion of the city and of the land; whose visionary powers derived by dreams and angelic visitations gave a new

Medieval depiction of King Brutus and family.

Relief depicting a Mthraic sacrifice from Walbrook Street.

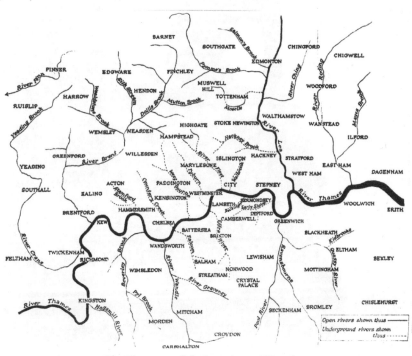

The Thames and the lost rivers of London.

Dragon marking the City boundary, Temple Bar.

Dr. John Dee.

Sir Christopher Wren and the Cadeuceus.

Doors on the side of the Bank of England.

Winston Churchill (centre, right) is initiated into the Druids.

Churchill's face at the centre of the Black Sun clock.

Livery Companies at St Paul's.

Aldermen at St Paul's.

Princess Anne at St Paul's.

The Lord Mayor and the Sword Bearer at St Paul's.

insight into human nature and the cosmos. London had found its Druidic thread once more through Blake. It would take some time to filter through, though. Blake brought the New Jerusalem mythos to life. His remains are buried in Bunhill (Bone Hill) near Old Street.

Some others involved with rebuilding the Capital had even more esoterically-based notions of grandeur. John Evelyn for example planned to reconstruct London on the basis of the Tree of Life from the mystical Cabala, using various churches and other landmarks to represent the points of the Sephiroth.

Evelyn had previously documented his Cabalistic convictions concerning a careful arrangement of the environment which could "influence the soule and the spirits of man and prepare them for converse with good Angells", the Angels' role in Cabalistic philosophy being that of emissary, operating between physical and metaphysical planes.

Wren himself used aspects of the Cabala in St Paul's, namely the ten domes corresponding to the ten spheres of the Sephiroth and the classical heavens.

During Roman times, oxen were regularly sacrificed on the site of the original Dianic temple. When excavation work was carried out in the 14th Century to lay the foundations of a chapel, more than a hundred oxen skulls were unearthed. The ancient ritual also continued in a Christianised form. In 1375 Sir William Baud was allotted some acres of land belonging to the Cathedral site, on condition that he supplied the annual sacrifice of horned beasts to Diana. The animals were brought into the old Norman church while the procession was taking place and were offered at the high altar. The church was destroyed by the Great Fire and replaced by St Paul's. It was here that a royal tradition spanning centuries was broken when in 1981, on a warm summer's day, HRH The Prince of Wales married Lady Diana Spencer instead of tying the knot in the customary Westminster Abbey.

St Paul's, the venue of Diana's marriage, where Brutus was said to have raised the first temple to Diana, is also connected to the mysterious London Stone. In one account of the stone's story, Brutus is said to have laid it as the central altar of a stone circle. Writing in the *Fortean Times*, David Hambling ponders that such a circle may well have existed at the St Paul's site, being that it was once a pagan site. John Wilcock writes "The stone is obviously of prehistoric derivation and must once have marked an important ritual site". Though some believe it to date from a later period in history, Wilcock describes it "A grubby limestone block about two feet square".

By the 16th Century, the stone had been set into the ground in front of what is now Cannon Street station. In 1742 it was moved to the north side of the street, before being set into the wall of another of Wren's churches, St

Swithin's, at the end of the 18th Century. St Swithin's was heavily damaged by the Blitz and later demolished in 1962 but miraculously the London Stone survived intact. The stone found a new home nearby in the wall of the Bank of China at 111 Cannon Street. However on the 22nd May 2006 amidst new demolition works, shop proprietor Chris Cheek noticed something wrong.

"When we were setting up shop, cowboy builders wanted to take a chisel to the stone" he said, "before disposing of it in a skip". Fortunately for London, Mr Cheek intervened in the nick of time and prevented them from doing so. The consequences for London's mystical legacy could have been dire indeed had the workmen succeeded. When Brutus first founded the stone, he decreed that London would remain safe only if the stone was not violated. It was at one time the sacred Pagan centre for London. In medieval times, it was used as a talisman for the city's safekeeping in keeping with the Brutus legend, where crowds would gather while the most important issues of the day would be debated, along with new laws and proclamations announced.

In 1450 Kentish rebel Jack Cade led a group of men to the City to protest against what they felt were corrupt government and laws. On the way, Cade stopped to strike his sword on the London stone as a gesture of strength. Cade formed his powerbase at the White Hart in Southwark. Here he planned the final revolt in order to take control of London, but the populace soon grew tired of the revolution and Cade along with his followers was dispelled.

A passage in William Blake's book *Jerusalem* alludes to the Brutus heritage: "At length he sat on the London Stone and heard Jerusalem's voice".

The Hawksmoor Alignment
At the centre of the New Jerusalem project, Royal Society members, Wren, Evelyn, Vanburgh, Hooke, Tompion and Newton were looking to create a new temple of Solomon in the form of St Paul's. These men of the Royal Society enjoyed the patronage of the King and were mostly men of wealthy beginnings. All were steeped in esoteric lore and believed in the spirit of the new scientific age. They encouraged learning and shared their own findings wherever possible in lectures, demonstrations and writings, using Gresham College to host much of this activity. In 1680 Wren hired a clerk, one 18 year old Nicholas Hawksmoor. Hailing from a Nottinghamshire farming family, the young Hawksmoor's undeniable talent earned him a position rebuilding London's churches in the wake of the Great Fire. In the spirit of the new Jerusalem project, Wren decided that the youthful clerk should learn Latin, a language that would be necessary to get on if one was serious about practising a profession and rebuilding London.

As we have seen, Wren and his contemporaries were a mixture of Freemasons, Rosicrucians and free thinkers, mostly attached to the Royal Society – England's new crucible of scientific and esoteric thought. Men like Tompion were producing complex timepieces and mechanical devices that transformed England's technological edge over their foreign competitors. It almost seemed as if the Great Fire itself had led to an explosion of creativity and scientific endeavour. One of the chief aspects of the vision of this new Jerusalem in London was the revisiting of classical themes, marking a departure from the former Gothic style. Wren and his contemporaries looked towards classical civilisations, as sketches of the architecture of Greece and Rome becoming all the rage. Later, Wren, Vanburgh, Hooke, Tompion and Hawksmoor were to use their knowledge in Greenwich, on a project quite separate from the rebuilding programme of the Great Fire. Here they crossed the river to transform Greenwich in south east London and to this day the fruits of their labours are found there, mostly around the Greenwich Naval College and on the hill above it, in the Royal Observatory.

As Hawksmoor progressed, he earned his first official post just three years after being hired. Wren declared Hawksmoor the Deputy Surveyor on Winchester Palace works. Hawksmoor went on to become Wren's principal assistant during the rebuilding of St Paul's Cathedral. As Wren advanced in years he relied increasingly on Hawksmoor to take on more of the workload. There is no doubt that Wren had every faith in his protegé who was more than capable of taking that trust. Wren had invested wisely in the genius of Hawksmoor, who eventually went on to design his own churches and buildings across London and also in other parts of England such as Oxford.

Hawksmoor was literally the poor relation amongst the grandees of the Royal Society and his name languished in relative obscurity, considering his important contribution to English architecture. There are many streets named after Vanburgh and Wren but not so many for poor Hawksmoor, who may well have become but a footnote in London's architectural history, were it not for modern resurgence of interest of his work.

In the mid 1970s poet and psychogeographer Iain Sinclair wrote *Lud Heat*, an obscure poetic piece that uses the backdrop of Hawksmoor-designed churches. *Lud Heat* connects Hawksmoor's designs with some of the darkest crimes committed in London's East End, including the Jack the Ripper murders and the Ratcliffe Highway killings. The poetry forges a link between the churches and the crimes through an invisible sinister geometry, a hellish alignment that draws murderous acts towards it. Obviously, Sinclair's work is pure prose, forged to conjure up an imagery or feeling in the setting of the East End. Later writers were to warm to the new theme such as Peter Ackroyd, who wrote a novel-cum-thriller entitled *Hawksmoor*, the story of which also flits between the Great Fire and the modern age, in which the character of Hawksmoor belongs to the latter. Comic book artist and self-professed magician, Alan Moore, collaborated with Sinclair and has also produced images and stories swirling around Hawksmoor, serial killers and so on. There seems to be some suggestion in certain quarters that Hawksmoor was, to coin a phrase, 'The Devil's Architect'. Recent articles featured in the *Fortean Times* have taken on mention of a dark Satanic ley line running through Hawksmoor's churches and fiction seems to have crossed over into fact, or what folklorists call ostention – in laymans terms, the making of a modern myth.

Hawksmoor's churches certainly lend themselves to a feeling that all is not run-of-the-mill and to the keen eye there seems to be very many peculiarities connected with their construction. Outwardly, much of their design seems to be non-Christian, as they contain strange obelisks, pyramids and unexplained 'sacrificial' altars. He himself said of his work that it followed 'The Rule of the Ancients'. Sinclair describes the alignment of Hawksmoor churches in the geometric landscape of the metropolis as forming "regular triangles and pentacles" which guard, mark, or rest upon London's occult origins. This poetic licence of Sinclair should not be seen as character assassination of Hawksmoor, from *Lud Heat* onwards we have seen a gradual revival in interest in the obscure architect, that may have in part led to the restoration of some his churches that had lain in a dilapidated state until relatively recently.

Looking at some of Hawksmoor's churches works such as Christchurch, Spitalfields, the very building that features so regularly in the work of Sinclair and others, we see they do not follow either the Gothic forms of pre-Fire churches, or the Baroque style so quintessentially Wren. In this respect Hawksmoor is unique. He also designed other churches near to Spitalfields in London's East End: St Georges-in-the-East, Stepney, and St Anne's, Limehouse. In South East London he built St Alfrege, Greenwich. In the City of London itself lies St Mary, Woolnath and St Lukes, Old Street. In South London near to Tower Bridge one of his churches St John's Horsleydown, was bombed during the War and demolished. If one cares to look more closely at these churches there is something very unusual about them, forgetting their alleged close proximity to dark acts or murders, they are like no other church seen before or since.

Hawksmoor collected travel books in order to learn more about distant lands and classical civilisations; a habit that he picked up from men such as Wren, Hooke and Vansburgh, all of whom read avidly about dimensions of ruined sites, meticulously studying travellers' sketches to learn what they could from these distant places. Looking at Hawksmoor's own studies we learn that he was very interested in the Temple of Bacchus in Baalbec. These sketches were published in a work by an Oxford educated scholar Maudrell, in his work entitled *A Journey from Aleppo to Jerusalem at Easter 1697 A.D.*. Another inspiration for Hawksmoor, as we now know from Hawksmoor's letters, was the mausoleum built by Artemisia the Queen, which was one of the Seven Wonders of the World. Other key influences on Wren, Hooke and Hawksmoor alike were Pliny and Vitruvius.

The commissioners of St Alfrege in Greenwich asked that the church be designed in such a way that it reflected primitive Christianity. Hawksmoor took this to mean that it was a revisitation to the early Church, not of Rome, but of Byzantine times. His treatments and submissions mention telling descriptions such as 'basilica' and 'temple', words more associated with the Church of Constantinople than Rome. He envisaged the early Christians wrecking, then rebuilding, the Temples to worship in amongst these ruins. It was romantic vision but may have been underpinned with more than just the wishes of the commissioners. His relationship with Wren had been a happy one but on occasion he did not always see eye-to-eye with the church commissioners. In one incident he commissioned sacrificial altars from a carver called Strong and fell foul of his paymasters. The commissioning authorities warned him to sign-off future additions with them first or pay the costs himself. Often as not, his designs were seen as too classical, as happened at St Anne's, Limehouse when in an early prototype that was rejected, he submitted a design showing Saint Anne surrounded by pyramids. His love of classical worship from all ages is clear.

Hawksmoor continually challenged the accepted order and used the esoteric ideas he had learnt from Royal Society members like Wren to augment his work. St Alfreges shows in stone the sacred geometric mathematical and alchemical discipline of 'squaring of the circle'. In another church, St Georges-in-the-East, he shows the history of primitive Christianity in the tower design, which is bewildering to gaze upon from the many influences it incorporates, rather like a puzzle in stone. A tower on top of a church in Bloomsbury shows allusions to the Temple of Solomon, so beloved of Freemasons.

Much folklore has built up since the 1970s surrounding the 'Devil's Architect'. If his churches were ever aligned to incorporate a Satanic alignment then surely it should be the commissioners who were responsible, as they sited the churches without any input from their architects. Most of the Hawksmoor churches in the City, and in the case of St Alfege, are built on particular sites for specific reasons, chiefly because they mark a spot that had already been dedicated to a former church. St Alfrege is built on the site of the former church that collapsed after a storm. As the appendix of this book confirms, the siting of more ancient London churches, particularly those in the City or 'Square Mile', most certainly have a secret alignment. Almost all are sited above blind springs and a great many are known to be pagan sites of some antiquity, such as St Brides (the church of journalists and writers). They were chosen many years before by geomantic means that would later be unlocked by Victorian scientist Thomas Lockyear (see Appendices). Whether Hawksmoor and Wren ever discussed the siting of the churches they were commissioned to rebuild is unknown, but given their deep esoteric leanings it is not too far off the mark to think they might have done so.

St Paul's is measured precisely in Egyptian cubits, pacing its distance from other buildings and Wren monuments. Wren realigned the axis of St Paul's to ensure it measured exactly 2,000 cubits from Temple Bar and the same distance from St Dunstan-in-the-East in the opposite direction. Hawksmoor definitely sought to incorporate the spiritual teachings of the age into the buildings he and Wren created, with the centrepiece of St Paul's as the crowning glory. Wren had excavated the ashes of the former St Paul's after the Great Fire, looking for evidence of Prince Brutus and had in some part restored the Trojan legacy by raising the mighty dome over the Temple of Diana. If the master architect had not divulged the true origins of the pre-Roman city to his second-in-command Hawksmoor, it would have been highly surprising. Hawksmoor, the talismanic architect, chose to cleave his occult thoughts in stone.

The Egyptian Connection

The British author Gerald Massey (1829-1907) published numerous works of poetry and spiritualism. After many years as an intellectual freethinker Massey turned his esoteric interest towards Egypt, producing an unparalleled and somewhat radical study on Egyptology. His observations have proved very prescient with the passing of time:

"And the final conclusion seems inevitable, that the universal parent of language, of symbolism, of early forms of law, of art and science, is Egypt, and that this fact is destined to be established along every line of research. If we find that each road leads back to Egypt, we may safely infer that every road proceeded from Egypt" says Gerald Massey in *A Book of Beginnings*, first published in 1881.

Early on in the book, Massey compares the English and Egyptian languages, listing literally hundreds of examples of similarity. For instance the word 'cart' in English corresponds to the Egyptian 'kart', meaning to carry. A 'gammon' cut of bacon is a 'kamh' joint of meat. He relates the words 'hero' and 'Ma-haru' and 'hey' is 'hai' with the same related definition in each case.

The county of Kent, often called the 'Garden of England' comes, he says, from the Egyptian 'Khent', meaning garden. Ma is Egyptian for mother which became assimilated by the British, Irish and American cultures as a slang term. 'Par' in Egyptian means to go round which, of course, became a golfing term with the same meaning. These are just a few of the examples listed in Massey's extensive work.

In yet another version Stone of Destiny story, this time emanating from Egypt, the Hes is the stone chair or throne identified with the great Egyptian goddess Isis, who was assimilated into the Celtic tradition, becoming Keridwen The Bard.

The Hes was originally called the 'Typhonian seat of stone'. Scota brought the stone from Egypt to Ireland where it became the 'Lia Fail' or 'Stone of Destiny'. This is virtually the same legend as that of the Stone of Scone, but with one basic difference. Instead of an Israeli seat of Solomonic stone, we now have an Egyptian, Typhonian, seat of stone, which re-examines the roots of the story and begs the question – did the legend begin in Israel/Palestine, or was the real source of origin Egypt itself?

Massey's assertions definitely point towards the latter as one might expect in view of his researches.

The ankh symbol is an Egyptian hieroglyph found in the UK, with several versions of it used in British society. Perhaps the most significant being its use in the great seals of England, albeit reversed, as a mark of power and authority. It also means to clasp: a sign of covenant. The Ankh is also used as a badge of office for the Inner Temple admittants of the Dragon Court. The symbol also gave its name to Ankou or Anjou, which according to De Vere is a type of 'Druidic death cult' of English Plantagenet Kings.

Covenants and great seals of England are related to law and the City. Another City custom was when a pair of white gloves was presented to the Magistrate sitting in the City of London when there was no one present to answer the defendant. Massey tells us "the glove is a hieroglyphic of the hand. The hieroglyphic hand is TUT (Egyptian), and the word signifies to give, image, typify, a type of honour, distinction, ceremonial."

One ceremony performed at St Lukes in Charlton, Kent and at Greenwich, London, was also linked to ancient ceremonies in Egypt. The traditional Horn Fair was eventually banned at the aforementioned venues owing to its licentious nature and worship of the old Horned God. At these events, women or men disguised as women were ritually beaten, probably with a sprig of plantagenista, the green broom of the Plantagenets. Ritual flagellation can be traced back to Ancient Egypt, and in all likelihood further back than that. The early Greek journeyman Herodotus said that the annual festival held at Busiris in honour of Isis, ritual beating was enacted by a whole assembly of several thousand men and women while sacrifice was being conducted. The ritual flagellation was part of the ritual proceedings but because it was also a constituent of the Mysteries into which Herodotus himself had been initiated, he was duty bound not to reveal the reason why the beatings took place.

However, Gerald Massey can shed some light on this darker background. The horn is generally perceived a being a masculine symbol but like many ancient representations it has several meanings and is not entirely the preserve of the male. The horns of the head are actually a mainly feminine mark, relating to both the cow and the moon. Massey says "In the hieroglyphics the cow and the moon are synonymous, as Kheri bound for the sacrifice. The horns of the Kheri, cow, victim, were wreathed and gilded for the sacrifice. And the horns figuratively applied to the cuckold have the same meaning; they are the hieroglyphics of the man who patiently bears, and who is the victim led to sacrifice by his wife."

The 'Kheri-heb' were the Priesthood, and in the Old Kingdom, they were drawn from the sons of the Pharaohs, destined for high office. The cuckold refers to a man who has become the object of scorn because his wife is having an adulterous affair, or at least that's the way that they viewed it in the ancient community. And it was this strange reversal that was symbolised in the old Horn Fairs, when the men dressed up as women and suffered for their actions. The horned man takes the women's place as the bearer, and it is this theme that was central to the Horn Fairs performed in London and Kent.

The Horn Fair began as a travelling procession at Cuckolds Point at Rotherhithe on the bank of the Thames, the start being marked by a pole, topped by a pair of horns. From here, the cortege wound its boisterous way through Deptford in Greenwich, before crossing Shooters Hill to Charlton where the men would dress as women and wear the horns of the willing sacrifice in a strong echo of the Egyptian rite. But in actuality the Horn Fair was quite a mirth-filled rite not to be taken too seriously, even if it was somewhat noisy. Some commentators such as De Foe suggested that proceedings were lewd and debauched, giving the authorities a reason to ban it, which they did in 1768. Despite a brief comeback a total ban was enforced by the Victorians. But this was not the end of the Horn Fair which has since been reinstated once more, albeit in a safe, sanitised family format held each year at Hornfair Park in Charlton. For those interested in the origins of the rite, a pillar marking the original start at Cuckolds Point is still in existence at Limehouse Reach by the Thames.

Much like the London of today, the city has always been the home of many religions; there was once a Temple of Isis at Southwark where a votive vessel was found bearing the inscription, "At Londinium by the Temple of Isis". In his book *Legendary London* Lewis Spence says of the worship practiced in

Londinium, "Cults from every clime, the strange gods of Syria, Egypt and Persia, the official deities of Rome and the native worship of Germany, Spain and Gaul, as well as the Celtic religion of Britain, which resembled the latter, all were represented and permitted to function with equal freedom."

While the project of London as the New Jerusalem contained all the imaginative grandeur of Wren and Hawksmoor, the Egyptian connection provides a much earlier Middle Eastern link. Jewish writer O.J. Graham comments in his work *The Six Pointed Star* saying "...the six pointed star made its way from Egyptian Pagan rituals of worship, to the goddess Ashteroth and Moloch...then it progressed through the magic arts, witchcraft (including Aran magicians, Druids and Satanists) through the Cabala to Isaac Luria, a Cabalist in the 16th Century, to Meyer Amschel Bauer, who changed his name to this symbol" (Rothschild). This means 'Red Shield', worn by the Egyptian Hyksos Kings as a protective talisman. Originally it was the old Phoenician/Canaan symbol of Saturn. Nathan Rothschild was tasked with bringing it, along with the family business operations – to London.

The City and greater London area continued to accommodate a diverse populace, a small number of whom were involved in occult practices, masked by orthodoxy, or indeed high office. London became a melting pot of classical and Biblical motifs underpinned by the myth of Brutus. But in the midst lay great corruption and dynastic ambition that was to set the stage for a mighty Empire, just as the Prince Brutus legend had predicted.

Captain Kidd and the City Traders

Under Royal Charter, the Stuarts had ushered in several powerful institutions after the Great Fire, such as the Bank of England and trading companies, but this had only been achieved after the deposing of the Catholic James II and the supplanting of the Protestant William of Orange to the throne in 1689. Following its massive rebuilding programme, London had begun to attract financiers, many of whom were of the Jewish faith. The rise of the Rothschild, Moccatta and Goldsmith families took place during this period.

Moses Moccatta, a diamond merchant from Amsterdam, was chosen to oversee the first national coinage system, based on gold reserves held by the Bank of England. Moccatta's issuing of 'promissory notes' was an immediate success, however the first notes proved to be an easy target for forgers, so a solution to the problem was presented by a printer from Hampshire called Henry Portal. It was his idea to watermark the notes that gave birth to the original pound note. Using paper currency that promised 'to pay the bearer' the amount stated on the note made trade easier and less risky than doing everything by gold, and with so much foreign trade being generated by exploration and the founding of colonies, dominions and off-shore commercial fiefdoms, the new system was a boon for the City financiers.

The rise of English fortunes was due as discussed before, to the rebuilding of London after the Great Fire of 1666. Key to this development was the formation of trading companies under Royal Charter, by which means investments made in London could succeed elsewhere. The idea was first floated by Londoners in 1600, when the East India Company had its inception. However in 1665, the year prior to the Great Fire, two Frenchmen perfected the idea. Monsieur Pierre Radisson and his brother-in-law Médard Chouart, Sieur des Groseilliers courted investment in the City. The gentlemen in question were finding it impossible to raise finances or interest in their own country, but found a more receptive audience in London. Their proposal of a share company to explore the new dominions abroad found an enthusiastic supporter in Prince Rupert, nephew of King Charles II. So the Hudson Bay Company was born with a remit to exploit opportunities in Canada. City financiers soon warmed to the idea and agreed to raise the necessary capital for an exploratory mission, principally to export furs. Soon, other trading companies sprang up in the wake of the success of the Hudson Bay Company, with City investors seeing plenty of opportunities to work in tandem with the burgeoning new British Empire. This expansion abroad became early template of corporate colonial capitalism. London acted as the hub, granting Royal Charters to the Hudson Bay, East India and Virginia Companies. In actual fact, the Frenchmen were not the first to use this business model, as the Dutch had already founded a Dutch East India Company decades before in 1600, but the City using royal assent, perfected the business model with the arrival of Radisson and des Groseilleurs.

The Stuart King William III had no qualms about enforcing this newfound trade, by using a system of privateers to protect British interests against rivals operating out of the Netherlands, Portugal and France. The use of private naval/merchant vessels had been developed by Queen Elizabeth I, in order to gain from the plundering of foreign powers on the high seas without direct involvement in the bloodthirsty deeds themselves. By using privateers the English establishment of the time was able to foster a plausible denial policy and defend themselves against charges of benefiting from acts of piracy, by saying that the attackers were private individuals who were not acting on instruction of the nation's Parliament. Here the expression 'perfidious Albion' came to the fore once again in order to describe these rapacious acts of piracy at the hands of the English seafarers. Privateers sailed around the colonies looking for booty by right of their Royal Charter called a 'letter of marque'. Admiralty law allowed those Captains holding the letter a lot of leeway on whom or how they attacked and on what terms they engaged at sea. Using privateer sea power was a policy adopted by all

European powers of the time and in some cases enabled them to supplement their official naval resources in time of overt war.

Investors in London backed not only respectable businessmen like Radisson and des Groseilleurs, but also men like Captain Kidd, a privateer from Scotland with much experience in international maritime trade. On January 26th 1696, King William granted the letter of marque to Kidd with one caveat. "We do hereby jointly charge and command you, as you will answer the same at your utmost Peril, That you do not, in any manner, offend or molest any of our Friends or Allies, their Ships or Subjects." Scotland and England were yet to be united and therefore Kidd had to be directed towards the business interests of the English and the City financiers, many of whom were high ranking and influential members of the Whig political party. Kidd was an experienced Captain who had been involved in questionable enterprises in the Caribbean in his past, he was no stranger to violent encounters, mutinies, taking ships and claiming booty. His name is now legendary as a villainous pirate steeped in tales of buried treasure and bloody acts on the high seas who was executed at Wapping Docks in a chained gibbet. Scottish author Robert Louis Stevenson based much of his pirate novel *Treasure Island* on events surrounding Kidd. But was Kidd's reputation as black and gruesome as his detractors made out, or was his legendary demise caused entirely by events leading back to City financiers and the murky world of the privateer system?

As his brand new ship *The Adventure Galley* left Deptford and sailed down the Thames passing Greenwich Naval H.Q., Kidd failed to let off the customary one gun salute. This was not well received by the Naval authorities, who let off a cannon blast across *The Adventure Galley*'s bows. Kidd and his crew did what might only be described as a 'group moonie' while slapping their backsides in disrespectful humour. The Naval response was to seize many of the crew and press them into Royal Naval service, depriving Kidd of his full ship's company. His reaction was to sail to New York and capture the crew of another vessel, while his crew in London were offered 25% of the booty at the end of the voyage. Upon enlisting to Kidd's service, new recruits swore an oath of allegiance on a Bible with a plaster skull placed nearby. Oddly he offered the newest crew members 60% of any booty seized, a vast increase from that offered to original crew members – an anomaly that subsequent historians have picked up on.

The pragmatic Kidd had well connected investors to satisfy, so on September 6th in the same year, with a full complement of crew, Kidd set sail again, this time for the Indian Ocean, to start his Royal mission to rid the region of pirates. *The Adventure Galley* was well equipped to deal with such an undertaking, fitted as it was with 34 guns and 150 crew of different nationalities. The vessel was stocked with enough oars to enable the ship to outmanoeuvre opponents in battle, even when the winds had dropped.

Meanwhile, as Kidd was ashore in New York, *The Fancy*, a ship captained by a notorious English pirate named Avery dropped anchor in Boston having sailed from the Caribbean. The two men were only two days apart by sea but their destinies would soon cross.

Avery had been very active in the months prior to reaching American shores. As a pirate he had attacked vessels in the Cape Verde Islands and captured two Danish ships near the island of Principe. After this attack Avery and his crew had headed for the Comoros Islands, located near East Africa. Here they dropped anchor and went ashore. Avery's plan was to lay in wait for the pilgrim fleet which sailed at regular intervals from the Indian port of Surat across to Mocha at the mouth of the Red Sea and then up towards Mecca. This fleet was a quite a substantial prize for any pirate, for as well as the pilgrims aboard, wealthy merchants were also travelling with them. The added bonus was that the Great Mogul had bolstered the pilgrim flotilla with a fleet with his own ships.

Aided by his 150 strong crew, Avery attacked the pilgrim ships, with the first prize yielding gold and silver bullion worth tens of thousands of pounds. The buccaneers were very enthused to seize more booty and chose to engage with the largest of the Great Mogul's ships the *Ganj-i-Sawai*. It must be remembered that the Great Mogul's ship did have some of the most powerful members of his court on board as well as one of his own daughters. The entourage would have traveled in the most sumptuous of style, this vessel would have contained diamonds, jewels, gold bullion, slaves and much other lavish booty. On account of its royal entourage the *Ganj-i-Sawai* defended herself stoutly in a bloody, two-hour battle, but eventually she surrendered and was boarded by Avery and his motley crew for the plunder. Their robbery was augmented by a number of atrocities and indignities, which, when reaching the ears of the Great Mogul, greatly incensed him.

The Great Mogul in his outrage, vowed to drive the English merchants from the East Indies altogether. Naturally such a pronouncement was far from welcomed, either by the East India Company or their City backers. Avery became a notorious pirate across the whole of Europe, not to mention the East Indies. Back in London the financiers were quick to enlist royal support against the man who might cause a costly war against Europeans in India and ultimately wreck the new, highly profitable trade of the East India Company.

Diplomatic efforts were made to appease the Great Mogul, with the English promising to find the pirates responsible for the humiliating defeat of his greatest ship. They pledged to deliver Avery into Mogul hands and help end piracy in the Indian Oceans altogether. To this end, the King hired the privateer Kidd and this was the real mission and his *raison d'etre* for sailing into the Indian Ocean.

In true pirate fashion, Avery hid the loot in buried chests on an undisclosed island and slipped away into Boston. From there it is said he went onto Ireland, whereupon he and the crew left the ship and parted company. All concerned were then supposed to retire to lives in England. Soon after, a small section of his crew were arrested, duly tried, but then acquitted by a jury much to disdain of the Admiralty judiciary. The crew members were freed only to be arrested again with new charges brought, gained on the evidence of a certain John Dann of Rochester. Mr Dann was allegedly arrested on piracy charges and had turned King's Evidence against the crew but on closer inspection the tale seems very spurious. Dann had not been involved in maritime activities at all; in fact he was a goldsmith by trade. Dann had serious City financial connections, with tendrils leading to the Admiralty courts. His employer was James Houblon (brother of Sir John Houblon, first Governor of the Bank of England) and Sir William Paterson (creator of the Bank of England). Dann saw to it that all concerned were hanged, while he himself was exonerated of all charges. Avery meanwhile went to ground – some say he gave up the crew as an act of treachery in order to save himself.

The perfidious double dealing of Avery is of great interest in the journey of Captain Kidd and has left many questions since. Some suggestions say that Avery offered to pay off the national debt (a recurrent theme: see Chapter Nine) through his activities in piracy in return for a King's Pardon, he merely offered up his crew as a bonus. Dann, according to some researchers, was the City's man to ensure the guilty verdicts so necessary in appeasing the Great Mogul who had been internationally humiliated by acts of English piracy.

Some searching questions have to be asked about Kidd's voyage. Why did he go to New York, some 3000 nautical miles out of his way, before going on such an important mission? It is true he had business and family there, but his close proximity to Captain Avery is also curious. Why did Kidd's journey closely mirror Avery's own route of two years previous? There are some suggestions that the two Captains may have met up and discussed where Avery's loot was buried so it could be retrieved by Kidd. Kidd would have been at sail in the Indian Ocean with the blessing and goodwill of the Great Mogul without attracting suspicion, while at the same time acting on a dual mission to dig up the remainder of the treasure.

Kidd was on a secret mission acting on the orders of others – men in the City of London. There was a lot of money at stake – perhaps even enough, as has been claimed, to pay off the national debt. His behaviour certainly was secretive towards the crew, who knew little or nothing about his offers and then again learned that he had changed the rules when he offered 60% of the booty to some men in New York. Was he actually on a secret mission to retrieve the rest of the Great Mogul's treasure, that had been buried on an island somewhere in East Africa? Kidd's route certainly lends itself to such a theory.

By the time he set off from New York bound for the Indian Ocean, the politics on the high seas were certainly against the English pirates but also privateers too. The East India Company was not happy to hear of an angry Mogul considering open war on English merchants from India. When Kidd arrived in the Indian Ocean he captured a French vessel without firing a shot. This was acceptable as it was part of his official mission at the behest of King; he was a privateer and the French were therefore fair game. He completed his mission and changed ships again. Upon arrival in the Caribbean the following year he learned of a warrant for his arrest issued by the King. To his shock and horror he was accused of acts of piracy in the Indian Ocean and several English men-o-war were searching for him. Going onto New York to unite with his family, he was arrested and slung in Stone Prison before being shipped back to England to face charges.

Kidd, along with his co-accused: Able Owens, Hugh Parrot, Richard Barleycorn, Robert Lamley, William Jenkins and Gabriel Loffe were placed on trial at the High Court of Admiralty in London. Kidd himself was left to languish inside the notorious Newgate Prison. However his arrest was not as cut-and-dried as some might have hoped. Tory politicians began digging for dirt on their Whig opponents who had backed Kidd's voyages, but the resolute Kidd had nothing to say. He did petition the King, proclaiming his innocence, but his pleas fell on deaf ears. His Whig backers also ignored the hapless Captain, depriving him of money and vital papers that might have proved his innocence – these papers eventually surfaced in the early 20th century. Kidd's ships and some of his loot recovered from chests on an island had been sold off, but this was not mentioned during his trial.

The City investors, particularly the East India Company, maintained a conspicuous silence during this period, leaving Kidd doomed. He and his cohorts were found guilty and sentenced to be hanged. All were pardoned except Kidd, who was taken to Execution Dock in Wapping on the bank of the Thames on May 23rd 1701. Kidd was carried through the streets to his execution on a cart, he was drunk. The ceremonial silver oar of the Admiralty Marshal's Office was carried to the execution as crowds jeered the doomed man. Kidd was hanged, but not before the first rope snapped, sending him crashing down into the mud of the Thames, requiring him to undergo the grim ordeal a second time. After the execution, three tides washed over the body, as was customary at Execution Dock, before it was removed. As part of his sentence, Kidd's cadaver was then dipped in tar, gibbeted in chains and displayed at Tilbury estuary for three years, as a warning to anyone who might be tempted to take up piracy. His body was not given a Christian burial in line with the ancient laws of Malmutius, 16th in line to Brutus (see Appendices).

The enduring mystery of Captain Kidd has been probed by the author Paul Hawkins, who has suggested a conspiracy at the heart of the City. When Kidd was commissioned to rid the Indian Ocean of pirates the supporting documents named those involved in the attacks on the Great Mogul's fleet – Ireland, Wake, Mace, Tew and Want. Conspicuous by its absence is the name of the principal criminal, Avery. Moreover he notes that virtually all involved who could testify otherwise were hanged by the dubious evidence of Dann, a man closely connected to the Bank of England and the City financiers. Then there is the matter of the seizure of Kidd's crew at the start of his secret mission, allegedly necessitating his arrival in New York only two days sailing from Avery, who was in Boston. Why did Kidd go thousands of nautical miles out of his way to pick up crew when he could have done that in other ports closer to the Indian Ocean and, as historians have noted, he paid nearly three times as much in success money to his new crew members? Then again, Kidd was in the region of the buried treasure belonging to the great Mogul (buried by Avery), a bounty which was recovered following Kidd's arrest. This same treasure was dispersed by City financiers while Kidd protested his innocence as he awaited trial. Papers that might have saved him because they showed he was a privateer contractor were deliberately withheld as Kidd languished in Newgate, hoping in vain that his Whig political backers would come to his rescue. The establishment of the day could not be seen to be overtly dealing with Avery unless they wished to jeopardise relations with the Great Mogul. Instead, they sent Kidd to do their dirty work and his disposal at the end of the job guaranteed no awkward stories would emerge later on.

The East India Company was the world's first multinational corporation and it came to symbolise the rise of the rapacious greed of the City of London. Kidd may have been an early victim, but he was certainly not the last. Ahead lay the annexing of free peoples, the slave trade, opium wars and appalling massacres of civilians in India. A new order of British Imperialism centred in the City had arrived.

CHAPTER EIGHT

London – The Hidden Hand of the Secret Societies

Bacon's Conception of a New Atlantis

The occult ideal of founding a new Jerusalem in London can certainly be traced to the efforts of Wren and the Royal Society, but the seeds of this revolution in thought must surely be found in the work of Sir Francis Bacon. Bacon's utopian vision was laid down in his fictional work entitled *New Atlantis*, which imagined a society in which equal rights existed between all religions – almost a prefiguring of the American Bill of Rights.

The London-born poet, Alexander Pope (1688-1744), once described Francis Bacon as "the wisest, brightest, meanest of mankind".

In his upgraded edition of *The Occult Conspiracy* entitled *Secret Societies*, Michael Howard writes "Columbus was the human instrument by which the New World was discovered – or perhaps rediscovered is the best word – but the next stage in the political development of America devised by the secret societies was to be the task of a true initiate of the occult tradition, Sir Francis Bacon (1561-1626)."

Bacon's futuristic views were pivotal, providing a guiding light which inspired the generation to come. His works such as *New Atlantis* were infused with esoteric thought and enlightened concepts that caught the imagination of wider society, including the Tudor court itself. During this time many academics were revisiting the early Medieval works of Geoffrey of Monmouth, chronicler of Brutus (see Chapter One). The Tudor monarchs, backed by their political advisers and viziers began to utilise the work of Geoffrey of Monmouth, especially the Brutus legend, to support their dynastic claims. Of course, they did so to support their legitimacy to rule England, but by default the Brutus legend was all-encompassing and involved the realms of the Scots and the Welsh too. Enthusiastic Tudor monarchs were keen on promoting their direct ascendency from the Brutus bloodstock and Elizabeth I, aided and advised as she was by court astrologer Dr John Dee, used this theory to invite colonial incursions into the North Americas. Centuries before Elizabeth I, the Plantagenet King Edward I, who was keen on legal reforms, had used the device to present his case to the Pope, in order that he might lay claim to the throne of Scotland. Geoffrey of Monmouth was cited as a legal authority by Tudor Edward VI in his rough seduction of Mary Queen of Scots. All three Henrys: V, VI and VII, reigned over their Kingdom under the shadow of Geoffrey of Monmouth, whose work held much sway over the politics of the day, as the House of Tudor relied heavily on the Brutus lineage to prop up its claim to the throne over all other claimants. During turbulent times the Trojan blood royal, with its ancient connection, was a political as much as royal prerogative.

Another Tudor to use this patriotic device was Henry VII, whose rather shallow claim to the throne was bolstered by a history that showed that the King's family tree was most certainly directly connected to Brutus.

The Brutus legend affected not only England but further cemented the historians of Wales and Scotland with English interests. This was a boon to ambitious and rapacious elements in the English royal circles who saw it as a chance to seize other thrones.

According to legend, Brutus had three sons: Locrinus, Kamber and Albanactus. The brothers were allotted different tracts of the British Isles to rule over. The eldest son Locrinus ruled Loegria (England) and Kamber oversaw Kambria (Wales), which is today known as Cymru actually pronounced Kamru. The last son Albanactus was sent to rule Albany (Scotland). Modern claimants to the defunct Scottish throne of the House of Stuart, such as Michael Roger Lafosse, still bear the title HRH 7th Count of Albany.

According to Geoffrey, the line of succession from Brutus in England starts with legendary King Locrinus who married Gwedolen, who bore him a son, Maddon. The line of Brutus in England after Maddon follows as such and we have used the indigenous spelling of the names: Mebryr, Efrawg/Efrog, Brutus/Darian Las, also known as Brutus Greenshield, Leil, Run Baladr Bras, Blaiddyd and Leir, whose modified story is retold by Shakespeare in his play King Lear. Geoffrey of Monmouth tells us that King Leir then gave birth to three female siblings: Regan, Cordelia and Gonorilla. Shakespeare casts the eldest daughter Gonorilla as a scheming pretender to the throne, but Geoffrey tells us she had a son with the Duke of Albany called Morgan who went onto to rule north of the Humber (Northumbria) but was later killed by Regan's son Cunedda, with the succession passing to Regan's line. These were the influences that Shakespeare weaved into his plays and perhaps, considering the politics of the time, he did so partly to curry favour with royal patrons.

The history presented by of Geoffrey of Monmouth is generally regarded as myth, a fantastic story wholly reliant on spurious sources, even outright inventions, long ago consigned by modern historians as delirious nonsense and nothing more. To the Tudors, the histories were presented as fact, perhaps out of political expediency or perhaps because they had access to knowledge we modern folk have discarded. It is certainly true that Geoffrey goes off into flights of fancy in one or two places. Cunedda's story is placed at around the 8th Century BC and treated with as much seriousness as the factual likelihood of the legend of Romulus and Remus founding Rome. But to the folklorist this too could be informing us that Romulus and Remus came after the founding of London. The London of Brutus is believed to have pre-dated Rome's origins by 150 years at least! Returning once more to Geoffrey of Monmouth, the ancient British line of succession continues, although details about the legendary British kings are scant.

He mentions other kings: Rivallo, Gorust, Seisyll, Cynfarch and Goronwy who gave birth to two sons Ferrex and Porrex. These two brothers warred with one another and brought the reign of the legendary Trojan kings to an end.

Besides Shakespeare, other playwrights of the Elizabethan age warmed greatly to the themes in the Brutus legend. John Day and Henry Chettle used the story of Brutus Greenshield and his alleged battles as the first Briton to found an Empire, to allow British influences to flourish. Edmund Spenser also mentions Greenshield's supposed exploits and battles in the *Faerie Queen*. There is also mention of Brutus being connected to Queen Elizabeth I in the same work:

> "A chronicle of Briton kings
> From Brute to Uther's reign,
> And rolls of Elin emperors
> Till time of Gloriane."

Gloriana being Elizabeth I.

Here Spencer clearly alludes to the bloodlines of ancient Britain, Arthur and the Welsh legacy, through the Elven inheritance to the Tudor monarch – pure Trojan legend with all its audacious notions of an ancient British civilisation. Other playwrights and intellectuals alive during the Tudor period, such as Francis Bacon and John Dee, may have had more subtle reasons, other than appealing to the dynastic politics of their age, for wanting to explore the works of Geoffrey of Monmouth.

It is Bacon's place in the occult tradition that provides us with the main focal point of interest.

The Freemasonic commentator Manley P. Hall said of Bacon, "He was Rosicrucian, some have intimated the Rosicrucian if not actually the Illustrious father C.R.C. [Christian Rosenkreutz] referred to in the Rosicrucian manifesto, he was certainly a high initiate of the Rosicrucian Order... those enthusiasts who for years have struggled to identify Sir Francis Bacon as the true "Bard of Avon" might long since have won their case had they emphasised its most important angle, namely, that Sir Francis Bacon, the Rosicrucian initiate wrote into the Shakespearean plays the secret teaching of the Fraternity of R.C. and the true rituals of the Freemasonic Order, of which order it may be discovered that he was the actual founder".

This throws up some points and theories that, if true, would have ramifications of seismic proportions for both the literary and occult worlds. In fact there are three candidates who are up for the role of Shakespear's ghost writer: besides Bacon and Marlow (see Chapter six), the third contender is Edward De Vere, the 17th Earl of Oxford, who arguably fits the bill more viably than Bacon himself.

Those claiming that the true author of the works attributed to Shakespear was actually one of these three men, point towards the Bard's plays' communication of secret knowledge, either through cipher or symbol. Such knowledge would have been available to high initiates such as Bacon, Marlowe and De Vere.

While most of the populace were illiterate and innumerate at this time, certain men of privilege and learning were using their knowledge and understanding to further the boundaries of human existence. Bacon is credited with being the father of modern scientific thought, while Marlowe being a member of the School of the Night pushed through new insights into literature, language and cryptography.

Shakespeare, on the other hand, did not have the background and learning of the other two. His parents were illiterate, as was his daughter. The first is perhaps unsurprising, but the second could be seen as somewhat peculiar for the offspring of the most celebrated English playwright of all time.

Whatever the truth of the matter, the authorship of Shakespear's plays will doubtless continue to be debated between alternative and orthodox historians.

Francis Bacon's influence and mystical prescience in laying the foundations for the New World Order cannot be overstated. This view is reiterated in George V. Thorpes book *Bacon Masonry* which examines the idea that the founding fathers of the USA were merely "outworking an occult plan envisaged specifically by Bacon in the 1590s."

As a young man Bacon became a keen student of Gnosticism and the Cabala. He later became initiated into a secret society known as the Order of the Helmet, a Templar type organisation dedicated to the worship of the Greek goddess Pallas Athena, who was depicted wearing a helmet and holding a spear. She was referred to in some texts as 'the Shaker of the spear', which was not lost on Bacon, whom, it is postulated, used the designation to create the name Shakespeare. The ancient Greeks placed statues of her upon their temples and it is said that when the rays of the Sun struck the spear, it gave the appearance of shaking, hence the name Spear-shaker.

There is also a mystery surrounding Bacon's genealogy, owing to a strong suggestion that being born of a relationship between Elizabeth I and her lover, Robert Dudley, Earl of Leicester, he was subsequently raised by Sir Nicholas and Anne Bacon as their own.

If true, this would account for his meteoric rise to prominence, both in politics and the occult-based secret societies. He was quite simply the most influential man in the country, both in a covert and overt sense.

Bacon's period of prominence in history coincides with that of John Dee and while evidence of the two men associating on a regular basis is scant, there is nonetheless an entry in Dee's journal, recording a meeting with the young Bacon at Dee's Mortlake home on the afternoon of 11th August 1582.

Bacon was accompanied by a certain Mr. Phillipes, who was a leading cryptographer in the employ of Sir Francis Walsingham, the head of the newly formed secret service. Walsingham was also a student of occultism who had used the underground movement of the remaining witch covens to help accumulate information for his spy network.

The purpose of this meeting between the foremost cryptographers of the age was to discover the truth concerning one the oldest cipher systems known to mankind, the Hebrew method of the Gematria, which dates from approximately 700 BC.

In his book *Francis Bacon Herald of the New Age* Peter Dawkins says "... Francis Bacon was intensely interested in and a master of cipher and symbol, and of rhythmic language... repeatedly throughout all his works in various cryptic ways... for he saw mathematics as a vitally important occult or mystical science, and used it accordingly."

In simple cipheric terms 'Bacon' enumerates to 33. However in complete Cabalistic methodology, 100 is the cipher of Francis Bacon, which is also the number of the goddess Hekate. She is the darker aspect of Diana/Artemis or Fortune, which Bacon was said to be very concerned with. Fortune was known to the Romans as Fortuna and to the Egyptians as the multifaceted Isis.

In the Latin edition of Bacon's *History of the Reign of Henry VII*, the goddess Fortune is shown standing on a globe, turning a wheel with her left hand while she holds a bridle and ceremonial salt over Bacon's head with her right. In her triple goddess aspect as Hecate Triformis, she is represented by the three 'weird sisters' or Fates, who turn up in Macbeth, as being swift as a horse, sure as a dog and implacable as a lion.

Shakespeare, of course, is known as 'the Bard', a term for a Druidic initiate who progresses slowly through the secret knowledge initiation time-cycle. However, it is intriguing to note that the word 'bard' is also used to describe a slice of bacon used to cover meat or game during cooking in order to prevent it from drying out.

On the 3rd February 1621 shortly after his 60th birthday, Bacon was created Viscount St. Alban by James I. Alban is yet another Druid term used in the naming of the equinoxes and solstices. (See Chapter four).

During the late 16th Century, Bacon had been a 'Grand Commander' of the Rosicrucian Order who conducted rituals that, in theory, dated back to the early Knights Templar. In fact, the origins of the Rosicrucians dated further back than that. The Sumerian Grant of Arms emblem was the Rosi Crucis or Dew Cup, a cup marked with a red cross within a circle – the Mark of Cain.

This is where the symbolism of the Grail Cup is derived from – the cup that symbolically caught the blood of Jesus whilst he was on the cross, except in all probability, it didn't. This is because the Grail Cup is symbolic of the womb in Rosicrucian and occult praxis and it is the cup, or rather the womb, that carries the purest bloodline, such as Brutus' lineage, which is protected by ancient secret societies such as the Dragon Court and the Knights Templar.

In his book *New Atlantis*, published in 1627, Bacon displays the Rosicrucian theme which underpins a fantastic tale about a family marooned on a strange island, governed by metaphysical scientists who have built flying machines and underwater vessels, thus more prescient than fanciful.

Bacon describes America as the New Atlantis with a scientific institute like the Rosicrucian Invisible College, which eventually became the blueprint for the Royal Society that was indeed founded by the Order of the Rosy Cross.

In 1646, Elias Ashmole, friend of Charles II and a Knight of the Order of the Garter, together with astrologer William Lily, founded a Rosicrucian Lodge in London that was largely based on Bacon's *New Atlantis* ideals.

Bacon's other books often contain pages with Masonic symbols such as the compass and square, the twin temple pillars of Solomon's temple and the burning triangle with its all seeing eye – an indication of his connection with secret societies.

One of the first deeds undertaken by James I was to grant Bacon a knighthood. Bacon was later assigned the roles of Solicitor-General, Attorney General, Lord Keeper of the Great Seal and Lord Chancellor, in 1618.

It was to Bacon that King James again turned to when commissioning the translation of his version of the Bible, which was also monitored by Robert Fludd who was the Grand Master of the Prieure de Sion between 1595 and 1637. Actually this version of the Bible contained a minimum of 36,000 errors in the translation according to one 19th Century study. It beggars belief that someone of Bacon's obvious intellect and command of language should have made such a shambles of the King's translation, especially when Fludd was the overseer, unless that was the intention all along.

Bacon edited out the two Books of Maccabees from the new version. These two Biblical Books contained texts that were ill-disposed towards a particular secret society known as the Nazarenes.

The Bacon legacy is perhaps the best summed up by the man himself when he wrote "so in learning there cannot but be a fraternity in learning and illumination, relating to the paternity which is attributed to God, who is called the father of illumination and lights". Note the word "Illumination" is said twice in the quote – its usage would become more pertinent in the centuries that followed.

The Esoteric Lodges

Rosicrucianism and Freemasonry continued to flourish and grow and by the 19th Century, the occult renaissance was in full swing in Victorian London.

Two significant Orders emerged from the general occult movement. One of these was the Hermetic Order of the Golden Dawn, the other being the Theosophical Society. Both went on to produce several significant individuals who rose up though their secret ranking systems to become influential figures, both within their respective orders and in wider society.

One such idiosyncratic personage was Annie Besant. She had once been a devout Christian, even marrying an English clergyman at the age of twenty, but this London born free-thinker soon began to challenge the dogmatism within Christianity, as she saw it, and divorced her husband, embarking on new adventures, combining politics with journalism, spiritualism, hypnotism, and secret societies.

In 1884 she chaired the Social Democratic Federation. Besant befriended Karl Marx's daughter Eleanor and was subsequently involved in the first meeting of the Fabian Society, founded in London during the same period in time.

This organisation became closely connected to the Labour Party in the years that followed, with leaders such as Tony Blair who is also a Fabian. Its logo is a wolf in sheep's clothing, its methods are concealed and like co-founder Annie Besant some of its current members are also drawn from the shadowy world of the secret society network.

After flirting with pioneer socialist movements, Besant moved completely into the occult after her editor at the *Review of Reviews* magazine sent her two huge volumes of Madame Blavatsky's seminal work *The Secret Doctrine* to review – it seems that none of the other young journalists on his staff wanted the task of appraising Blavatsky's epic book.

The work had an immediate effect upon her. She sought out Blavatsky for an interview and after that first meeting, Besant's whole life changed.

She became Blavatsky's disciple and was placed in direct contact with an 'adept', known only as "Master M", who was one of the Theosophical movement's two secret founders.

In physical terms it was Blavatsky herself who inaugurated the Theosophical Movement in New York during 1875, along with her American promoter Col. Henry Olcott, who became the head of the Order. Besant joined the Theosophical Movement in 1889. At the core of their belief system was, and still is, the existence of a hierarchical priesthood of 'Secret Chiefs', also referred to as the 'Hidden Masters' or the 'Great White Brotherhood'. According to Theosophical doctrine, these secret occult adepts reside in Tibet and have clandestinely influenced world affairs for centuries. Blavatsky claimed that they could only be contacted telepathically, through concentrating the mind.

Some authors are of the opinion that belief in the existence of these secret Chiefs was the initial driving force that lay behind the inception of the Sufis, Knights Templar, Rosicrucians, Hermetic Order of the Golden Dawn and the Theosophical Society. Other researchers go a little further by claiming that this secret brotherhood were directly responsible for the creation of these occult orders.

Either way, Blavatsky was the first person to commit this concept to print, which had such an influence over the likes of Annie Besant. But Blavatsky latter admitted in private correspondence with her sister that she had invented the names of the Great White Brotherhood by using the nicknames of the Rosicrucians and Freemasons who were financially subsidising her.

The other major influence upon the Theosophists was a novel entitled *The Coming Race* by Lord Edward Bulwer-Lytton, himself a successor to John Dee and Francis Bacon as the Grand Patron of the Rosicrucians. Bulwer-Lyton was also a Grand Master of the Society Rite of Freemasonry and the Head of British Intelligence.

One of his recruits was Blavatsky herself, apparently, and Lytton is mentioned on several occasions in her book *Isis Unveiled*. Lytton's own fictional work *The Coming Race* was published in 1871. It centred upon an underground race of superiors who ruled a socialist state using mastery of the life-force or 'Vril' power. This mysterious Vril energy manipulated by these Asian adepts could be used telepathically for healing purposes, or as a weapon, a lethal death ray not dissimilar to a present day laser or microwave technology. But it wasn't only the Theosophists and Blavatsky who became significantly influenced by Bulwer-Lytton's work.

Writing in his book *Secret Societies* Michael Howard comments "One of the German mystico-political groups called itself the Vril Society and took its philosophy from Lytton's novel. The Vril Society was originally founded as the Luminous Lodge, combining the political ideas of the Illuminati with

Hindu mysticism, Theosophy and the Cabala. It was one of the first German nationalist groups to use the symbol of the swastika as an emblem linking Eastern and Western occultism".

Blavatsky's notions about racial origins and the surfacing of a new esoterically armed human during the Age of Aquarius, were readily adopted by German nationalist orders, who used it to justify their own agenda of Aryan racial supremacy.

Thus the seeds had been sown for the flourishing of something far more sinister and malign in 20th Century central Europe.

HPB, as Blavatsky was known, moved to London in early May 1887 where she inaugurated a new Theosophical Lodge at 'Maycott'. But after a four month stay there it was obvious that the Blavatsky Lodge required more spacious accommodation, so it was relocated at 17 Lavisdown Road, Holland Park W11.

Three years further on and in the summer of 1890, there was yet another move to another London property, this time close to Regent's Park. 19 Avenue Road, NW8 comprised three separate houses joined by a garden where HPB planned to build an Eastern style lecture hall made from polished wood, that would accommodate approximately 300 people.

But by this time Blavatsky's health was fading, and she died the following year. Her husband Col. Henry Olcott remained President of the Order until his own death in 1907, whereupon Annie Besant was elected president for seven years and was re-elected three times as Chief of Theosophy.

Besant was also instrumental in bringing Co-Masonry (which admits both male and female members) into Europe and the English speaking countries, using her Theosophical connections to set up lodges all over the world. In 1912 Besant inaugurated a Rosicrucian organisation within Theosophy called the Order of the Temple of the Rosy Cross, which was disbanded in 1918. However most of its members became involved in the formation of a new group, the Rosicrucian Order of the Crotona Fellowship in 1920 which was headed by none other than George Alexander Sullivan, the same Alex Sullivan that would later take the Crotona Fellowship into the theatre and the New Forest Coven, which we have already documented in Chapter six in 'The Windsor Royal Coven'.

Early in this chapter we also referred to the Fabian Society, which was partly created by Annie Besant. A more indepth look at the Fabian Society soon reveals that it is a secret society at its very heart.

Early leading Fabian, George Bernard Shaw wrote "This new and complete revolution we contemplate can be defined in a very few words. It is outright... world socialism, scientifically planned and directed".

It was Shaw who designed a muralled "Fabian Window" which shows two leading Fabians pounding the earth with a raised anvil above a mounted globe. Alongside the anvil, situated directly above the globe is the familiar Fabian logo of the wolf in sheep's clothing.

This window was mysteriously lost to the world for a quarter of a century, before its equally strange appearance in Phoenix, Arizona, after which it was brought to England and unveiled at the Fabian society's, London School of Economics in 2009 by a certain Tony Blair. Its motto reads "Remould nearer to the hearts desire". Fabians use a method that they call 'permeation' which involves arriving at a consensus via means of manipulation – underhand deals once again.

The use of the Blacksmith's anvil hammering into the world globe, has a mystical legacy of its own. In *The Element Encyclopaedia of Witchcraft* by Judika Illes there is a substantial section on metalworkers, in which we find "The history of the modern magical practitioner is intertwined with the history of smithcraft...". The Smith's art was kept secret for centuries. Those who possessed its secrets were able to craft weapons and tools by which they could completely dominate their neighbours – world domination indeed.

Molten iron is the Earth's menstrual blood, the witch blood, which has associations with primordial female power, as in the great goddess figures.

The ancient Phoenician Cabiri (meaning 'Mighty') colonised the Mediterranean island of Samothrace and turned it into a haven for the dark mysterious worship of Hekate – the infernal underworld goddess, prior to their arrival on British shores. Some of the earliest depictions of the Cabiri show them complete with hammer and anvil.

The Fabian Society's window reveals deeply occult connotations.

The seminal 1960s TV spy drama *The Prisoner* written by and starring Patrick McGoohan encompassed a combination of George Orwell's book *1984*, published in 1948 and Aldous Huxley's 1932 novel *Brave New World*.

In the original ITV series *The Prisoner*, a high-ranking government agent (Patrick McGoohan) resigns from his post, thinking that he is going on vacation but instead, he wakes up one morning to find himself in a mysterious controlled environment simply called "The Village". In the Village there are no names, everyone has a grade and number and they exist in a cashless society using credit notes provided by the community's controllers. Mind control techniques are employed on some inhabitants to ensure that they fit in and, of course, there is no escape. The underlying climate of fear means that no one asks any questions, surveillance cameras are everywhere and the movements of the Village's inhabitants are closely monitored by those in control.

Sound familiar?

George Orwell and Aldous Huxley were personal friends and Fabians, indeed it was Huxley who introduced Orwell into the Fabian Society.

However there was more than just a suspicion that *Brave New World*, *1984* and *The Prisoner* which was heavily inspired by them, offered not so much a fictional vision of things to come, as an actual portent of what was just around the corner.

It is certainly true to say that leading Fabian, Tony Blair and his New Labour administration introduced more laws designed to restrict our civil liberties than any other previous administration and increased the amount of CCTV surveillance on an unprecedented level.

George Orwell, whose real name was Eric Blair, (no relation to Tony) became disillusioned with the Fabians, leading some to believe that *1984* was indeed an expose of the real Fabian agenda, using the title as a symbolic centennial commemoration of the Fabian Society's founding in 1884.

When Orwell's second wife died, his entire estate fell under the control of the Fabian society. They apparently control the copyright of *1984*, and will continue to do so until 2025. They also seized and sealed up Orwell's documents along with other archive material. Clearly they do not want any of this material to be released into public domain.

The wolf in sheep's clothing logo could not be better illustrated by the behaviour of the Fabian Society which Annie Besant helped to found in 1884.

Besant herself was not averse to acquiring material from others and incorporating into her own Order. Such was the case with John Yarker's Masonic Rite of Memphis and Misraim, which Annie Besant and Josiah Wedgwood wanted to assimilate into Co-Masonry upon Yarker's death in 1913. This was resolutely resisted by Aleister Crowley, who did everything in his power to ensure that Yarker's authority transferred to him. Owing to problems with the legitimacy of Crowley's own Masonic credentials, he was unable to wrest control of the Rite of Memphis and Misraim from his Theosophical rivals, although the O.T.O. which he went on to lead, still claims that it is in part a continuation of Yarker's Masonic Rite.

Crowley was a member of what was probably the most important magical order in recent history, The Hermetic Order of the Golden Dawn, described as a hothouse of schism, scandal and intrigue, with a membership of diverse initiates such as the poet W.B. Yeats, the actress Florence Farr, tea company heiress Annie Horniman, Dracula author Bram Stoker, and of course occult dangerman, Aleister Crowley himself.

The Golden Dawn was founded upon the 'Cipher Manuscripts' – a strange set of documents written in English using the Trithemius Cipher. These mysterious manuscripts gave detailed outlines of the Grades and rituals attributed to the Order. They encompassed alchemical and occult sciences along with astrology and the Qabalah.

They were apparently unearthed by a Masonic scholar, Kenneth

Mackenzie, who handed them on to the Rev. A.F.A. Woodford, said by occult writer Francis king to be the fourth founder of the Golden Dawn.

Woodford in turn sent them to London Coroner and Freemason, William Wynn Wescott. However, this is just one of four versions of how the Golden Dawn rituals ended up in Westcott's possession. One account has it that he found them in the dingy archives of the library belonging to the Societas Rosicruciana in Anglia (S.R.I.A.), a Masonic side Order with Rosicrucian pretentions of which all the founders of the Golden Dawn were members. In another account he was handed them by Mackenzie's widow. The final tale has Woodford finding the papers in a London bookstall and handing them to Wescott. Whichever way around it was, Wescott had them, and he knew what he needed to do with them.

Like his fellow Freemason Mackenzie, Wescott also had obtained the *Trithemius Polygraphie* (1561) that contained the Cypher used in the manuscript, which he duly decoded in 1887, following the deaths of both Woodford and Mackenzie.

Westcott then requested the help of fellow Mason Samuel Liddell 'MacGregor' Mathers (1854-1918) to assist in developing the Cipher Manuscript ritual blueprint into a coherent magical system.

Mathers in turn asked another fellow Mason, Robert Woodman, if he could provide further assistance with the task and Woodman duly accepted.

In the course of his own decoding of the manuscript, Westcott discovered the name and address of one Freulein Anna Sprengel. He wrote to her and in her reply, she bestowed honorary grades of Adeptus Exemptus on Wescott, Mathers and Woodman. This enabled Wescott to conceive plans denoted in the manuscript.

In London during 1888, this process came to fruition with the formation of the Isis-Urania Temple where the rituals decoded from the manuscript were first conducted. This became the 'Outer' or 'First Order' of the Golden Dawn, which existed purely in this format until 1892.

During this period, Mathers was already working on the creation of the neo-Rosicrucian 'Second Order' which he named 'Rosa Rubae et Aureae Crucis' (Ruby Rose and Cross of Gold).

The main influences and philosophy behind what was to become the 'Inner Order' were the Qabalah, the religion and magic of ancient Egypt, Theugy, Alchemy, Freemasonry, the Enochian magic system of John Dee and the various works of the early 19th Century French occultist Eliphas Levi, who reconstituted the now infamous Baphomet, or 'Goat of Mendes' image.

When news of Anna Sprengel's death reached the adepts of the Golden Dawn in 1891, Mathers claimed that contact between himself and the Secret Chiefs had been made, sealing his status as chosen leader of the Order.

Talk of 'hidden masters' brings us into more familiar territory, namely Blavatsky and the Theosophists, and as with Theosophy, there is much controversy surrounding the identities of the key influential figures in the foundation of the Golden Dawn. For example, many researchers dispute the existence of Fraulein Sprengel, the German representative of the German magical order from which the Cipher Manuscripts were said to have originated, who supposedly granted Wescott the licence to create the Golden Dawn.

Many researchers think that it is highly likely that she was merely a fabrication that legitimised Westcott's plans. However, it is possible, if not probable, that the Cipher Manuscripts did exist even if the real story of how they were discovered remains forever elusive.

Similarly intangible is the story of the tomb of Christian Rosenkreutz, which was symbolically pivotal to the Golden Dawn's Second Order rituals.

The mysterious semi-mythical figure of Christian Rosenkreutz supposedly founded the Rosicrucian movement some time in the 14th or 15th Century after acquiring secret knowledge during his travels in the East (where else!).

In 1614 a manuscript called *The Declaration of the Worthy Order of the Rosy Cross* was published at Kassel in Germany, which revealed the existence of the Rosucrucian Brotherhood. This publication was followed by another in 1615 called the *Confessio Fraternitatis*, which further boasted about the all powerful knowledge held by the secret brotherhood which would one day go to overthrow the established church and thereby change the world.

This trilogy was completed in 1616 when a strange story entitled *The Chemical Wedding of Christian Rosenkreutz* appeared in print. This tale is supposedly told by Rosenkreutz himself and in it he speaks of a royal wedding between King and Queen in a lavishly furnished castle. However, this joyous event suddenly takes a far more sinister turn as the wedding guests are subjected to a series of tests to determine their worthiness, after which several are killed and then brought back to life by means of an alchemical operation.

There is much occult symbolism in this story and it has been suggested that this uncanny fictional tale could possibly be an allegorical allusion to the Royal Dragon Court bloodline and alchemical ritualistic activities associated with Royal Witchcraft.

As we have already seen, the connections between the Rosicrucians and the Royal Dragon Court are indeed quite close.

There is also much debate and controversy over the real identity of Christian Rosenkreutz. Was he a real person or just another coded mystery reference?

The author of the three works is generally reckoned to be one Johann

Valentin Andrea, who has been named as the Grand Master of the Prieure de Sion between 1637 and 1654.

Rosenkreutz's legend maintains that he was born in 1378 and died in 1484 at the age of 106. His body was then said to have been interred in a mysterious tomb with instructions given to the Brotherhood to open the tomb after 120 years. The story tells us that this was duly done, upon which Rosenkreutz's body was found to have been perfectly preserved.

It is this curious narrative that underpinned the Golden Dawn ritual curriculum drawn up by Mathers.

The Golden Dawn continued to flourish with a clientele which had risen to over a hundred initiates drawn from all facets of Victorian society.

But in 1897, Westcott, who was a respected coroner, got into hot water when his employers became aware of his occult activities after a batch of the Golden Dawn's secret papers and other related documents were discovered in the back of a hansom cab, supposedly left there mistakenly by Westcott himself.

The finger pointing began with Mathers, who some sources say wanted Westcott out, and had thereby arranged for the papers to be planted where they could be found. If this was a deliberate ploy on Mathers' part, it certainly worked. Wescott's superiors simply could not tolerate someone who dealt with dead bodies by day and attempted to summon spirits by night. An ultimatum was given – it was either the Golden Dawn or his job and his reputation. Wescott chose the latter and duly broke with the Order. Mathers got what he wanted at last – total control of the Golden Dawn.

One of his firsts acts as Master was to appoint actress Florence Farr as Chief Adept in the region of Anglia.

Together with other Golden Dawn Adepti, Farr had formed the Spear Group in 1896. This Order within an Order was heavily involved with rituals focused on the centre of a spear, wherein the group were convinced that the astral form of an Egyptian adept could be contacted. They claimed to have first made contact with the Egyptian through a piece of his mummified casing.

This splinter group within the Order proved problematic for Mathers. While he was keen to maintain his cherished status by keeping the contact and identities of the Secret Chiefs to himself, others such as Farr and her associates were stretching out in the astral plane for themselves.

They wanted to make contact with the Secret Chiefs in their own right, rather than continue with the sole Mathers monopolisation of the Order hierarchy. Mathers had imposed his dictatorial rule over the Golden Dawn, but like all dictators he had to be careful to maintain it.

He relied heavily on funding from Annie Horniman, the wealthy tea company heiress. Horniman (1860-1937) was born in Forest Hill, London where she also founded the Horniman Museum in 1897. Acknowledged as a pioneer of British repertory theatre, she was initiated into the Golden Dawn in 1890. Her brother was the Liberal MP Conslie Horniman, and her grandfather, a wealthy tea merchant was the inventor of the tea bag.

It was from this background that Annie Horniman had acquired her wealth, some of which subsidised Mathers, who was able to develop the Golden Dawn entirely through her patronage.

When Horniman emerged as a leading opponent of Dr Edward Berridge's occult sexual theories also subscribed to by Mathers, this presented huge problems for both the Golden Dawn's overlord and the Order itself. Berridge and Horniman were suspended and summarily expelled from the Golden Dawn. With his finances gone Mathers was soon to follow. In the meantime, looming large and waiting in the wings was the figure of a certain Aleister Crowley – Mathers' staunchest ally at this time. But in fairly typical fashion, Crowley soon fell out with Mathers for daring to go public with the Order's secret rituals. The Golden Dawn was probably best described by Martin Short, author of *Inside the Brotherhood*, a book essentially about Masonry, when he describes the Golden Dawn as "Freemasonry with the occult lid off". Certainly this uncapped well of magical ritualistic activities became the cornerstone of the modern occult revival.

As for Crowley, he soon got bored the Golden Dawn and its politics, leaving to continue his journey of exploration into ritual practices embracing the weird, the wonderful and downright dangerous, in order to boldly, (or perilously) go where no occultist had gone before.

Entering the Eye of Horus

It was at London's Mark Masons Hall, on the evening of November 18th 1898 that a young man, robed in black, petulantly waited to be admitted into what he sincerely believed would be the ultimate hidden knowledge, embracing the secrets of the occult, the universe, life and even death itself.

The 23-year-old postulant was blindfolded and led into the Temple, before being steered into a kneeling position facing an altar containing a red cross and white triangle. He was then commanded to swear an oath that he would "Keep secret the order, its name, the names of its members and the proceedings that take place at its meetings…". After swearing further that he would not allow any person or power to cause him to lose control of himself, the young man was directed into making the following chilling closing commitment that "If I break this, my magical obligation, I submit myself, by my own consent, to a deadly and hostile current of my will set in motion by the Secret Chiefs of this Order, by which I might fall slain and paralysed without visible weapon as if slain by a lightning flash".

After an invocation of 'the Lord of the Universe' was read over him, the young man's blindfold was finally removed to reveal three robed magicians, two of whom held sceptres, the other a sword, directly over his head. They all spoke together saying "We receive thee into the Golden Dawn". The young man taking his first tentative steps into the occult world was none other than Aleister Crowley, who would go on to become the 20th century's most revered, and reviled, practitioner of the magical arts. The influence of both the Hermetic Order of the Golden Dawn and the group's leader, Samuel Lidell 'MacGregor' Mathers, never really left Crowley, even after he had long since left them.

The young idealist Crowley joined the Golden Dawn with the highest of hopes, truly believing that he was finally being admitted into the shadowy group of adepts that had been governing the development of humanity for centuries. The romance soon faded however, once he discovered that many of his new found 'Fratres and Sorores', far from being hidden masters, were more the type of Victorian bohemian who had a penchant for the theatre of ceremony, if possessing little in the way of true occult knowledge. Yet one or two members impressed Crowley enough to cause him to stay, most notably Allan Bennett, who went on to become the first western Buddhist monk and who is largely credited as a key figure in bringing Buddhism to a western audience, and of course, the group's brilliant if somewhat peculiar leader, Mathers, with whom Crowley became close.

Under his new magical motto, 'Perdurabo' (I shall endure unto the end), the young Crowley set to the Order's syllabus of magical work with characteristic zeal and rapidly rose through its ranks. The young man's meteoric rise through the grades of the Golden Dawn's initiatory system began to alarm many of his more senior brethren, who saw that Crowley represented a threat, not only to the stability of the Order itself, but to their own increasingly flimsy authority over him.

The events leading up to Crowley's departure from the Golden Dawn are both baleful and bizarre. On March 29th 1900, the Adepti held a meeting at the London Temple, 36 Blythe Rd, Hammersmith W14.

Here the rebel Golden Dawn Adepti voted to oust their leader Mathers, who responded with an astonished communiqué in which he threatened to send a punitive a magical current after the dissidents, as he claimed in the final paragraph of his letter which read "And for the first time since I have been connected with the Order, I shall formulate my request to the Highest Chiefs for the Punitive Current to be prepared, to be directed against those who rebel should they consider it (after examination of the Status of the London Order) advisable."

The loyal Crowley was called to assist his friend Mathers and after scampering off to Paris, Crowley was requested to return to London in order to help Mathers take back the London Temple from the rebels, but they had their own ideas about launching a pre-emptive occult strike upon Crowley. Most of them hated him through his continual and unabated support for Mathers. They thought Crowley to be "a mad unspeakable person" according to poet W.B. Yeats, who was himself a member. He also said that the rebels' most capable magicians had inaugurated a combined occult attack on Crowley via the astral plane, influencing a former mistress to turn against him, which she did by going straight to Scotland Yard and laying a charge of torture and medieval iniquity against him. Unsurprisingly, he saw it differently. His own accounts reveal that when he left Paris on 13th April, Mathers warned Crowley to expect a psychic attack and to watch out for mysterious fires and ones that refused to burn.

As a protective talisman, Mathers gave Crowley a Rosicrucian cross. On his return to the London temple strange things did indeed happen to Mathers' magical hatchet man.

Whilst riding in a cab, the paraffin headlights ignited, causing the cab to immediately halt its journey. Crowley flagged down another cab, but shortly after he had boarded the carriage, the horse bolted for no apparent reason. Later, at the London home of one of Mathers' supporters in the Order, Crowley observed that the fire in the open hearth was seriously struggling to stay lit, while at the same time his rubber mackintosh which was well away from the fireplace suddenly and inexplicably burst into flames. Crowley recalled the warning given by Mathers when he left Paris. Crowley was indeed experiencing precisely what Mathers had predicted would happen when he returned to London.

Crowley clasped the Rosicrucian cross entrusted to him by Mathers, and as he did so he noticed something strange about it. Its colour had begun to fade and by the next day it had turned nearly bleach white.

By this time Crowley had seemingly had enough, and exited swiftly from the whole Golden Dawn affair setting sail for New York, but before he did so, he made one last visit to Paris to see Mathers. Whilst there, Crowley persuaded Mathers to release the punitive magical current and direct it towards the rebels. This Mathers did, by using bizarre symbolism involving the most common of green vegetables. Crowley expended an entire Sunday afternoon observing Mathers use a food sieve containing green peas. Each of these peas were allotted the name of one of the rebels who were attempting to take over the London Temple of the Golden Dawn. Mathers would then shake the sieve and by the "formulae of the Great Enochian Tablet of Spirit " he would summon the demons Beelzebub and Typhon-Set, calling upon them to work on the rebels and create chaos. Mathers' vegetable magic histrionics left Crowley decidedly underwhelmed, as did the lack of noticeable results from the operation. He wrote later of the rebels under Mathers' attack, "nobody seemed a penny for the worse".

In the years that followed, Mathers unsuccessfully tried to get an injunction against Crowley in order to prevent the publication of Crowley's periodical *The Equinox*, No.3 in March 1910. By that time, Crowley no longer felt under any Golden Dawn control and had decided to publish several of the Order's secret rituals, much to the remaining members' chagrin.

But Crowley had moved on, this time to a secret society of German origin, called the Ordo Templi Orientis, or the Order of the Eastern Templars, better known by its initials, O.T.O. which is said to contain a secret meaning hidden in the abbreviation.

One of the most significant figures in the formation of the O.T.O. was a Freemason called Theodor Reuss, described by Francis King in his book *The Magical World of Aleister Crowley* as a "very odd character indeed". Reuss was a paid-up German secret agent and he was far from being the only head of a secret society to have such a connection. Crowley, his acolyte Jack Parsons and originally John Dee, also enjoyed similar links to intelligence and high-ranking military circles. In the main the O.T.O. claimed a lineage from sects such as the Bavarian Illuminati, the Templars and the Albigensians who were alleged carriers of the Elven bloodline, so important to the Prieure de Sion, the Templars and the Dragon symbolism.

Reuss had a number of occult titles on his CV. One of his prime interests was instigating the revival of the Bavarian Illuminati as a modern day institution, a project which failed. Reuss employed his own Masonic affiliations to appropriate the 90th and 96th degrees of the Ancient and primitive Rite of Memphis and Mizraim along with the 33rd degree of the Ancient and Accepted Scottish Rite from leading English Masonic scholar John Yarker. It was Yarker who inducted Crowley into the same degrees. Crowley joined the O.T.O. in 1910 and by 1912, taking the title Baphomet, he became Grand Master of the English speaking world, operating out of the order's London HQ.

When Reuss died in 1923, Crowley proclaimed himself the order's sole leader or O.H.O. (Outer Head of the Order), a position that he would hold right up until his death in 1947. The student had finally become the Master.

Through Crowley the O.T.O. claimed to have received heretical knowledge from numerous secret societies such as the Order of the Temple, the Knights of Malta, the Rosicrucian Order, the Golden Dawn and the Order of Illuminati, to name but a few. The latter's name was also incorporated by Crowley into the lower Masonic degrees of the O.T.O. named 'Mysteria Mystica Maxima' or M.M.M. for short. The eighth of the nine degree initiatory system is called 'the Perfect Pontiff of Illuminati', 'Epopt of the Illuminati'. The fifth degree, 'Sovereign Prince of Rose Croix: Knight of the Pelican and the Eagle', takes its name from the 18th degree of the Ancient and Accepted Scottish Rite of Freemasonry. In an earlier, rather fanciful illustration, showing the initiation of a candidate into this degree we are shown the candidate being carried aloft seated in a chair, wearing a Satanic goat's head mask similar to Eliphas Levi's 'Goat of Mendes' illustration, the large horns and bearded portrayal of the face forming an inverted pentagram. Yet it has to said, this depiction of the rite bears little relation to the real 18th degree ritual, which is based squarely on Christian symbolism, albeit unorthodox in nature.

The O.T.O. then, has drawn its ritual process from a plethora of Masonically inclined secret societies, although in common with its Rosicrucian parent, it does claim to incorporate mystical teachings drawn from both eastern and western sources. The O.T.O.'s philosophy under Crowley and subsequent leaders, is underpinned by the *Book of the Law*, a short book of three prose poem chapters, that announces a new spiritual law for humanity called 'Thelema'. After a bizarre series of events that culminated in Crowley being contacted by a 'praeterhuman intelligence' named Aiwass, the book, so Crowley maintained until the end of his life, was dictated to him on three successive days in April 1904. Thelema is expressed in the statement "Do what thou wilt shall be the whole of the Law" which was presaged by one of Dee's angelic channelling sessions when he received the words "Do that which pleaseth you ... wherefore do even as you list". Other precursors to the Thelemic law can be found in Francois Rabelais' religious satire, *Gargantua and Pantagruel*, and even in Saint Augustine's "Love, and do what you will."

The Invisible Illuminati
The Order of the Illuminati, which Crowley claimed formed part of the O.T.O.'s occult genealogy, first arose in the late 1760s when Mayer Amshel Rothschild formulated the directional programme for the Order's inception. This concordat began in Frankfurt and consisted of Adam Weishaupt, Mayer Amshel Rothschild and Jacob Frank, who was part of the Frankfurt spin-off of the Jewish Sabbatain sect. It was the Jesuit educated Weishaupt who finally founded the Masters of the Illuminati in 1776.

According to some sources, Weishaupt was just a front man for a pre-existing occult cabal, originally called 'the Brotherhood of the Snake'. His chief role was to restructure the bloodlines of this brotherhood under a new name, the Order of the Illuminati, or 'the illuminated ones', meaning that its admittants had been initiated into the occult knowledge appertaining to Lucifer in his guise as Light Bearer, and thus elevated to a divine status. In actuality Weishaupt said "The true purpose of the Order was to rule the world".

To achieve this lofty ambition it was necessary to destroy all religions, overthrow all governments and abolish private property.

Weishaupt also wrote "One must speak sometimes one way and sometimes another...so that, with respect to our true line of thinking, we may be impenetrable". However, a different form of divine intervention came into being when an Illuminati courier, Herr Lanze, was struck by lightning while travelling through the German city of Regensburgh. Lanze was *en route* from Frankfurt to Paris, carrying important instructions for the Chiefs, when tragedy struck. The secret Illuminati papers were recovered from his lifeless body and passed to the German authorities, who subsequently swooped upon the Illuminati HQ, seizing all their papers.

The contents of these documents soon spread around the rest of Europe, with some falling into the hands of Scottish Freemason and scientist, John Robison. A man of integrity, Robison was shocked to read the dastardly Illuminati plans to infiltrate Freemasonry and manipulate the Lodges for their own benefit. Robison set out to investigate the Iluminati by gathering more information, his exposé is still regarded as one of the most accurate renderings of the Illuminati. Robison's paper is entitled *Proofs of a Conspiracy Against All Religions and Governments of Europe, carried on in Secret Meetings of the Freemasons, Illuminated and Reading Societies*, the book is still in print today.

It contains one key quote that stands out, which is taken directly from the Illuminati's own documents:

"The great strength of our Order lies in its concealment, let it never appear in any place in its own name, but always concealed by another name, and another occupation. None is fitter than the lower degrees of Freemasonry, the public is accustomed to it, expects little from it, and therefore takes little notice of it. Next to this, the form of a learned or literary society is best suited to our purpose, and had Freemasonry not existed, this cover would have been employed; and it may be much more than a cover, it may be a powerful engine in our hands...A Literary society is the most proper form for introduction of our own Order into any state where we are yet strangers...".

This document reflects perfectly what happened when the Bavarian Government banned the Illuminati in 1785 and attempted to round up the ring-leaders. Some were prosecuted for attempting to overthrow the State but most, including Weishaupt himself, got away by fleeing to other countries where they assimilated into the culture and infrastructure of society. Just because a secret order or secret society is banned, exposed or purged it does not mean that it ceases to exist. Individual members of resurrected groups with the right connections can merely re-identify themselves and operate with a new mask. It is highly likely that the Templars were able to do this. The purge of the Templars in Britain was much less severe than that of France and many think that the City of London Livery Companies became a haven for the routed Templar order, leaving those behind the scenes to remain very much active.

As for the Illuminati, their alleged policy of structuring the bloodlines would seemingly be apparent in the legacy of Mayer Amshel Rothschild, which would be so dominant within London.

Mayer Amshel Rothschild (Bauer), was the founder of the Rothschild dynasty. Before he died on September 19th 1812, Mayer drew up a will in the form of a dictum upon the future of the Rothschild family structure. The precise contents remain secret, but one edict did emerge. That the importance of the family bloodline which they claim can be traced back to Nimrod (including that of Brutus, founder of London) takes precedence over all other matters. In this respect Mayer decreed that the family's daughters and their husbands and heirs must be excluded from the family business, the running of which was to be a completely male-controlled prerogative. The will also ruled that the male heirs continued the policy of procreation by first cousins intermarrying, in order to keep the bloodlines pure and to effect control over the children. Mayer had five sons who all carried his name as their middle names, so they were known as the Mayer brothers. The cleverest of these sons was Nathan Mayer Rothschild, whom Mayer senior sent to England to establish the UK House of Rothschild, which he did by going first to Manchester and then moving to London in 1804, where his wealth increased markedly along with his reputation.

Mayer sent each of his five sons to different European capitals for the same purpose. At least one of his sons was known to be a member of the Illuminati, but it is not known whether Nathan was among them.

Mayer Amshel Bauer-Rothschild died in 1812, and his sons each voted that Nathan should become the next head of the family from his operational base in London. Nathan was also a member of the London Lodge of Emulation, which was only open to Master Masons, and operated more like a Lodge of ritual instruction based upon the notion of the old pagan Temple of Solomon and the removal of all traces of Christianity from the rites. This movement within Freemasonry met at Freemasons Hall, London, where plans were mooted to change the dedication of Masonic Lodges from Holy Saint John to King Solomon. The Rothschilds had begun to become powerful within the various Masonic Lodges at this time.

Among their secret plans was a plot to appropriate and avail themselves of the ancient laws and customs that had been first instigated by Brutus and the ancient Britons, in order to hijack them to serve their own agenda.

CHAPTER NINE

London – Ancient Paths, Shadow Powers and Covert Connections

Malmutius – The Brutus Bequest

Both the Tudors and Stuarts had grasped at any supporting evidence that would demonstrate their Trojan heritage, if only to protect their realms and seize the lands of other rulers, but there were those who understood the Brutus mythos in an altogether different way.

The foundation of London as a major city in Europe followed the publication of Bacon's *New Atlantis*, which later gave birth to the concept of a New Jerusalem rising like a phoenix from the ashes. Wren and the Royal Society were acutely aware of Brutus and his London connection: their work, albeit Christian, made Wren's Temple of Diana (St Paul's) the hub of the City. Scholars and academics of the period were happy with the notion of an ancient British heritage, even if, on occasion, the odd King or Queen took liberties with its usage.

This mood suddenly changed upon the arrival of the Germanic House of Hanover, who rose to the throne in 1714. King George I, formerly called George Ludwig, spoke only German and understood little of his new subjects. George faced a hostile audience in his new Kingdom and within a year of being crowned the old ruling House of Stuart had started a rebellion in Scotland, which was both religious and political. This Jacobite uprising was fuelled by ancient claims to the throne, and demonstrated the volatile nature of George's new position as monarch. The Scottish Jacobite rebellion, aided by the French, caused great concern for George I and his supporters for it fanned the flames of ancient alliances going far back in history. The Brutus legend, with its unifying links to English, Welsh and Scottish histories was now something distinctly unsettling to the Hanoverian court of George I. Geoffrey of Monmouth and his eccentric histories of the ancient Britons may have been tolerated a few years earlier but now the Brutus mythos would be intellectually suppressed. The rebellious Scottish, along with their Stuart pretender to the throne were *persona non grata* in Hanoverian eyes and their claims nothing short of heretical. Although the military side of the rebellion was soon put down, the Stuart Jacobite plot simmered in the background. Another Scottish rebellion in 1745 only worsened the situation, and was heavily linked to Masonic, Tory and French circles that were unhappy with the Hanoverian succession. There were three King Georges in succession and they oversaw an age in which the upper classes were linked to excess and debauchery, yet the rights of the common man were being eroded.

By 1789 when the rather shattering news of the French Revolution arrived, the monarchy in Britain was already wary of secret societies that harboured the recently forbidden history of the British Isles. The legend of Brutus and his Trojan lineage, along with his ancient laws, immutable rights and British history, was something of a powder keg ready to explode. The Brutus mythos had the power to give credence to certain enemies of the House of Hanover, challenging the legitimacy of their claim to the throne and was therefore something not welcome in Georgian England.

Nearly a century later Queen Victoria married another Germanic royal, Prince Albert of the Saxe-Coburg-Gotha aristocratic line, who like George I, spoke only German. The heritage of Prince Albert was clearly Saxon in origin and after the wedding the Victorian establishment did all in their power to promote the vision of an Anglo-Saxon England, and by cultural default, under the all-encompassing title of Great Britain, imposed this history on the rest of the British Isles.

One of the remaining Celtic tongues still spoken at that time in Britain was Welsh. In 1846 there was a Government Commission raised to look into it being taught in Welsh schools. They reported unfavourably on this and so the teaching of their native language was banned all over Wales. Similarly the teaching of the Welsh folklore, much of which supported the Brutus mythos, was ethnically cleansed from the classroom and elsewhere, in the English public school system, the focus was entirely placed on the study of classical civilisations with little or no mention of the ancient Britons.

The Victorians, obsessed with the notion of Anglo-Saxon England, chose a person to rewrite British history. He was a clergyman called Stubbs, who was duly appointed as Regius Professor of Modern History at Oxford in 1866. His view of British history was firmly Anglo-Saxon in origin with little or no time for ancient Britons, who from that point on became lowly savages in the view of academia with little or no cultural input into the islands' history. His chosen discipline to support his new theories was the fledgling science of archaeology and the result was a very pro-Roman history of London, leading of course to the Anglo-Saxon hegemony. It suited the Imperial mindset of the Victorian Establishment, who had hailed from public schools and been fed on classical literature, to treat the notion of a civilised ancient Britain as below contemplation. This attitude of considering other cultures as inferior was extended to the hundreds of indigenous peoples of the British Empire, who were looked down upon as mere un-Christian savages and thus treated as such.

Victorian Britons often compared themselves to the glory of Rome and grandeur of Greece, while much of their own roots stemming from the ancient British and Welsh myths were actively suppressed during this period. A London emerging from a Trojan legacy was seen as being the most absurd of all the myths and was abandoned completely. To this day conventional historians are still quoting the history edited by Stubbs, and schoolchildren fed the canon of this history, that the Romans founded London. However one should be mindful of the many claims that historians have made, and then had to back down from in light of later discoveries.

For example historians initially told us that the pyramids were eroded by sand, until a new science called geology proved that this was not the case at all, and that in fact the pyramids were eroded by water. Once historians stood corrected by science, history then had to be rewritten to catch up with facts. Similarly, the Theological historians who derided Charles Darwin upon publication in 1859 of his *Origin of the Species* faced the great leveller that man sprang from the ape not Biblical Adam.

The inference that Brutus the Trojan was the founder of London, throws up several anomalies to the conventional historians' theories that the Romans founded London, and thus they have not addressed these anomalies but have ignored them. However, these irregularities present tantalising clues to the civilised nature of the ancient Britons, and tend to show Stubbs' history as wholly inaccurate, based solely on pro-Roman propaganda.

One of the greatest anomalies is to be found in English Common law, which could not be changed as this would lead to direct confrontation with the judiciary of the land. It is likely that Stubbs was entirely ignorant of the obscure byroads of these laws, which were known to only a few. Stubbs in his re-writing of history left behind him the mistaken construct that the ancient Britons were illiterate barbarians who were civilised by the Roman invasion.

The Saxon King Alfred (849 AD – 899 AD) commissioned a study of law and came across the Malmutius Code, which was a set of old British laws compiled by Martia, wife of Guithelin, great-grandson of Malmutius (whose name in Welsh is Dyvnwal Moelmud), an ancient British King. Alfred translated these ancient British edicts into Saxon-English and they became the basis for English Common law. The story however becomes more intriguing when we learn more about Malmutius himself. On closer inspection we find that Malmutius had not only been an ancient British King but was a direct descendant of Brutus of Troy. Malmutius was in fact only re-establishing the ancient Trojan laws left by his forebear Brutus. According to Geoffrey of Monmouth, Malmutius was credited as being a lawgiver and a monarch who standardised weights and measures, as well as being a road-builder of some repute, building the first straight roads in Britain.

This is another point of British history that conventional historians of the Stubbs camp, attribute to the Roman influence on Britain. It must be noted that Alfred was king of the Britons over a hundred years before Geoffrey of Monmouth was born and his study represents very fecund evidence for the Trojan legacy. Esoteric author, the late John Michel, rightfully qualifies the Malmutius Code as "...the foundation of English law today".

One prime example of the Malmutius Code that survived until 1623 is the Law of Sanctuary; whereby a fugitive from authority could take refuge in a sacred or holy place and remain free of arrest, as long as they remained within the boundaries of that sanctified place. Saxon King Aethelbert brought back into the English statutes the Law of Sanctuary as codified by Malmutius. Even today some churches have a chair known as a peace-stool or Sanctuary chair placed beside the altar on which those who had committed a violent act could place themselves and claim their ancient right to Sanctuary. Westminster Abbey was no exception having been granted rights under Edward the Confessor (King of England from 1042 – 1066) and several historical characters took refuge there though not always for violent crimes. These included poet John Shelton, who had offended Cardinal Wolsey through satirical verses and went there to avoid arrest.

Today the law of Sanctuary is no longer in force but one remnant of its presence remains in the official office of 'Searcher of the Sanctuary', which is held by a semi-ecclesiastical worker whose duty was once to challenge loiterers in the precincts of Westminster Abbey to see if they were genuine Sanctuary claimants and though there is still someone employed in this role today, it is an honorary title that goes under the banner of 'High bailiff and searcher of the sanctuary.'

Malmutius had two sons, Kamber and Belinus, who it is recorded was the founder of Belin's Gate (Billingsgate, although there are alternative etymologies offered for this name). On this spot according to Geoffrey of Monmouth, Belin built a Temple dedicated to the god of peace. Belin continued his father's work by building straight roads, and he decreed that the travellers upon these constructions were entitled to protection in sanctified places along the way, including the roads themselves, as Malmutius intended. A last survival of this idea may in part explain the draconian sentences passed on Highwaymen who were often hung in gibbets and prevented from receiving a proper Christian burial as their crime was seen as a sacrilegious offence having violated the peace of the King's or Queen's Highroad. Alleged pirates such as Capt Kidd, as we have seen, also met their end in this manner.

It is interesting to note at this stage, that the Saxon King Alfred reinstated the Malmutius Code and is an earlier source than Geoffrey of Monmouth whom later historical revisionists criticised. As for the clergyman Stubbs, who rewrote British history in 1866 to promote Anglo-Saxon values, we must assume that he did not of know of Malmutius and the ancient laws laid down by him which still impact on the British legal system today.

The most learned Jurists refer to the original Institutes of the British Isles as products of the Trojan laws, brought here by Brutus. Lord Chief Justice Coke (Preface to Vol. iii. of *Reports*), affirms, "The Original Laws of this land were composed of such elements as Brutus first selected from the ancient Greek and Trojan Institutions." Lord Chancellor Fortescue, in his work *On the Laws of England* justly observes, "…concerning the different powers which Kings claim over their subjects, I am firmly of the opinion that it arises solely from the different nature of the original institutions. So the Kingdom of Britain had its original from Brutus and the Trojans who attended him from Italy and Greece, and were a mixed Government compounded of the regal and democratic." (See Appendices for examples of the original Malmutius Code).

London's Infrastructure and the Ancient Britons

After Stubbs revision of history in 1866, the Trojan origins of London, the Welsh myths, Geoffrey of Monmouth or any other than the accepted view of the ancient British as savages became academically unfashionable. Victorian academics as a whole did not attribute anything positive to the ancient Britons. Children were now taught that it was the Romans that had built London, constructed straight roads, enacted laws and civilised the barbaric ancient British tribes. Names of the ancient British tribes and characters from their history, if ever they were mentioned at all, were duly Latinised. Descriptions of them were taken from largely derogatory Roman historical accounts, never the indigenous records of the Welsh triads. Roman chroniclers painted the ancient British as wild savage people with little or no culture of their own.

The Roman viewpoint is not supported if one cross-references them with the ancient British sources describing the same times and events, but then there is the convenient canon of historical assumption that the British sources are, after all, fictitious histories. How could the ancient Britons, who had no learning and were an inferior culture to the Roman legions, accurately record their own history?

Returning once more to legendary King Malmutius, in addition to being one of the founders of British Legislation, Dyvnwal (or Malmutius) designed and partly made the Royal British Military Roads through the Island. These were nine in number:

The Sarn Gwyddelin (corrupted into Watling street), or Irish Road, in two branches, from Dover to Mona and Penvro.

The Sam Iken (Iknield street), the road from Caer Troia (London), Northward through the Eastern districts.

Sam Ucha (Iknield street), from the mouth of the Tyne to the present St. David's.

Sam Ermyn, from Anderida (Pevensey) to Caer Edin (Edinburgh).

Sam Achmaen, from Caer Troia to Menevia (St. David's).

Sam Halen, from the Salt Mines of Cheshire to the mouth of the Humber.

Sam Hàlen, from the Salt Mines to Llongborth (Portsmouth).

The Second Sam Ermyn, from Torbay to Dunbreton on the Clyde.

The Sam ar y Môr, or military road, following the coast around the Island.

From evidence cited by the indigenous chronicles of the time we learn much about the Britons' vision of their own history. As they are independent of Roman input, these accounts make for fascinating reading. They are of course peppered with stories of giants, fantastic events, visions and magical powers and cannot be regarded as strictly factual to our modern understanding, however if one reads with an open mind you can see the reality woven in the myth, and as an experienced folklorist would say, folk memory is often more accurate than conventional history. Take the Middle Eastern records that preserve their experience of the Great Flood thousands of years ago, an event that spans many cultures including its mention in the Bible. If we stick to the current thinking there can be no dates attributed to this and if we look at it from a conventional historical perspective it would appear this cataclysm never happened. However if you take into account the history of Egypt and the erosion of the pyramids by water it would tend to back up the theory that thousands of years ago there was a deluge. Therein lies the danger of being fixed or following the dogmas laid down by others in one's approach to unlocking the past.

If we cross-reference the British indigenous records with the alternative histories of the Romans who often speak about the same events, a picture can be built up. Even the Roman Lucan, on one occasion employed sarcasm to speak of what he could not report i.e. the defeat of his own emperor, Caesar.

Emperor Caesar's Downfall

One has to read between the lines with the ancient British sources, think beyond a search for chronological explanation and enter into the cultural mindset of the time. When one does so, it is clear that much of the islands' history has been lost to those seeking dates for everything. In these ancient accounts we are told that London was a substantial capital and they attest to the building prowess of the British tribes. *The Mabinogion*, translated by

Lady Charlotte Guest, describes that an ancient British King called Lud, who existed in circa 70 BC, prior to the Roman invasion, "…bade the citizens build houses therein, such as no houses in the kingdom could equal. And, moreover, he was a mighty warrior, and generous and liberal in giving meat and drink to all that sought them."

The Mabinogion described London as a mighty city, well fortified and prosperous, and Lud as founder of the city Caer Lud. The alternative account of Geoffrey of Monmouth does indeed agree that the city was ruled by King Lud and was called Caer Lud but that in fact, Lud had changed the name of the city from its former name Trinovantum, which was a corruption of the name New Troy given to the city by Brutus. Geoffrey tells us that one trace that is left of King Lud is the area in the City named after him, Lud's Gate (Ludgate). Interestingly, the indigenous account states that Lud changed the City's name from New Troy to Caer Lud, which translates to Lud's castle from the Welsh.

A man referenced frequently in Welsh literature and by Geoffrey of Monmouth who is connected indelibly with London is Cassivalanaus (Welsh for Caswallon). These stories vary from pure myth to what might be sober historical chronicles of his life. *The Brut Tysilio* (attributed to the 7th Century Welsh Saint Tysilio) makes no equivocations of the Trojan that lived with the ancient Britons, while Geoffrey states he is the brother of Lud a lineage firmly rooted in the city Caer Ludd. These accounts are a rare glimpse into the sophisticated diplomacy that existed between the agitator Caesar who wanted to invade and seize Britain, seemingly aware that Brutus easily conquered the British Isles, and Caswallon who saw the ancient Britons as rightful heirs of Brutus and relations of Rome by virtue of the Trojan connection.

The Emperor Caesar, in his replies to Caswallon, suggested being paid off with slaves or payments to prevent the invasion, but this suggestion was tersely rejected. In the letters between Caswallon and Caesar, he said that Caesar had no legal right to invade the islands as both the British and the Romans were of the same noble stock, namely the Trojans. It is an interesting point that the legality of Caesar's invasion was something of a sore point back in Rome as he only had permission to go as far as Gaul in his invasions, and when the diplomacy broke down, the Romans invaded Britain and there was a mighty battle, which Roman historians attest happened at the Isle of Thorns, a place of law making.

We know from looking at street names in London today exactly where Thorney Island is: Parliament is now built on it, though at that time there was a Druid college. It was originally a ford in the estuary of the Thames and therefore the ideal place to cross the river. Both the British and Roman records agree that a fierce battle took place. In the indigenous accounts Caswallon's brother Nennius engaged Caesar himself in a sword fight. Caesar plunged his sword into Nennius' shield so deeply that it became lodged there but not before Caesar managed to deliver a mortal wound to the head of Nennius. The British accounts say the fighting continued with Nennius and Caesar having to be separated by their respective sides. The sword of Caesar was captured by the British, by virtue of remaining in the shield of Nennius and they kept it as a trophy. The indigenous accounts say that Caesar was routed that day and a great feast was held for three days with a hundred thousand beasts slaughtered to feed the celebrants. The legendary sword, that became known as the Mors Crocca, often translated as the Yellow Death or even Red Death, is however more properly translated as the Saffron Death. Nennius, although victorious in battle, actually died as a result of being struck by the Mors Crocca at the hands of Caesar, albeit a death that came after the heat of battle.

The Welsh records tell us that the greatly prized trophy, the Mors Crocca was displayed in Caer Lud (London). Such a trophy could only serve to remind the British of their momentous victory over their oppressors. Today the City of London flag looks almost identical to the flag of St George, except for one small difference. In the left hand quarter is a small red sword. Some researchers have suggested it is the dagger used to kill rebel leader Watt Tyler but since the design of the flag predates Watt Tyler's birth by 60 years this is not feasible. Some authorities say it is the sword of Saint Paul, the Patron Saint of London, but without citing much evidence to support this theory it seems unlikely. The third suggestion, which is seldom mentioned since the Brutus histories have become forbidden subjects, is perhaps the most alluring. The sword is that which Nennius took from Caesar, to remind Londoners of their victory against tyranny and the regaining of City's independence. Two modern Welsh researchers interested in Arthurian legacy and Welsh myths, Barram Blackett and Alan Wilson, go further still. They suggest that the Mors Crocca was known in Welsh as the 'Hard Cleft' (Caledvwlch), which is also evidence of its being cleft into Nennius' shield and the means by which it was captured. Sarcastic poet Lucan returned to Rome but said of the battle, employing a certain amount of witticism and craft to describe Caesar's humiliation at the hands of Caswallon:

"In haste he turned and showed his back to the British he had attacked."

Apart from Caswallon and his diplomatic entreaties suggesting a deep, educated, civilised ancient Briton, another anomaly which becomes distinctly uncomfortable for conventional historians, who would have us believe that the British Isles were inhabited by savages, is taken from the Roman, Tacitus. This is not so easy to dismiss as it comes from traditional

Roman historical sources, and Tacitus leaves us with the surest evidence yet of a civilised, diplomatic and eloquent ancient British leader named Caractacus (Welsh name Caradoc). Caradoc can be found in the ancient Welsh myths too but we shall concern ourselves with the Roman account to take a conventional historic account at this point. Caradoc led a successful guerrilla campaign for many years that halted the Roman advance into South Wales, often enlisting the help of other tribes from other regions loyal to him. His military genius defeated the Romans on many occasions. He was only captured after an act of betrayal by a female leader of the Brigantes tribe and handed over to the Romans, who wasted no time shipping him and his family back to Rome.

Tacitus tells us that crowds flocked to see the famed rebel and his family who were led through the streets in chains. According to the account at no time did Caradoc look downcast or subdued by events, the ancient British leader every bit as regal, civilised and learned of diplomatic discourse as any Roman he encountered. When he was brought to trial at the senate he stood and spoke, using the most reasoned of arguments, appealing for the life of his family. His speech at the Senate of Rome was recorded by Tacitus and could not have been made by any other than a highly gifted and extraordinary person possessed of leadership skills and diplomatic experience. Both the Senate and Roman Emperor Claudius were suitably impressed by his highly reasoned diplomatic rhetoric.

Cardoc's fame spread far and wide and he was granted clemency to live in exile in Italy for seven years with a promise to not raise arms against Rome again in his lifetime. The Romans provided a comfortable villa for their captured Briton in respect of his status as a chieftain and leader of his people. This is contrary to the treatment meted out to captured Gallic leaders, who were dragged to Rome and executed, in the most downtrodden of circumstances, being labelled as mere detritus by the conquering Romans. According to modern researchers Baram Blackett and Alan Wilson, Caradoc was a direct descendent of the Kymri, who took their name from Brutus' son Kamber, Blackett and Wilson also state that some of the tribes that flocked to help Caradoc in his fight against the Romans came from London and that this fact is recorded in the Welsh myths. The pair also believe that it is likely that these Londoners would have taken the sword of Caesar or Mors Crocca with them.

Most of the material connecting Brutus to London is recorded in the Welsh language, as the Romans were unable to penetrate much of Wales during their time in Britain. The Druid stronghold in Anglesey, containing much of the knowledge about the island's past, despite the Roman massacre of the Druids there by Paulinus, remained intact, even the Normans were held back and it was not until the medieval period during the reign of Edward I (1272-1307) that any outsider managed to get a serious military foothold on Welsh lands. Therefore the Brutus myths were impenetrable both to Roman legions and English speaking revisionists such as Stubbs.

Much has been said about the anomalies from which certain questions may arise but there is other evidence for Brutus and the Trojan origins of London. While digging the foundations of St Paul's Cathedral, (a survey of London states that these works were carried out in 1316), a man called Stow states that:

"...more than a hundred scalps of oxen or kine" were found; "which thing confirms greatly the opinion of those which have reported that of old times there had been a temple of Jupiter, and that there was daily sacrifice of beasts."

Over the years there has been unearthed in the environs near St Paul's a head of Diana, Roman remains, including a bronze image of Diana, and as recently as 1830, a stone altar bearing a carved figure of the goddess was unearthed on the site of the present Goldsmith's Hall in Foster Lane, near to St Paul's Cathedral which was where the animal remains that had been left there as votive offerings in centuries past had been found. More recently archaeologists announced that they had uncovered bones left as sacrificial offerings which suggested the worship of Diana in that they contained stags, an animal sacred to the goddess, among other creatures linked to worship of the lunar deity. A knee-jerk reaction might be to say they must be Roman but the balance of probability weighs in favour of Brutus, who we are told founded a temple to Diana at this site. According to the London Museum, the Romans, as was their habit, borrowed local deities from countries they resided in, hoping that this would increase their luck. Therefore, the discovery near St Paul's of Roman religious artefacts dedicated to Diana, further strengthens the theory that a pre-Roman Temple consecrated to Diana already existed on the site and that the legionaries and Roman colonists simply went along with the former Trojan customs already in place.

Queen Boudicca (indigenous Welsh spelling Buddug), Queen of the Iceni tribe, sought revenge against the Romans, to avenge the rape of her daughters at Roman hands and the betrayal of an agreement they had made with her late husband. Boudicca attacked the Romans in Colchester and in London. The fierce warrior-Queen led 100,000 disaffected Britons and razed the Roman occupied Londinium, as it was called at that point, to the ground. During her rebellion Queen Boudicca slaughtered nearly 70,000 Romans. She remains one of the few ancient Britons to be recognised during the Victorian period largely because her name means Victorious. It is only in the last ten years that her name has been de-Latinised when spoken of, such is the cultural stranglehold over ancient British history by the Stubbs style historians. What is interesting for our study of London is that professor Grimes, a Welsh archaeologist, succeeded Mortimer Wheeler in 1945 as the director of London Museum, then based in Lancaster House. He was involved in the programme to excavate Blitz sites in London before they were developed and it was at one such excavation at the former site of St. Swithin's church on Cannon Street that he found some features that cannot easily be explained. One must remember that it was at this site until the time of the blitz that the London or Brutus Stone was housed.

Prof Grimes discovered Roman deposits at a level of around 4-6ft below pavement level. The Roman building Grimes discovered was placed on a layer of ashes from an earlier time. Could this be the conflagration of the Iceni overrunning London? To further this theory, in 1840 across the street from this discovery, nearer to Cannon Street station, 15-20ft thick stone walls had been discovered while workmen were digging to establish a sewer. These walls however were discovered at a much deeper level than the Roman deposits of Grimes' archaeological discoveries and well below the burnt layer. There are those who have postulated that these walls, now under the street, may well be the evidence for the existence of Caer Ludd. The location close to the original London Stone site and the strength of their construction very much match the descriptions we have found for Lud's city, and because the walls are positioned considerably deeper than the burnt layer, which is only some 6ft below ground level, it is quite possible that these walls date from a time way before the Iceni incursion of circa 60 AD.

The Brutus legend covers not only the City but South London too. For many years it was said that the etymology of Camberwell, South London was taken from the Old English word camber meaning crooked. However, in 2007 the Telegraph featured an article on the rediscovery of Camber's Well in the area, which had been lost during Victorian times, when the Bronze Age site was built upon. The newspaper's article reignited some older research by suggesting another alternative etymology for Camber, for it tapped into the Brutus legends. A local historian, John Chaple from South London, was quoted in the Telegraph piece, and has also shared his own investigations into the matter online. In his research he has explored a great wealth of new and old material, about the Camberwell area and its environs. It was said that Roman coins were found at the bottom of the well, which if true, means that the well is at the very least 2,000 years old. Mr. Chaple considers that this of course is a date that corresponds to the time of Kamber, son of Brutus, and he points out that the alternative meaning of Camber's Well is linked to this mythos. The authors note that there is further evidence of Trojan influence in nearby Peckham where the modern street name Troy Town, SE15, is said to be named after a turf cut maze whose pattern was based on the walls of Troy. Today all that stands there is a typical Victorian terraced road.

Some researchers have pointed out that London in Brutus's time was a marshy estuary and that there existed a raised road that navigated this difficult territory leading out of the City heading south. The first point of high ground it arrives at is the location of Kamber's well. Today this road is known as Walworth Road. Professor Walter Skeat gives his own etymology of the name Walworth that hints at the original meaning of the name. In Anglo-Saxon the word Wal means Welsh and the Professor states that there was once an ancient British settlement where Walworth village was. All of this is interesting yet cannot prove conclusively that Kamber lived there. However one definitely gets the feeling that the area is most certainly pre-Roman.

Forbidden History Revisited

A German businessman named Heinrich Schliemann (1822 – 26 December 1890), who had travelled the world working on ships and making a fortune in South America, came to use his newfound wealth by following his life-long interest in Troy. As a child he had been enthralled by the tales his father had read him from books on Homer, Troy and classical myths. From accounts of his life he was a polymath who could pick a language in just six weeks. Fascinated with searching for the mythical city of Troy he began to excavate an area known as Hissarlik in Turkey in 1871. He had already had some disappointments at another site but this did not dissuade him in his search for the elusive ruins of the fabled Troy.

Archaeology was in its infancy and the results of digs at this time published in academic papers. There was a man called Calvert, also at the dig, who Schliemann had a falling out with and who afterwards declared that there was no evidence of Troy at all at the site. This declaration hardly came as a surprise to historians of the time. Schliemann however was not one to give up easily continuing to excavate the site and in 1873 he discovered a cache of gold artefacts which he named Priam's Gold. The news reached academia via his papers, one of which was called *Troy and Its Ruins* published in 1875. Academics read this and with great excitement declared that Troy of the *Iliad* did exist after all, and that in turn led to a re-evaluation of many of the myths left to us from classical accounts. One of the unexpected results of Schliemann's findings was that people began to question the notions of Brutus of Troy and the possible sea voyage leading him to Britain. Stubbs and the naysayers had not entirely won the day as they had supposed. There were of course attacks aimed at Schliemann, to discredit him. Firstly, critics pointed to his destructive methods of excavation, which incidentally would not be acceptable today in the archaeological community. Secondly, to preserve his finds Schliemann smuggled the treasures out of Turkey. Today these actions remain a bone of contention and Turkish officials would like to see the treasures returned to their national custodianship.

Leaving these controversial issues aside, his discovery did however lend much credence to Homers *Iliad* and the notion of sea borne voyages at this time, therefore Brutus coming to Totnes was placed firmly back into the realms of historical possibility. Schliemann was made a member of the Society of Antiquaries in London in respect of this find. During Victorian times when ancient British history had been the poor relation, the Brutus mythos was preserved mainly by secret societies; the Masons certainly backed the Stuart claims in Scotland, as had some Tory sympathisers within in England, who were acutely aware that the Hanoverians had laid claim to the ancient title Duke of Albany, a resolutely Stuart-Scottish preserve. Albany (the name for Scotland) was also part of the Brutus legacy.

During the reign of the Germanic House of Hanover, the civil liberties and ancient traditions of the British people had been curtailed. This trend had abated slightly post industrial revolution and into the Regency period (1811-1820), the worst excesses such as the Peterloo Massacre of 1819, had gone with its passing. The last king and penultimate monarch of Britain's Hanoverian dynasty was King William IV, whose reign oversaw many reforms such as the abolition of slavery, electoral reforms, sensible budgeting and the beginning of an end to child labour, a new era began to take shape with some semblance of social order.

Oddly, while Stubbs in 1866 was busy publishing his revision of the British histories and the new Liberal Chartist movement was trying to reform all manner of English politics to help the disaffected proletariat, the Brutus mythos had an unlikely champion in Prime Minister Benjamin Disraeli.

Prime Minister Disraeli was a Jewish Tory who championed protectionism, although he was a reformer too. In 1866 the same year that Stubbs was publishing his new histories, Disraeli made a famous speech in Parliament arguing for the ancient rights of the British to be upheld. His politics ranged somewhere between the protection of the landed gentry and the rights of the working man against the increased mercantile interests of the Industrial revolution. Disraeli wanted to preserve the ancient beliefs and customs of the British Isles and was a great supporter of Queen Victoria, who, greatly upset by the early death of her beloved Prince Albert, was becoming a recluse. Disraeli saw the dangers of Teutonic based history and urged the Queen to undo the damage to royal interests caused by unpopular monarchs preceding her from the Hanover reign and engage once more with pomp and circumstance.

Much of this underground movement towards British myth was preserved in the poetic and artistic movements of the time. Those who studied law and jurisprudence ignored the folly of abandoning the ancient British customs and kept up the notion that Brutus was the bringer of the first laws.

Disraeli had been encouraged to study law and held his articles, and for a while had thought of joining the Bar as a young man but had eventually worked in the City at the stock exchange. Within a decade Disraeli began to show his true colours by starting a new policy against Russia known as 'The Great Game'. Essentially it was a power struggle between Britain and Russia for much of central Asia but the prize was India, the British Empire's jewel in the Crown.

Disraeli, securing a loan from the Rothschild family without permission from Parliament, secured controlling shares in the Suez Canal. Prime Minister Disraeli began a period of unabashed Imperialist expansion. He clashed with parliamentarians again over his foreign policy in the Balkans and then promoted Queen Victoria as Empress of India. Disraeli was again using the age-old arguments used by Tudor viziers in the 1500 and 1600s to promote British acquisition of territory. Disraeli was no longer working for Parliament but the private interests of the City or what is known as the 'Crown', a power quite distinct from the Monarchy.

The British Crown Affair

"I care not what puppet is placed on the throne of England to rule the Empire. The man who controls Britain's money supply controls the British Empire and I control the money supply" – Nathan Rothschild (1777-1836)

As we have discussed earlier the City of London Corporation is a private company quite separate from the British State. It is run by the 'Crown', which is not to be confused with the Royal Family. The City of London is not to be mistaken for London the metropolis, but is essentially representing the so-called 'Square Mile' and has almost the same borders as the Roman Londinium. Like its counterpart, Vatican City in Rome, the City of London operates as an independent state, a country within a country. Even her Majesty the Queen must acquiesce to the Lord Mayor, again not to be confused with the freely elected Mayor of London, when entering the hallowed precincts of the City. Symbolically St George surrenders to the Dragon – England gives way to the City of London Corporation in this last ceremonial act.

At the centre of the City of London Corporation organisation is the Lord Mayor elected by and in league with the 108 Livery Companies. Some of these Liveries (trade guilds) have residual powers under laws that have been in place since Medieval times. The Liveries, in some cases, set standards and control their given trade within the City. One example is the Scriveners Company, whilst being forty-fourth in the strict pecking order of precedence within the liveries the Scriveners for many years dominated

156

the provision of notaries public, in London as a whole, a notary public being an officer constituted by law to serve the public in non-contentious matters usually concerned with estates, deeds, powers-of-attorney, and foreign and international business. Nowadays that mandate is limited to how another might ply their trade and other Liveries are just names of past trades of a bygone age.

The Lord Mayor as titular head of these 108 Liveries is but a public or ceremonial title, a figurehead who liaises between the Livery companies and the City of London Corporation and whose election at Guildhall before Gog and Magog proclaims him as such. All of these good folk who are involved in Livery business, including the Lord Mayor himself, can little suspect that they are drawn together like pawns in a gigantic worldwide chess game, wherein the scheme of things, the sum of the parts are greater than the whole. The Liveries came into being to protect their rights and trade fairly, as well as safeguarding their respective occupations. When, in some cases, their trade fell into obsolescence or decline, they became exclusive fraternities. The Lord Mayor was, and still is, the ceremonial figurehead and one can only congratulate these fine upstanding people for continuing their noble traditions in the face of relentless modernisation. But there is an underlying malaise that few can suspect. The hard working, honest and very charitable Liverymen and their highly esteemed Lord Mayor are completely ignorant of the mystical basis from which this powerbase is formed and from where it is controlled. Few of them would suspect the global implications and enormous secret financial portfolio of the Crown. In this regard it would be clearer to say that the City of London is not only financially independent of the rest of the country but controls it completely. Some may say that the City of London's financial grip extends to the entire world capitalist system. It is clear that this power is not in the hands of a few quaint old fashioned Medieval Livery companies even though some of the officers such as the Remembrancer do carry some real responsibility and power with them (covered in the Chapter Three), so in whose hands is this power?

An obscure stone hidden by a grille marks the 'Omphallus', or navel, of this independent state. The London Stone or Brutus Stone as it is sometimes referred to is the sacred centre or mystical hub of London as a whole, as it underpins the true origins of the City and is the very stone on which, according to Legend, the capital's fortunes depend. It seems to have no owner and has been generally ignored in modern times by passers-by and our grand museums alike, yet despite what conventional historians may say, the London Stone holds its own in Cannon Street to this day. Nearby in King William Street the world HQ of Brutus' alleged ancestors, the Rothschilds command their vast financial web; they dominate the City, perhaps even the globe. Their unimaginable wealth is beyond estimate and they have studiously avoided inclusion in the world's richest list, but their wealth is put, in some estimates, at trillions. They have certainly played a pivotal role in British history since the Battle of Waterloo which they helped finance.

Each and every successive Government has had to deal with the Rothschilds, who in each age increased their sway over business, society and the populace and lead the British Empire onto the global stage. To accurately assess the true scale and magnitude of the Rothschild wealth one only has to look at their influence over the City in order to gauge its true importance and mystical significance. By coincidence their HQ is in King William Street, as it was during this monarch's reign that the Bank of England was formed by a Royal Charter, paving the way for British emergence in Europe. The formation of the first bank was based on private finance using a new model of trade 'debt-finance capitalism'. No longer did the state produce coinage based on the national trade but this new money was based on confidence or expectations of future trading conditions. It plunged the ordinary man in debt for the first time in English history but allowed the new merchant classes to trade internationally.

The Rothschild rise to ascendancy was through this debt–finance mechanism – lending capital to kings and Governments in return for interest on that money, often gained from peoples' taxes. King William badly needed capital to hang onto his power. In order to do this his Government raised enough private money in twelve days to finance a new navy to take on the French. Effectively he gave the Bank of England over to private hands and as a result the nation was plunged into debt within a few years. The selling of debt based on 'confidence' has been adopted almost everywhere since. A Government can borrow money at a percentage interest, print new notes and then the debt is levied on the populace in the form of taxes.

Today the Bank of England stands near to the ancient Druidic stream of Walbrook on the ancient site of the Temple of Mithras, fittingly a god of contracts amongst his other attributes. Ask any British citizen who owns the Bank of England, the lynchpin of the City, and the reply will probably be, Parliament, The British people or the Monarch. However in truth, no one knows who owns the bank, or more accurately, no one is allowed to know. The bank is privately owned and there are strict statutes of anonymity for its nominees covered by the Official Secrets Act. It has long been suspected that the Rothschilds are the real power behind the bank, however, this is just conjecture and cannot be proven.

For most of the 20th Century, part of the Rothschild family business has been setting the world gold price, assaying its quality, marking each and every gold bar in Britain with their family hallmark bearing the Rothschild name and controlling the Royal Mint Refinery. Meeting twice a day, five members of the gold pool, chaired by a Rothschild, fixed the world gold price inside the sacred precincts of the City, the very City they claimed to have founded. The Rothschild dynasty eventually decided to relinquish control of gold in the City in 1968 when London trade prominence went into decline under Europe. Many of the large British stock exchange companies also had Rothschild money invested in them. The current head of the Rothschild dynasty, Jacob Rothschild is married to the Sinclair family, the custodians of Rosslyn Chapel, Scotland, which is a marriage that must surely stimulate the interest of anyone who has an interest in mystical unions and secret societies.

The Sinclairs are the descendents of the 8th Century Nobleman Guillaume de Grellone, who had strong connections with the Languedoc region in southern France, particularly its capital Narbonne, which became the centre for Medieval Cabala. It was these practitioners who were said to be among the leading protagonists in fomenting the Crusades, which enabled the Templars to operate under the veneer of Christianity in order to defeat the armies of the Muslim leader Saladin. The truth lay in the resulting rubble of the Holy Land where Templars excavated for quite a while searching for ancient artefacts and texts, but a war based on religious preference gave them the excuse to go there. One such text which they were said to have retrieved was the *Sepher ha Bahir*, a Cabalistic work that generated the inception of the Medieval Cabala. The *Bahir* fell into the hands of the early sages of Ashkenaz – the German Cabalists who hungered after all manner of written records of supernatural and mystical knowledge. But they apparently only had part of the text. The rest of the ancient writings appear to have been split up, with some facets finding their way into the *Book of Secrets*. More recently there have been further suggestions that some passages of *Bahir* are based on Babylonian teachings – so some answers may lie in artefacts buried there.

The Ashkenaz Jews from Kharzaria are, of course the ancestors of the Bauer-Rothschild dynasty. The current head Jacob Rothschild inherited the title of fourth Baronet from his father Victor, who was the instigator of the notoriously unpopular Poll Tax. In 1987 at the time of the Libyan bombings, the BBC broadcast a *Panorama* programme linking the ruling Conservative Party with some far right groups and organisations. This whole matter was so detrimental and disturbing to the Prime Minister and leader of the Conservative party at that time, Margaret Thatcher, that she contacted her close friend and staunch ally Victor Rothschild, who was strongly connected to intelligence circles. He leaned on the former BBC Chairman Duke Hussey, to sack Director-General of the BBC Alistair Milne. Victor's son, Jacob Rothschild, is chairman of the Rothschild Foundation, Yad Hanadiv, which gave one franchise for, and also built, various Government monuments including the Supreme Court of Israel, that contains Masonic symbolism as well as the pyramid topped with the All-Seeing Eye.

Coming back to the Bank of England, in recent years the British Government have given autonomy and control to this private company to fix mortgage rates, a much more important factor than gold at the moment. This power is outside of Parliamentary control and in the hands of a faceless cabal that is unaccountable to government Ministers or indeed the people it serves. This leads to the conclusion that the City of London is beyond the constraints of democracy, a powerful organisation not only within national boundaries, but also globally and is controlled by a quasi-mystical elite tracing their roots to Brutus and similarly allied bloodlines. It was reported in 1977 via a Parliamentary question that the Bank of England had established a special nominee company, the Bank of England Nominees Ltd (BOEN). This was, in part, claimed to obscure investments made by HRH Queen Elizabeth II, as well as other people recommended by the Royal Household. One can hypothesise that the BOEN includes the Saudi Royal family, the Sultan of Brunei and other Commonwealth leaders, though this is conjecture as no accounts are available for public scrutiny.

The BOEN is also covered by the Official Secrets Act which, if broken can lead to life imprisonment. Phillip Beresford stated in his book, *The Book of British Rich* written in conjunction with the *Sunday Times*, that the Queen held substantial shares in named companies such as Rio Tinto, GEC, ICI, Dutch Shell Oil and BP, to name but a few. Her obvious personal stake in the North Sea oil fields is unquestioned but her stake in other energy fields caused embarrassment in a court case during the 1970s in America. Rio Tinto were accused in a US court of fixing the price of nuclear material such as uranium but several directors were not named due to protecting British national interest. The City had stepped in to block publicity in the case and shielded one of the most powerful investors in the Square Mile.

But as we have said, the Crown is not to be confused with the Monarch. Under the auspices of the Crown, there is a council of thirteen members chaired by the Lord Mayor. They oversee a vast portfolio including the deeds to the Crown lands in former colonies such as Canada, New Zealand and Australia. Also there is land from other countries by rights of spoils of war. In Japan it has long been rumoured that prime lands have secretly been confiscated, and in Canada 94% of British Columbia is considered to be Crown lands owned, at least publicly by the Monarch of England. However it is more correct to say that the Crown oversees it. This is just an example of this enviable global property portfolio, and the web that has its hub in the City.

To Whom We Serve

"Six or seven men can plunge a nation into war without consulting Parliament". – Andrew Carnegie (Victorian rail and steel magnate and philanthropist)

It seems that the Brutus bloodline, that stakes its claim to having founded London, is still in charge of the City and using as its mechanism of ascendancy the City of London Corporation to play the world stage too. Romanov gold was shipped clandestinely out of Imperial Russia to help pay for the First World War, and later to aid the flight of Czar Nicholas. In 1917 it simply disappeared. At the time the Romanov gold reserves were estimated to be the largest gold deposits in the world, above and beyond that of the British Empire. Subsequently, after being shipped out of Russia by the British Navy, via Canada and Japan, the gold simply disappeared into the British banking system.

The Bank of England handled part of these shipments and British merchant banks such as Barings handled others. Successive Russian Governments have negotiated in vain for its return but no one can seem to account for it because there is no trace of it. When a Russian Imperial pretender tried to claim the Romanov throne as well as the gold reserves, there was a court battle in Germany. Lord Louis Mountbatten (Prince Charles' uncle) paid legal teams to contest the claim in court, though it was not his gold, nor the British Royal Family's fortune either (their family name being Saxe-Coburg or as they are known today, Windsor). Although he was a distant relative of the Tsar, and a family intimate of the doomed Romanovs, Mountbatten's involvement may have betrayed his true motivation. He had married into the Cassell banking family and thus into the heart of the Brutus bloodline of the City. No subsequent Russian Government has ever been able to trace the world's largest gold reserve, which appeared to vanish into thin air via British, or more accurately, City hands?

Since the 'credit crunch' that has seen millions plunged into debt, national economies teetering on the brink of collapse, redundancies, repossessed properties and record bankruptcies, *Forbes* magazine have reported that the super-rich have increased their personal wealth by at least one third. Much of that wealth has been acquired by the inevitable property sales at the lower end of the chain as people attempt to survive the coming depression. Reading the City companies' index carefully one can see a hydra of international family connections. The Rothschilds hold Directorships in De Beers Consolidated Mines Ltd., Eagle Star Insurance, The Economist Newspaper, IBM UK, Le Banque Privee, United Race Courses Ltd., Alliance Assurance, London Assurance, Sun Alliance, Tokyo Pacific Holdings, Rio Tinto and the list goes on and on. In much of this business they keep close ties with other banking families such as Cassells, Barings, Hambros, Warburgs, many of whom are on the same boards of the above firms. It makes the various City boardrooms a very tight and cosy arrangement. This web begins to unravel as City names come up time and time again in interlocking groups of people who are sometimes Directors on different boards: Directors such as Lord Shackelton, Lord Privy Seal, who is Chairman of RTZ Dec Corp, Lord Charteris of Amisfield, grandson of the Earl of Wemys, married to Viscount Margesson, private secretary to HRH Queen Elizabeth II. This tightly knit group has been referred to as 'The Club of the Isles'. According to writer E.N. Knuth:

"...the international oligarchy uses the allegoric 'Crown' as its symbol of power and has its headquarters in the ancient city of London....the giant Bank of England, a privately owned institution ...is not subject to regulation by British Parliament and is in effect a sovereign world state."

The above book was first published after World War II when the Bank of England had supposedly been nationalised, yet its content is still current, when one considers the Bank of England's nominee company status, operating as it does as a shadow private holding company within the City confines.

The City covers just 677 acres of land, yet this 'Square Mile', as it is known, houses the biggest concentration of wealth on Earth. It has a population of little more than four thousand souls, though this population is swelled during the hours of trading, Monday to Friday, leaving it little more than a ghost town at weekends. It is ruled by the Lord Mayor and his cabal of thirteen, yet like many other carefully manicured fronts in Britain, not all is what it seems on the surface. Benjamin Disraeli was known to have said, "... so you see...the world is governed by very different personages from what is imagined by those not behind the scenes."

The origins of the Committee of 300 can apparently be traced back to the British East India Company's Council of 300, founded in 1727 by the British aristocracy. It was reckoned to be an influential body even during the early 18th Century, challenging the strength of numerous countries in the process. Following the exposure of the Illuminati Order in the latter part of the 18th Century, the Council of 300 sustained its secret agenda along with some newly assimilated 'Illuminated Ones'. It developed into the Committee of 300 in its current guise during the latter half of the Victorian era. Membership is said to have been comprised of people such as Lord Rothschild and George Bush and to have included European royalty and big business moguls, who collectively own corporations in practically every industry, including banking and oil.

The original British East India Company began life on 22nd September 1599, (the autumnal equinox, Alban Elfed), when one hundred and one investors, led by the Lord Mayor of London, Sir Stephen Soame, who was the

162

leader of the original founding group, raised £30,000. However, the Company did not start trading until the following year. Then nearly a hundred years later, in 1698, King William of Orange was bribed to the tune of £2,000,000 by adversaries of the sitting stockholders, for his hand in making their rival bid successful. It is recorded that, a hundred years later in 1799, forty-six out of forty-nine major stockholders of the British East India Company lived in the London area, and many of these seem to have inherited their stocks as certain names re-occur on the board, such as Baring and Thornton.

Whomsoever was at the heart of the British East India Company became very rich indeed, so much so that by 1858 its debts had risen to a staggering £100,000,000, prompting a Government bailout and take-over. Nonetheless the British East India Company was instrumental in chartering other trading monopolies, becoming a major player in the global markets. In this respect, genealogist Fritz A. Springmeier cites the British East India Company as being the predecessor of the Fabian Society. It begins to get even stranger when Springmeier, referring to the Boston Tea Party, goes on to say: "While the 342 chests of tea (valued at £18,000) destroyed by the Boston Tea Party was Company property, the American flag that was created in the Boston area, and became the American flag was a duplicate of the official East India Company flag. Why did the Americans adopt a flag that had been the Company's flag for about two centuries? It is clear that the founders of the USA knew the history of the flag."

Is it possible to sense the furtive hand of the City or the Crown at work here? At this juncture the Council of 300 was firmly established at the heart of the British East India Company. In a little over a century, it would become adopted into the Committee of 300 in its present day form.

The arcane mysteries of international finance are dispensed by the Chancellor of the Exchequer, one of the Chief Ministers of Government, but he is not expected to understand fiscal dynamics, only to recommend and explain them to public and Parliament alike. In reality, he is informed by permanent advisors of the Treasury, and these officials take their stance directly from the City. If a Chancellor and his Prime Minister are under the illusion that they are in control, events can backfire very quickly, as Prime Minister Sir Anthony Eden discovered in 1956 during the Suez Crisis. Events had hardly unfolded before he was informed that the City did not intend to finance his international crusade, and that hostilities must cease or the Pound would collapse. He stopped the war but was shortly after removed from office, his own party turning against him, such is the lot of anyone unwise enough to oppose the City. Because the City pays the piper it also calls the tunes, although it is a song inaudible to the man in the street and the hand that pays is invisible too.

The rise of the merchant banking classes led to the inevitable rise of such families as the Rothschilds who, as we have discussed, created central banks and then hooked each and every nation on the opiate of debt. With the end of the Napoleonic wars the British Empire had dispensed with their main rival, the French. By the early 19th Century, Britannia ruled the waves through her superior naval firepower. She patrolled and policed the high seas using Admiralty Law, founded, of course, by the Templars, exacting taxation on lesser foreign powers and other merchant lines. This set the stage for the formation of the British Empire that was to engulf a quarter of the world's land and gave dominion over almost every ocean. It was the largest empire the world had ever seen and comprised of dominions, colonies, protectorates, mandates and other territories each being administered in a different way. By Victorian times these various British colonial outposts were placed into two categories: the colonies ruled directly by Parliament which tended to be those populated by white settlers and the colonies ruled by the Crown that were populated by indigenous people. Parliament controlled Canada, Australia, New Zealand and South Africa while the Crown managed territories such as Grenada, Bermuda, Jamaica, Gibraltar, Ceylon (now Sri Lanka) Hong Kong, Malaya (today Malaysia and Singapore), and India – described at the Empire's height as the 'Jewel in the Crown'. India in Empire terms comprised of today's Pakistan, India and Bangladesh. There were many other Crown colonies and all ruled over by Admiralty Law.

The Crown sponsored enterprises such as The South Sea Company, the Virginia Bay Company, London Assurance, the famous East India Company and many others. Often the Crown appointed rulers to these private fiefdoms such as Viceroys, Governor-Generals or nominated councils. It is interesting to note that the East India Company became the foundation for India as a Crown colony. The Crown colonies were important financial investments and guarded by British military might, paid for by the taxpayer. Much blood was spilled founding and protecting the Crown's lucrative ambitions. The wealth was funnelled back down the Thames to the City and the noble edifice of the Bank of England. Despite these huge trade surpluses the ordinary person in Victorian London did not see a penny of this wealth; much of the urban sprawl was festering slums, where people passed their days in semi-starvation sinking into wretchedness. E.N. Knuth in his *Empire of the City* says it best:

"Loans to foreign countries are arranged by the City of London with no thought whatsoever of the nation's welfare but solely in order to increase indebtedness upon which the City thrives and grows rich...today we see through a glass darkly; for there is so much it would not be in the public interest to divulge."

However in the House of Lords in early November 2010 Lord James of Blackheath proceeded to turn policy right on its head and beyond, with his own devastating disclosure. Lord James said the Bank of England had appointed him to "deal with problems" created by the laundering of IRA (Irish Republican Army) funds. His job was to run down the companies containing IRA money and liquidise whatever assets were left. Lord James stated, "I have had one of the biggest experiences in the laundering of terrorist money and funny money that anyone has had in the city. I have handled billions of pounds in terrorist money." Amidst the gasps from the assembled Lords, Lord James continued, "My biggest terrorist client was the IRA and I am pleased to say that I managed to write off more than a billion pounds of its money". The following day Lord James made a statement saying that he never intended to imply he had done anything improper. "I'm a money washer not a money launderer," he further stated.

Perhaps the most intriguing part of his story is what Lord James also revealed to his fellow shell-shocked Lords in the second Chamber. He confessed that he had been contacted by a secretive organisation, which he referred to only as 'Foundation X', a group that he claimed has more gold on hand than all the world's bullion reserves combined. Lord James also revealed that one didn't contact this group, "…they contact you." Lord James maintained that they had already pledged £22 billion that was to be injected into the UK economy, £5 billion to made available immediately. Lord James added that he had been investigating this strange covert organisation for the previous six months and concluded that Foundation X is absolutely genuine and sincere. But he would give no further clues as to exactly who Foundation X might be, if indeed he knew at all. Perhaps the last time that a supposedly benevolent secret society had access to wealth equivalent magnitude was the Knights Templar prior to their purge, but there was more to the Knights Templar and their true occult role than has been previously revealed.

Cracking The City Cauldron

We have previously spoken about the City of London's most effective and notorious corporate activity, finance. What, some may ask, do the banks and financial corporations have to do with London's mystical legacy?

Perhaps the answer comes from a most unexpected source, a Victorian American Baptist preacher known as L.B. Woolfolk. The preacher made a point of tracing the strands of the banking cartel in the years following the American Civil War. This activity involved tracking down members of the cartel and making contact with them – a move that brought Woolfolk to London. During the course of his researches, which included several visits to the City, Woolfolk discovered that the cartel had bought the entire US economy via agents, many years prior to the existence of the US Federal Reserve and were controlling it. Woolfolk wrote:

"The Imperialism of Capital to which I allude is a knot of capitalists...who make their headquarters in the Money Quarter of London, in Threadneedle Street, Lombard and other streets in that vicinity, where bankers have their habitat...They own almost all the debts of the world, the debts of nations, states, countries, municipalities, corporations and individuals...They hold possession of all the great lines of trade and business of all kinds, and they regulate all prices by their own arbitrary methods".

This quote could easily be updated to encompass the City uranium price fixing scandal of 1977, the recent Libor rate fixing scandal, or indeed Lord Blackheath and his shadowy Foundation X.

The symbol of the money power according to Woolfolk is the the 'Great Red Dragon'. This is echoed in Pierre Sabak's seminal work *Murder of Reality – Hidden Symbolism of the Dragon*, who tells us that, "the red serpent, (emblem of the City of London), is a depiction of the fox, (Arabic Ta'alib), an initiatory device of the student, (taliba), cognate with the Theban Priesthood, signified by the brazen cobra". One such Priest of Thebes was Ankh-fn-Khonsu, whose 26th Dynasty funerary stele plays such an iconic role in Thelema, the religion founded by Aleister Crowley. This unusually brightly coloured wooden stele is referred to in the *Book of the Law* (the central Holy text of Thelema) as the 'Stele of Revealing'. We have already referred to Ankh-fn-Khonsu earlier in Chapter two as the founder of the Dragon Court circa 2170 BC.

We have already looked at the mysterious document of *Le Serpent Rouge*, which has been labelled as the codename for the bloodline of Cain. This series of documents from the Priory of Sion revealed the equally enigmatic 13th sign of the zodiac corresponding to the Dragon, London's lost symbol. The relationship to the number thirteen and ancient moon worship is attested and affirmed by Jules Cashford. In her work *The Moon* she says, "Thirteen is the number of days from the first crescent to just before the days of the full moon – the period of waxing; thirteen is also the number of cycles that make up an observational lunar year (a solar year of 365 is measured by the 13 moons)." Contained within *Le Serpent Rouge* in relation to the secret astrological sign of Serpent/Dragon, it should be noted here that while the serpent text falls as number eleven in the Priory of Sion's pecking order of astrological houses, it is still known as the 13th astrological sign. However, most of the Dragon/serpent text concerns references to the six-pointed star or Seal of Solomon used by Amshel Mayer Bauer-Rothschild in Frankfurt. There are also references to 'Arcadia' in *Le Serpent Rouge*, which in ancient Greece was the legendary home of the Gods and Titans and the Trojan bloodline that includes Aeneas and indeed Brutus. The Kymri or Welsh extract of the Brutus lineage is to this day represented by the Red Dragon.

While Geoffrey of Monmouth was the most well known Brutus chronicler there are others. These include some earlier manuscripts as we have mentioned in Chapter One, which go to predate Geoffrey's account of the capital's founder. There is a strong indication of a conspiracy conducted by those determined to deny Brutus his rightful place in history. One such English historian Gwylin Bach, who was refused the post of Lord Bishop of Llandaff by Dafydd ad Owen who was Prince of Gweneed in 1169. The previous Bishop was Geoffrey of Monmouth and Gwilyn (William) was desperate to be appointed his successor but it was not to be. Gwylin returned home a bitter man determined to take revenge, not just against Dafydd, but also on the work of Geoffrey. This by default exacted its toll on the Welsh people, as he wrote his own book damning the Brutus history. Even so, the Brutus tradition was never really questioned until the 19th Century when some men such as Stubbs, decided in their wisdom that Brutus was fable and not fact. Their pronouncement is now canon to conventional historians, despite earlier evidence to the contrary.

But genealogists say the British Kings are traceable through Beli the Great to Aeneas and Dardannus. The first leader of Britain was said to be Hu Gadarn, who led the first migration from the Caucasus to the Southern Babylonian province of Arcadia, which gave its name to the Greek province of the Gods. Hu Gadarn brought with him someone called Gomeridae, and it was he who some believe first introduced the Druidic religion into Britain from the aforementioned Eastern regions. In her book *Prehistoric London: Its Mounds and Circles*, E.O. Gordon maintains that the original British colonists came from Arcadia, Babylonia:

"The earliest recorded history of the British race takes us to Central Asia, the fertile district watered by the Tigris and Euphrates, lying between Mount Ararat on the north and Persian Gulf on the south. To this country of the ancient Chaldees, the cradle of the human race, the earliest settlers in Britain trace their origin."

Hu Gadarn's successor Aedd Mawr is reputedly credited with founding the first Druid Order in Britain, containing the first proper triad infrastructure consisting of three grades. There were three Arch-Druids of Britain who were leaders, and their seats of power were Caer Troia – London, Caer Evrok – York and Caer Leon – Monmouth.

Gordon advances the theory that originally the City of London Mile consisted of two hillocks both thirty-five feet in height that stood either side of the Walbrook stream. St Paul's now stands at the highest point of the Western hillock and Gordon postulates that this was the seat of the London

Arch Druid, and that it was once surrounded by a Druidic stone circle, now lost forever in the heady mists of time. St. Swithins' church was built on the apex of the Eastern hillock and was once a resting place of the London or Brutus Stone. The earliest mention of this stone according to Miss Gordon was in the time of King Athelstane circa 895 AD. We have already mentioned the Druid College on Thorney Island next to Tothill, which is a sacred mound (tot means mound. In Winckcliffe's translation of the Bible he applies the word tot or tote to Mount Zion). But Thorney Island was not the only Druid College in ancient London – there was another close to Cannon Street station, its name survives as College Street where the Druidic inhabitants were known as the Guardians of the Circle.

At the heart of the Druid worship was the devotion to the serpent, which they used in their magical grades such as the adder: something that was definitely not lost on Dr John Dee. He believed that both he and Queen Elizabeth I were descended from the tribe of Dan, to whom Jacob attributed the qualities of the serpent during his deathbed address in Genesis 49. Dee maintained that both himself and his Queen, were part of the Brutus bloodline and of Trojan lineage. Whether or not he truly believed this, or simply propagated the story out of personal and political expediency is unclear. Dee also linked himself strongly with the Pendragon legends, which again would certainly do no harm to a man of such standing within the English Royal Court. All the while, Dee was developing a geo-political agenda for the planned imperial ordainment of Elizabeth I, which involved the religious responsibility to conquer the globe. Centuries later, Dee may have had his intentions fulfilled, since the current Queen Elizabeth II is the largest landowner on Earth. According to Kevin Cahill in his book *Who Owns the World*, the Queen owns a staggering global acreage of 6,698,146,531 acres, which amounts at the time of valuation to US $33,490,732,655,000. This is all overseen and administered by The Crown, within the confines of the City of London.

In ancient civilisations the wearing of the Crown symbolised high rank within the serpent cult. In ancient Britain E. O. Gordon tells us in her book *Prehistoric London* that, "The whole island was considered to be under the Crown – the Crown itself to be the 'Voice of the Country', hence the maxim 'the country is higher than the King', which runs through the ancient British laws, and was directly opposed to the feudal system, in which the country itself was dealt with as the property of the King."

The origins of the Crown can be further traced back to the first wearers of this regal artefact, King Nimrod and Queen Semiramus of Babylon. The latter is depicted wearing the Crown surrounded by twelve stars or heavenly bodies, imagery which was later embodied into that of the goddess Europa.

Today the EU flag contains the same twelve stars but they do not represent the original founding member countries, of which there were only six – they represent the Crowned Goddess. The wearing of the Crown was the mark of high rank within the Dragon and Serpent cult. King Nimrod ruled his subjects with all the ferocity of a fire breathing dragon, and he is seen as a significant figure within the secret cloisters of Scottish Rite Freemasonry through his organisation of labour in the legend of the Tower of Babel. The world's largest landowners are thirty-four monarchs, all wearers of their respective Crowns. 85% of the global population own nothing at all.

Since Tony Blair took it upon himself to eradicate the Magna Carta rights that since 1215 all free people had by birthright, perhaps now is the time to revisit Common law and the ancient British laws accorded to all people. Today the Crown weighs heavily on the shoulders of mankind but if we can once again avail ourselves of the ancient British law, that the Crown is under the voice of the country, this should be the inheritance bestowed upon man in London's mystical legacy.

APPENDIX

1. Sacred Mounds and Alignments in London

Using an alternative scientific system founded by Thomas Lockyear, K.C.B., who first discovered the gas helium, the right Rev. John Griffiths, claimed to have been able to interpret what he referred to as the "interrelation of mound and alignment of ancient roads in the District of London". Griffiths was an early archaeologist influenced by Lockyear. The latter had been one of the first to realise that Stonehenge was an advanced mathematical structure.

Griffiths pointed to Stanmore, for example, as forming the apex of an equilateral triangle which includes Windsor Castle and Salt Hill as its base.

The Rev Griffiths produced a series of figures, measurements and calculations which he claimed amounted to the "numerical symmetry" of the Stanmore-Windsor-Salt Hill grouping. He advanced a theory that that the sites had correlations with three matching stellar dates that suggested that their formation began at around 1500 BC.

Griffiths maintained that some of these alignments related to the solstices, sunrises and sunsets in May (Beltane) and November (Samhain) of Druidic calendar system. In 1500 BC these dates pointed to the position of the stars Capella and Sirius in connection with the geometry of the Stanmore grouping.

Another collection of mounds and triangular corresponding alignments were the White Mound of the Tower – Penton and Parliament Hill, which all connect in a straight line, showing Tothill from the base of the triangle along with White Mound, rising to Parliament Hill as the apex.

The legend of Bran is also relative here according to Griffiths, who says that the "legend of Bran is undoubtedly largely astronomical". He also refers to "Bran's injunction about keeping a door in a certain direction closed" (presumably North).

Griffiths also claims that once he saw the diagram of London's mounds, he could see that "the burial has reference to the leading astronomical measure worked into legend...". What is seemingly beginning to emerge here is the stellar rather than lunar understanding of alignments of London's ancient roads.

Griffith comments "Mounds and straight roads should be studied together. Signal stations preceded long straight roads, and the mound builders were the pioneers of road makers. The positions of mounds, individually and relatively were determined by astronomical requirements. The astronomy of the rods is now duplicated in related roads."

Griffiths then proceeds to give examples of 'Clock Star Alignments' and 'Rectangular Alignments' which we have reproduced and included here. He further claimed that each of the mounds was also an astronomical observational platform, citing Streatham Church as one such example amongst other parish churches which also served as observatories. Where two streets converge, he says, this jointly forms a 'Star Clock'. It is worth remembering that conventional historians are uncertain of the origins of the shaft or well found at the White Mound found at the Tower today, which is clearly an astronomical platform of Druid origin.

From what Griffith advanced, one can see that in the same way a 'blind spring' marks the convergence of two ley lines as energy points, and many of London's early roads were seemingly built on such lines.

London Mounds

Tower Hill-Parliament	46° 45' NW-SE
Tower-Tothill	72° 30' NE-SW
Tothill-Parliament	19° 15' NW-SE
Tothill-Penton	17° 30' NE-SW
Penton-Primrose Hill	76° 45' NW-SE
Tothill-Primrose Hill	28° NW-SE
Primrose Hill-Parliament	2° NW-SE
Angle at Tower	60° 45'
Angles at Tothill	(1) 91°, (2) 9°, (3) 55°

2. The Malmutius Code

Examples of Malmutius Code laid down by King Malmutius (Dyvnwal Moelmud). It is said that King Malmutius died in the 40th year of his reign, and was buried in the White Mound of the Tower, which also contained the remains of Brutus and by legend, Bran. One history concerns itself that Malmutius' final resting place was Blackwell Hall (defunct) which stood southwest of where Guildhall now stands. Both sites are clearly linked to the Brutus mythology. His laws, at the bequest of Prince Brutus are the basis of English Common law today:

"There are three tests of Civil Liberty; equality of rights, equality of taxation, freedom to come and go.

There are three causes which ruin a State; inordinate privileges, corruption of justice, national apathy.

There are three things which cannot be considered solid longer than their foundations are solid – peace, property, and law.

Three things are indispensable to a true union of Nations; sameness of laws, rights, and language.

There are three things free to all Britons, the forest, the unworked mine, the right of hunting wild creatures.

There are three things which are private and sacred property in every man, Briton or foreigner, his wife, his children, his domestic chattels.

There are three things belonging to a man which no law of men can touch, fine, or transfer, his wife, his children, and the instruments of his calling; for no law can unman a man, or uncall a calling.

There are three persons in a family exempted from all manual or menial work; the little child, the old man or woman, and the family instructor.

There are three orders against whom no weapon can be bared; the herald, the bard, the head of a clan.

There are three of private rank, against whom no weapon can be bared; a woman, a child under fifteen, and an unarmed man.

There are three things that require the unanimous vote of the nation to effect; deposition of the sovereign, introduction of novelties in religion, suspension of law

There are three civil birthrights of every Briton; the right to go wherever he pleases, the right, wherever he is, to protection from his land and sovereign, the right of equal privileges and equal restrictions.

There are three property birthrights of every Briton; five (British) acres of land for a home, the right of armorial bearings, the right of suffrage in the enacting of the laws, the male at twenty-one, the female on her marriage.

There are three guarantees of society; security for life and limb, security for property, security of the rights of nature.

There are three things the safety of which depends on that of the others, the sovereignty, national courage, just administration of the laws.

There are three things which every Briton may legally be compelled to attend, the worship of God, military service, and the courts of law.

For three things a Briton is pronounced a traitor, and forfeits his rights, emigration, collusion with an enemy, surrendering himself, and living under an enemy.

There are three things free to every man, Britain or foreigner, the refusal of which no law will justify; water from spring, river, or well, firing from a decayed tree, a block of stone not in use.

There are three orders who are exempt from bearing arms; the bard, the judge, the graduate in law or religion. These represent God and his peace, and no weapon must ever be found in their hand.

There are three kinds of sonship; a son by marriage with a native Briton, an illegitimate son acknowledged on oath by his father, a son adopted out of the clan.

3. Admiralty Law

Admiralty Law is distinguished from the so called Law of the Sea which governs coastal rights, mineral ownership and navigational issues between private owners. Admiralty Law is quite different in that it affects maritime commerce, whether conducted wholly on sea or not and also marine trade, shipping and sailors. Admiralty Law was introduced to England by Eleanor of Aquitaine, one of the most influential and powerful women of her age. Eleanor ruled as Regent over England while her son King Richard the Lion Heart fought the Crusades. She had come across the law while accompanying her husband on a Crusade, with the first European rendition known as the 'Rolls of Oleron', dating from 1160. Admiralty Law was formed of an amalgam of earlier Southern European edicts such as the Rhodes Sea Law (Nomos Rhodion Nautikos), itself a product of some Roman maritime edicts combined with those laid down by Byzantine Emperor Leo VI. Admiralty Law also includes elements of Islamic seafaring legislation too. Much of the legislation is to be expected such as: salvage rights, basic law while aboard a vessel, maritime lien or claim upon property, the treatment of cargo, including slaves, a ship's mortgage, care to passengers, the duties of sailors to guard lives, salvage rights and so on.

It is believed that Admiralty Law was ultimately the legacy of the Knights Templar, the most powerful bankers of the Medieval period. It is believed by some researchers that many of these Christian warrior monks set sail from France in their desperate flight from persecution under their flag of convenience - the skull and crossbones. The actual title 'Jolly Rodger', the name for the black skull and cross bones flag, has its origins in the French 'Jolie Rouge' ('pretty red') denoting the earlier Templar flag adorning their vessel's masts which was plain red. The Knights Templar are said to have flouted their sacred Admiralty Law obligations and taken to piracy, flying their skull and crossbones, after their own Templar livelihoods were usurped and their lands plundered by the authorities of the day.

The High Court of Admiralty was started during the reign of English Monarch Edward I. The basis of this law was in the Rolls of Oleron, but developed over time by the English into the 'Black Book of Admiralty.' It was the highest form of law on maritime matters, including torts, ownership rights and setting out all maritime related crimes, offences and their prescribed punishments. Admiralty courts were formed quite separately from other courts, with special judges sitting on them. Some of the terms used in maritime law will be familiar to the reader, although their legalese remains obscure now – flotsam, jetsam and wreck.

4. London Etymology

The origin of the name London is unclear and hotly disputed with several etymological theories being advanced. We include a few below but this is by no means an exhaustive list.

Luddun – or 'King Ludd's wall' is often mentioned.

Llandin – translates as 'sacred eminence'.

KaerLudd – comes from the early account given by Geoffrey of Monmouth, who says that the city was seized by King Ludd who ordered it to be renamed in his honour, that gives us 'Caer Lud'.

Lhwn Town – William Camden advanced that the name derives from 'Lhwn' meaning 'grove' in Welsh.

Glynn Din – meaning 'city in the valley' advanced by Jackson in 1792.

Lan-Dan – denotes Tribe of Dan.

Luna-Din – 'Moon Fortress' taken from Cambro Briton 1821. There are variations of this theme such as 'Luandun' meaning 'City of the Moon'.

Lan Dian – is allied to the above theme as this translates as 'Temple of Diana' which is of course where St Paul's Cathedral stands and is a direct reference to Brutus' founding of Diana's temple at this spot.

Lyn Dain – meaning 'pool of the Thames' given by Jones in 1855, in a work called *The Cymry* of '76.

Lyn Din – meaning 'Lake Fortress'.

Lond or Lont – this is a very different etymology suggesting that the name is of a Ligurian root, not Celtic, and means 'marsh, or mud town'.

Lohna – suggested by a Frenchman Gigot and taken from a Germanic root.

Plowonida – is even more obscure and is derived from old European language roots, those allied to Indo-European 'plew' which gives the meaning 'to flow' or 'to swim'. Therefore '(p)lowonidonjo' would have become corrupted to. 'Lowonidonjon' and either 'Lōondonjon' or 'Lōnidonjon'.

5. City of London Churches and Sites of Great Antiquity

i) Conventional authorities on history claim that a shaft that sits below the White Tower was placed there by the Romans, although there is little or no evidence to support this unchallenged theory. The shaft is more likely an observational well, such as found at the Pyramids, to observe the constellations by daylight. Such a shaft would have been necessary to the practices of the Druids who may have required it for their astronomical observances and religious festivals. The site was considered so sacred by the ancient British people that they buried several of their kings there, including, as folkore has it, giants such as Bryn/Bran (Guardian of the British Isles), it would suggest that the place was a key site within Druidic London – and ideal for the placement of an astronomical platform.

174

ii) Most of the City churches are built over far older ruins of sacred places, some are Saxon but almost all are of ancient (pre-Roman) origin. To augment this theory, ley line enthusiasts such as Paul Devereaux and others have suggested that those responsible for founding these churches/ pagan sites have aligned them in some way, and that these alignments must be, even to the casual observer, more than co-incidence. Most of Wren's churches designed in the wake of the Great Fire are built upon former churches, themselves built upon ancient British pagan sites. One can draw a straight line through their relative positions on a London map. Examples given by Paul Devereaux and Ian Thompson are: St Clement Danes, the Templar Church, St Paul's Cathedral, St Helen of Bishopsgate, St Dunstan, Stepney – all of whom are oddly aligned but why? St Paul's of course is a site founded by Brutus as we have said before, or did he simply identify a sacred enclosure known to the local inhabitants and conform to the ancient knowledge available to him? Conventional historians are unable to offer even a remote explanation of this phenomenon, if indeed they acknowledge the blatantly obvious alignments at all.

iii) Sadly, much damage was inflicted on the City churches, firstly by the Great Fire of 1666 and then by the Blitz, with London, the 'City of Steeples' losing a lot of its mystical heritage in the course of these two conflagrations. Quite a few churches were not rebuilt after the Great Fire and are now just forgotten designations recorded in local borough wards or obscure street names. This physical destruction, coupled with the pronouncements of certain historians such as Stubbs, who in their hubris declared Brutus no more than a mythical figure, have distorted what we know today of London's ancient British/Trojan past. The rest of the damage, particularly to the grand vista of St Paul's has been left to tasteless property developers. Thankfully, modern researchers such as John Michell, Alan Wilson and Baram Blackett and more recently Peter Ackroyd and Iain Sinclair, have opened our minds to new possibilities about the City's foundation. If this Trojan connection is accurate it makes London 150 years older than Rome!

Mystical writer John Michell says of these magnificent sanctified buildings "The City churches are hidden shrines of London. Each has its peculiar character and atmosphere, developed over many centuries. Their individuality is not impaired by the fact that they were designed by one man, Sir Christopher Wren. His policy was to rebuild on their old foundations the churches destroyed by the Great Fire, often reproducing their old features."

Michell was aware that the placement of City churches, often described as being Saxon or Norman, were actually built upon already sanctified places, some of these being of great antiquity and most definitely pre-Roman origin.

iv) The greatest, if the most controversial, evidence in the mystical importance of the placements of London church and cathedral buildings is given to us by dowsers or what are termed 'water-diviners'. Guy Underwood, an author and researcher who was one of the early pioneers of 20th century dowsing, discovered as he learned his craft that this knowledge was certainly known to prehistoric man and those who built Medieval churches. He came to this conclusion because all prehistoric monuments such as Stonehenge, Woodhenge, Avebury, hill figures, dolmens etc are all found to mark the siting of so-called 'blind springs' that emit invisible streams of energy. He cites dowsers who are sensitive enough, being overcome by an unseen force at the convergence of two streams.

Coming to the placement and alignment of Medieval churches built by the Masons, he says, "As for the selection of those sites, the early Christian missionaries were charged by Pope Gregory the Great, and by other churchmen, to take over sacred places whereupon to build their churches. [...] when the site had been selected, the first step would have been to make a plan of the geodetic lines or blind springs". Underwood surveyed a great many Prehistoric and Medieval sites including Southwark Cathedral, Westminster Abbey and St Paul's. He found that most side chapels are built in close proximity to main altars and nearly always had diagonal geodetic lines, Lady chapels he found marked a place where a terminal spring occurs approximately in line with the structure of the building, but an altar spring, he tells us, "is always indicated by a step in the chancel".

In describing his dowsing survey of Westminster Abbey he informs us "The shrine and tomb of Edward the Confessor, Henry V, Henry VI, Henry VII, and Queen Elizabeth I are all located above important blind springs". Underwood also managed to locate the path of the ford taking one from the Druidic Thorney island across the Thames.

7. City of London 'Crown' and the use of covert power over sovereign rulers
William the Conqueror – Once William had conquered the Saxon Harold to seize the English throne at Hastings, he did not take hold of London as might have been expected but rather promised that the City could continue in her independent sovereignty. William gave assurances in which he guaranteed the legal rights of London as before and as such he entered the City as joint enterprise. Nor did William interfere or impose Norman law on his new city.

Henry I – gave further legal definition to the office of Portshrieve, giving charter to the City Sheriffs. He had in effect recognised the City's legal independence by creating this tenure.

Richard I – his ransom was raised and paid for by the City.

Longchamps – acting Regent while Richard I was fighting the Crusades, Longchamps entered into a dispute with his Liege. The City and the English Barons sided with the King against Longchamps, who was later ejected from both the Tower and the City precincts.

King John – who at first was allied to the enemies of Longchamps with the aforementioned Barons, later imposed both his pro-Catholic religious views and unfair taxation on his people. He soon came unstuck, as the City and the Barons rebelled, forcing King John to sign the Magna Carta – one of the first human rights charters in history. The document guaranteed basic rights to all Englishman, which stand to this day, but also protected the City of London with clauses enshrining the liberties, independence and customs of London.

Edward I – reaffirmed the Magna Carta using wise counsel in his words "the City of London should have all the old customs which it hath been used to".

Richard III – garnered the full support of the City Livery Companies during his reign.

Tudors – Henry VIII, Elizabeth I – garnered the support of the City by promoting war and expansion to make London wealthier. Their claim to Brutus' lineage may have cemented this great success, particularly with the Liveries. Elizabeth's great-grandfather was Lord Mayor Boleyn.

House of Stuart – rode roughshod over liberty and freedom. These monarchs tried to impose unfair and illegal taxation and were generally anti–City. When events came to a head between Parliament and the Stuart monarch Charles I, the City chose to support Parliament, via the decrees of the Common Council. Parliament won and the City independence grew ever stronger as a result, literally as Kingmakers.

Cromwell – Once the Commonwealth Government itself tried to oppress the people by force of arms the City orchestrated its own move to restore the House of Stuart but only as a Constitutional Monarchy which is the same today. His main crime seems to stem from the fact that he thought himself above the City instead of in partnership with his former backers and financiers. This connection has rarely been considered let alone explored by conventional historians.

Charles II and his successor James II – both Kings from the House of Stuart tried to forfeit Livery/City wealth but upon their exit the new monarch William III restored their position by way of Royal charters. The attempts of the House of Stuart to restore to the monarchy during Protestant William's reign were firmly out outmanoeuvred by the staunch financial support of the City who remembered the Stuarts' assault upon the City sovereignty.

William III (House of Orange) – signed a significant Bill of Rights which in large part prevented the monarch from ever again levying unfair taxation upon the people, raising an army during peacetime and effectively banned Catholics from the Throne. This last clause was almost certainly a reaction to the House of Stuart and their continued claims upon the throne. The Bank of England was formed during William's reign.

8. Offices of the City

i) **Lord Mayor** – Elected by the Livery Companies to hold sovereign power over the City. As such, the Lord Mayor automatically becomes Viceroy of the City precincts as well as Chief Magistrate, holding jurisdiction over the ancient laws and customs of the Square Mile. He is also privy, along with the reigning monarch, to the secret passwords issued quarterly for accessing the Tower of London. Other automatic titles conferred upon the Lord Mayor during his tenure include Admiral of the Port of London, Trustee of St Paul's and Lord Lieutenant of the City.

The Lord Mayor enters office with great fanfare, being elected each Michelmas (September 29th). Prior to his installation all present celebrate a pre-Reformation Mass. Anyone who is not a Liveryman must depart before Mass or expect to be imprisoned. The ancient ritual begins with the words of the Cryer "Oyez, oyez, oyez". Herbs and flowers are strewn about to perfume the event and symbolically ward off the plague. The election of the new Lord Mayor is announced by his Aldermen who vote as a legal court and announce their verdict. The new incumbent is then seated to the left of the outgoing Lord Mayor as his newly elected successor summons his new officers, with the Sword Bearer overseeing events.

Upon election the Lord Mayor is presented with a chain of office some five and a half feet long, consisting of twenty-eight letters 'S', fourteen Tudor roses, thirteen knots and a portcullis. It is known as the 'Collar of Esses' and is believed by some scholars have a connection with loyalty to John O' Gaunt of the House of Lancaster. Both the S symbol and the Tudor roses may have direct inference to the Brutus bloodline and Kingship values. The origin of the S has many theories but one has the meaning 'Sovereign whose rights are ancient'.

The Lord Mayor's regalia includes four ceremonial swords, a mace, a chain as mentioned above and the distinctive red robes of office. Other perks of office include an ornate golden coach used for transportation during special occasions and an official residence called The Mansion House, located near to the Druidic Walbrook.

ii) **Sword Bearer** – The senior officer of the Lord Mayor's household and very esteemed in his position as one the four principal officials of the City charged with carrying the Lord Mayor's sword. His impeccable character is as important as his role. He wears a fur hat in sable, black robes and strikes a military bearing in ceremonial. He may read Royal Proclamations at the Exchange among other elect duties. His sword will point downwards when in the presence of the Royal Family.

iii) **Common Cryer and Sergeant-at-Arms (Mace Bearer to some)** – Bearing the Mace dressed in black robes and stockings, this may be the oldest of the positions created within the Lord Mayor's household. As his title suggests the Cryer makes announcements and pronouncements of the City to both Aldermen and the Sheriffs. In essence the Sergeant-at-Arms is a descendent of the King's bodyguard, armed with a mace for the personal protection of the Lord Mayor. As such the office is military in bearing, although the mace is effectively a diamond encrusted sceptre, part of which dates back to Medieval times. The Mace Bearer carries it as an emblem of City authority rather like the Beadles of the Livery Companies but in higher office.

iv) **City Marshal** – Another principal officer of the household. The office is a survival of an early proto-police force. This mounted officer is charged with protecting law and order within the City. He ushers processions and rides ahead of the Mayor.

v) **City Solicitor** – Although the title of City Solicitor may only stretch back to the 16th Century, it is of considerable antiquity according to some sources. A clue to his antiquity may come from the Quit Rents Ceremony conducted with the aid of the Remembrancer. This judicial ritual is mentioned elsewhere in this book, and where the City Solicitor holds the billhook and hatchet which may have its origins in the scythe of ancient Druidry. The duties connected with the post are varied but naturally all legal frameworks affecting the City Corporation go through this official. He is City Prosecutor and should he be required to do so may act against any City Magistrate. In another capacity he is also a Draftsman of the Common Council of the City.

vi) **Remembrancer** – As mentioned above the Remembrancer is involved with the Quit Rents Ceremony, fully decked out in his judicial attire he takes away the billhook and hatchet to the reigning King or Queen. In effect the office involves being a conduit between the Lord Mayor and the monarch, as such he is also the officer between the City and the Government. In essence he is the Head of Protocol. To describe him more specifically one might be to say he is an off-shoot of the Exchequer and some of his duties reflect that role. As part of his duties the Remembrancer reports Bills to the Common Council of the City and is charged with the responsibility of protecting the interests of the City, being present for the Trial of the Pyx – a centuries old ceremony to assay the quality of coins in the Kingdom. He advises both courts and committees in the nomination of High Sheriffs with the exception of a few Sheriffs nominated by the Royal Household themselves. The Remembrancer also enjoys the privilege of sitting in the House of Lords (the second chamber of Parliament).

vii) **City Comptroller** – The Comptroller of the Chamber (the Chamber of London) is placed in charge of the Bridge House Estates. In times past under King Edward I the post may have been known as Clerk of the Chamber or even at other times as the Contrarotulator. The title confers authority over the deeds of the Corporation of London including leases, property documents and so on but also overseeing property owned by the Corporation or conveyancing property that may be of interest to the said body. He is one the three officials entrusted with guarding the City Seal.

viii) **Sheriff** – Originating from the title and office of Portrieve this office is older than that of Mayor. The Portrieve eventually became Shire-reve, and then Sheriff. The title was democratic although outside of London in Lancaster & Cornwall, there were Sheriffs whose titles became hereditary. Scholars will not fail to pick up on these last two locations, both being firmly linked to the Brutus lineage.

Nowadays only two Sheriffs are elected for the City. The election is made by the City Livery Companies, with nominees being announced by the Remembrancer prior to election. The office of Sheriff is an exulted one, making this select group among the most privileged of the City.

The election of Sheriffs at Common Hall, made by Aldermen on June 24th each year, observes the ancient rite of placing a sword on top of roses. This is in respect of Harpocrates, Lord of Silence, who was presented by Cupid with the rose so that he would not betray the armours of Venus. The legal term 'sub rosa' takes this legend on board in the code of silence and integrity in legal matters.

The Sheriff wears a red robe, a chain of office, entertains feasts such as the 'Sheriff's Breakfast' and may often earn a Knighthood from his endeavours in years to follow.

ix) **Chamberlain** – Like the City Comptroller the Chamberlain has the honour of guarding the City Seal. Over the years the method of his appointment has varied but the date was originally set just after the Autumn Equinox, Sept 21st (the Feast of St Matthew) but that has now been changed to Midsummer's Day according to modern accounts. His inauguration takes place at Chamberlain's Court, Guildhall – the Temple of Brutus. The Chamberlain was in years past a kind of proto city banker. At one stage the Chamberlain and his Chamber of London dispensed loans to the King or Queen, taken from City coffers, in much the same way the Bank of England does today. The financing of the rebuilding of London after the Great Fire was one such scheme organised by the Chamberlain, on City finances.

Essentially the Chamberlain is a Treasurer of the City and in his ancient role paid for entertainments to visiting potentates, rulers and dignitaries entering the City in an official capacity within the Lord Mayor's remit. The Lord Mayor may request an audience with any monarch but only through the Chamberlain. Today he still may grant Freedom of the City to certain individuals. There is also a Chamberlain's Court which has powers of tribunal through existing courts. His attire is an ermine trimmed gown.

x) **Town Clerk** – The Town Clerk is one of the three officers entrusted with guarding the City Seal. His title may seem mundane to some but his ancient title is really Common Clerk and herein lies his real remit. He attends the Court of both Common Council (in modern times a Police Authority for the Police Force) and Common Hall (a City electorate body) and oversees business, carefully recording minutes of their meetings. He is Executive Officer of the London Corporation. His high office requires him to be privy to all codes of practice, every privilege of the City and as one City historian Col. Blackman put it "the guide, philosopher and friend to every member of the Corporation from the Lord Mayor downwards".

xi) **Secondary** – The Secondary is the Under Sheriff of the City. His duties include acting in his capacity of keeper of the Old Bailey and he also has duties within the Guildhall and High Bailiff.

xii) **Alderman** – The Aldermen comprise of the Common Council which is the oldest municipal in the country which actually predates Parliament. At one time the court of Aldermen had power to reject admittants to their ranks or anyone they considered unfit for office. The Aldermen currently meet nine times a year at Guildhall and can confer Livery status on organisations and give Freedom of the City.

9. The Red Dragon and Brutus
i) An intriguing link exists between the Tudor Rose, the Brutus bloodline, the dragon motif, the Tarot 'Atu' (Trumps) and the Luciferian tradition. The authors stumbled upon in this information 1996, but only after researches concerning the 'Crown', did the full implications of the link become clear.

Madeline Montalban, a.k.a. Dolores North (see Chapter Six), was private astrologer and psychic to Lord Louis Montbatten. Madame Montalban founded a magical fraternity called the Order of the Morning Star, whose practices partook of the Luciferian tradition, an ancient belief system concerning Lucifer, Angel of Light and the Morning Star (Venus), who is considered an angel of salvation by virtue of his bringing light or enlightenment to man. In many respects, Lucifer is a parallel to the figure of Prometheus, who stole fire from heaven and brought it to earth for the use of man. Lucifer in this tradition was a force encouraging evolution and spiritual development by providing 'light', or in Latin, 'lucis'. The Order of the Morning Star, which was founded and headed by Madame Montalban as an attempt to revive the teachings of the ancient Babylonian and Egyptian Priesthoods, counted among its members the late Nicholas Tereschenko, Russian aristocrat, prominent Freemason, ritual magician and Gurdjieffian.

Tereschenko spoke to the authors of this book (during 1996) about his esoteric work and theories. It has latterly been discovered that Tereschenko's esoteric interests were extremely diverse, even disparate, making it extremely difficult to ascertain direct sources. It is likely that Tereshenko was not only a student of Madame Montalban, but also of the Golden Dawn, at the Ahathoor Temple No. 7 in Paris. In talks with one of the authors, Tereschenko insisted that the Tarot system was incomplete as was generally known, since there actually existed 24 Major Arcana as opposed to the generally accepted 22 Atu. He stated that the 24th card was actually known as the Dragon. He said that the Dragon card may have had links with the idea of the Red Dragon symbolism which he intimated may have suggested the 13th sign of astrology – the Serpent Holder.

Madeline Montalban, who was also an expert on astrology and Tarot, wrote a private document for distribution only to initiates of the Order of the Morning Star, in which she explained her thoughts on the secret Luciferian tradition. The secret text, known as the *Book of Lumiel* (a name she ascribed to Lucifer), contained details about the guardians of angelic magic in ancient Egypt, of whom she said "The rich did the ruling, and kept the knowledge to within a small circle of kings and priesthoods, the priests being sworn to the king". The book also stated that it was Lucifer's destiny to incarnate in human form at certain key points in history, as a saviour or redeemer of humanity.

During the Wars of the Roses, a series of civil conflicts between two Plantagenet families and their supporters over the claim to the English throne, rival Houses Lancaster and York both took the rose as their symbol, with the House of Lancaster choosing red, while the Yorks plumped for white. The final victory was claimed by Henry Tudor, who was of the House of Lancaster. Henry then married into the House of York, bringing both white and red roses together in to a single national symbol that became known as the 'Union Rose'. The colours red and white have many alchemical attributions, including those of a sexual nature. It isn't, we hope, too difficult to grasp why this might be so. It is also worth bearing in mind that the rose itself is used to symbolically represent the female sexual organ in many systems, especially those originating in the Middle East. It is perhaps easy to forget, for readers living in the 21st Century surrounded by corporate logos and a myriad of other visual devices, that symbols such as the rose were not simply used in an arbitrary fashion prior to the modern era. If we look at the rose as perhaps being indicative of a family lineage, from its allusion to the reproductive organs, it suddenly becomes clear as to why the Lancasters and the Yorks, both strands of the same Plantagenet line, adopted it as their symbol, with the white and the red possibly indicating male or female succession. Their final amalgamation in the Rose of Union may well have been a symbolic device used to shore up the legacy of the Brutus bloodline and to lend legitimacy to Henry's divine right to rule.

Later, during the reign of Henry Tudor's daughter, Elizabeth I, court astrologer Dr John Dee also seized upon this Brutus/Tudor connection to lay claim to the Americas and extend British interests abroad. With his notion of the Americas belonging to the Crown, he effectively formed the ideological foundations for what would go on to become the British Empire.

ii) Lucifer in his capacity as 'light-bearer', was a Latinised form of the Hebrew angel Uriel, the 'light of god'. The angel Uriel was the angel of salvation, but he was also depicted as the keeper of the keys of hell, a quality commensurate with his status as the chief of the fallen angels. However Lucifer was used as a Latinised form of the Greek name for Venus as the morning star, Phosphorus. Lucifer as the light-bearer (Phosphorus) was sometimes depicted as the key-bearer (Kleidouchos) which was the goddess Hekate. Therefore the Red Dragon/Luciferian symbolism which underpins the Crown can also be equated with Goddess Hecate.

10. The Crownship of Britian
"This Crown was called "the Crown of Britain," and the Sovereignty over the whole Island vested in it, - the Crownship of Britain, Un Bennaeth Brydain."
History of Britain From the Flood to A.D. 700 by Richard Williams Morgan 1933.

BIBLIOGRAPHY

Ackroyd, Peter; London – The Biography (Vintage 2001)
Ackroyd, Peter; Thames – Sacred River (Vintage 2008)
Alexander, Marc; Enchanted Britain (B.C.A 1981)
Amaru Pinkham, Mark; The Return of the Serpents of Wisdom (Adventures Unlimited Press 1997)
Ashe, Geoffrey; Mythology of the British Isles (Methuen, London, 1994)
Baigent, Michael; Leigh, Richard; Lincoln, Henry; The Holy Blood and the Holy Grail (Jonathan Cape 1982)
Baigent, Michael; Leigh, Richard; The Temple and the Lodge (Jonathan Cape 1989)
Baring, Anne; Cashford, Jules; The Myth of the Goddess (B.C.A. 1991)
Barrett, David. V; A Brief History of Secret Societies (Robinson 2007)
Barton, Nicholas; The Lost Rivers of London (B.C.A. London 1984)
Benson, Michael; Inside Secret Societies (Citadel Press 2005)
Beresiner, Yasha; The City of London Masonic Guide (Lewis Masonic 2006)
Berresford Ellis, Peter; The Druids (Constable 1994)
Black, Jonathan; The Secret History of the World (Quercus 2007)
Boulay, R.A.; Flying Serpents and Dragons (The Book Tree 1997)
Branston, Brian; The Lost Gods of England (B.C.A. 1974)
Buffery, J.; London Witchcraft (James Pike Ltd 1977)
Bulfinch, Thomas; Myths of Greece and Rome (Viking 1979)
Cahill, Kevin; Who Owns the World (Mainstream Publishing 2006)
Cartier, John; Sex and Rockets (Feral House U.S.A. 2004)
Cashford, Jules; The Moon, Myth and Image (Cassell)
Cicero, Chic; Cicerco, Sandra, Tabatha; Self Initiation Into the Golden Dawn (Llewellyn 1995)
Cohen, Tim; The Antichrist and a Cup of Tea (Prophecy House 1998)
Coils Masonic Encyclopedia, H.W.Coil (Macoy Publishing 1961)
Collins, Andrew; The Black Alchemist (ABS Books 1988)
Cotterell, Arthur, Storm, Rachel; The Ultimate Encyclopedia of Mythology (Hermes House 1999)
Cranston, Sylvia; H.P.B. (G.P. Putnams Sons, New York 1993)
Davidson, Gustav; A Dictionary of Angels (Free Press 1967)

De Vere, Nicholas; The Dragon Court Legacy (The Book Tree 2004)

Drury, Nevill; Dictionary of Mysticism & the Occult (Harper and Row 1985)

Duncan, Andrew; Secret London (New Holland 1995)

Encyclopaedia of Witchcraft and Demonology (Octopus 1974)

Freemasonry, A Celebration of the Craft; Edited by John Hamitt and Robert Gilbert (Greenwich Editions 1993)

Gardner, Laurence; In the Shadow of Soloman (Harper Element 2005)

Gardner, Laurence; The Magdelene Legacy (Element 2005)

Gilbert, Adrian; Alan, Wilson; Baram Blackett; The Holy Kingdom (Corgi 1999)

Gilbert, Adrian; The New Jerusalem (Bantam Press 2002)

Gilberston, G & A, Roberts; The Dark Gods (Rider 1980)

Gooch, Stan; Guardians of the Ancient Wisdom (Wildwood House 1979)

Gordon, E.O.; Prehistoric London (Covenant Publishing 1932)

Grant, Kenneth; Cults of the Shadow (Frederick Muller 1975)

Graves, Robert; The Greek Myths (Penguin 1948)

Graves, Robert; The White Goddess (Faber & Faber 1948)

Greene, Liz; The Astrology of Fate (George Allen & Unwin 1984)

Greer, John Michael; The Element Encyclopedia of Secret Societies and Hidden History (Harper Element 2006)

Grimal, Pierre; Dictionary of Classic Mythology (Presses Universitaire De France 1951)

Harrison, Michael; London – Beneath the Pavement (Peter Davies 1961)

Heironim us, Robert; Cortner, Laura; Founding Fathers, Secret Socities (Destiny 2006)

Hill, William Thomson; Buried London (Phonenix House 1995)

Holmes, Ronald; Witchcraft in British History (Tandem 1976)

Howard, Michael; The Occult Conspiracy (Rider 1989)

Icke, David; And the Truth Shall Set You Free (Bridge of Love 1995)

Icke, David; Children of the Matrix (Bridge of Love 2001)

Icke, David; Human Race Get Off Your Knees, The Lion Sleeps No More (Bridge of Love 2010)

Icke, David; Infinite Love if the Only Truth, Everything Else is an Illusion (Bridge of Love 2005)

Icke, David; Tales From the Time Loop (Bridge of Love 2003)

Icke, David; The Biggest Secret (Bridge of Love 1999)

Icke, David; The David Icke Guide to Global Conspiracy And How To Bring It To End (Bridge of Love 2007)

Illes, Judika; The Element Encyclopedia of Witchcraft (Harper Element 2005)

Jackson, A.C.F.; Rose Croix (Lewis Masonic 1980)

Jackson, Keith, B.; Beyond the Craft (Guild Publishing 1990)

Jones, Kathy; The Ancient British Goddess(Ariade 2001)

Kaczynski, Richard; Perdurabo, The Life of Aleister Crowley (North Atlantic Books 2002)

Keay, John; Keay, Julia; Hibbert, Christopher; Weinreb, Ben; The London Encyclopedia, Completely Revised Third Edition (Pan MacMillan 2008)

King, Francis; The Magical World of Aleister Crowley (Weidenfield and Nicholson 1977)

Lawrence, Rev. John. T.; The Prefect Ashlar (A.Lewis 1912)

Lethbridge, T.C.; Gogmagog – The Buried Gods (A.B.C. London 1975)

Lord, Evelyn; The Hellfire Clubs (Yale University Press 2008)

Marrs, Texe; Codex Magica (River Crest Publishing 2005)

Masse, Gerald; A Book of Beginnings (Cosmos, New York 2007)

Matthews, Caitlin; Sophia, Goddess of Wisdom (Mandala 1991)

Maxwell, Jordan; That Old Religion (The Book Tree 2000)

Mc Cintosh, Christopher; The Rosicrucians (Samuel Weiser Inc 1997)

Mitchell, John; Sacred England – Guide To (Gothic Image Publications)

Murray, Dr Margaret; The Divine King In England (Faber & Faber 1954)

Murray, Dr Margaret; The God of the Witches (Faber & Faber 1931)

Mythology – An Illustrated Encyclopaedia; Ed. Richard Cavendish (Black Cat 1987)

Nabaz, Payam; The Mysteries of Mithras (Inner Traditions 2005)

Naundon, Paul; The Secret History of Freemasonry (Inner Traditions 2005)

Newton, Toyne; The Dark Worship (Vega 2002)

New Larousse Encyclopedia of Mythology (Hamlyn 1959)

Pennick, Nigel; The Pagan Source Book (Rider 1972)

Pepper, Elizabeth; Wilcock, John; Magical & Mystical Sites (B.C.A. 1977)

Peel, J.H.B.; Along the The Green Roads of England (Cassell 1976)

Picknett, Lynn; Prince, Clive; The Sion Revelation (Sphere 2008)

Piggott, Stuart; The Druids (Thames & Hudson 1975)

Ridley, Jasper; The Freemasons (Constable 1999)

Roberts, J.M.; The Mythology of Secret Societies (Watkins 2008)

Robinson, John. J.; Born In Blood (Guild Publishing 1990)

Robison, John; Proofs Of A Conspiracy (Forgotten Books 2008)

Rohl, David; The Lost Testament (Century 2002)

Ross, Anne; Druids (Tempes 1999)

Ross, Anne; Pagan Celtic Britain (Sphere 1974)

Ross, Anne; Robins, Don; The Life and Death of a Druid Prince (Rider 1989)

Rowse, A.L.; Simon Forman (Purnell Book Services 1974)

Rowse, A.L.; The Tower of London (B.C.A. 1972)

Rutherford, Ward; The Druids and Their Heritage (Gordon and Cremones 1978)

Sabak, Pierre; The Murder of Reality (Serpentigena 1989)

Shepard, John; The Temple of Mithras London (English Heritage 1998)

Spence, Lewis; Boadicea (Robert Hale 1937)

Spence, Lewis; Legendary London (Robert Hale 1937)

Spence, Lewis; The Encyclopedia of the Occult Bracken Books 1994)

Springmeir, Fritz; Bloodlines of the Illuminati (Ambassador House 1999)

Sutton, Maya Magee. PHD; Maan, Nicholas.R.; Druid Magic (Llewellyn 2008)

Symonds, John; The Great Beast (Granada 1973)

The Druid Source Book; Ed. John Matthews (Blandford 1997)

The Halls of the Livery Companies of London; Ed Peter J.A. Lubbock (Morrison and Gibb 1981)

Twyman, Tracy R.;The Merovingian Mythos (Dragon Key Press 2004)

Valiente, Doreen; An ABC of Witchcraft Past and Present (Robert Hale 1973)

Wallis Budge, E.A.; Egyptian Magic (Bell 1991)

Wallace, Murphy, Tim; Hopkins, Marilyn; Rosslyn (Element 1999)

Wilcock, John; A Guide To Occult Britain (Sidgwick and Jackson 1976)

Wooley, Benjamin; The Queen's Conjuror (Harper Collins 2001)

#0297 - 210518 - C0 - 229/152/11 - PB - DID2202310